Sam Jo
and the
Remaking of Ashanti

For Ross and Christine

Sam Jonah
and the
Remaking of Ashanti

A. A. Taylor

MACMILLAN

First published in 2006 by
Pan Macmillan South Africa
1st Floor, The Pavilion, Wanderers Office Park
52 Corlett Drive, Illovo, Johannesburg, 2196

www.panmacmillan.co.za

ISBN 1770100245 (TPB)

Edited by Andrea Nattrass
Typeset in 11.25/15pt Bembo by Triple M Design & Advertising
Cover design by Donald Hill of Studio 5
Cover photograph courtesy of Elmond Jiyane of GCIS
Printed and bound in South Africa by CTP Book Printers

Contents

Author's Note

While researching my doctorate thesis, 'An Economic History of Ashanti Goldfields Corporation, 1895–2004', the influence of the firm's last chief executive, Sam Jonah, intrigued me. I was curious about this African miner who had transformed a single, ailing gold mine into one of the world's largest multinational gold producers. As a Ghanaian myself, the spectacular growth of the firm at the helm of a compatriot motivated an Internet search for his email address and I audaciously asked for authorisation to write his biography.

My boldness paid off, but what I had initially envisaged to be a straightforward business leadership biography transpired to be an altogether more complex tale. Jonah's story not only maps a private life's journey, it is also an account of the fitful evolution of a corporation, a nation and a continent. Peering into Jonah's life-world reveals the crux of Africa's problems: all the debt relief, foreign aid, even the attainment of equality in global trade will make no long-lasting difference to Africa's masses without a radical transformation of the continent's political and judicial institutions. Ghana, regarded internationally as an exemplary African country, is exposed through Jonah's story as having a very long way to go in healthy institution-building.[1]

On the positive side, Jonah's story shows that Africa's mineral wealth could do for the continent what the Industrial Revolution did for Britain, and what railways did for the United States of America. A mine is a crucible of economic activity: the on-site geologists, engineers, chemists, physicists and a myriad of skilled technicians are supported by accountants, lawyers, doctors, transport companies, construction firms, food growers and food sellers. It is obvious to me that the balanced exploitation of mineral resources to incentivise investors adequately while replacing the depleted assets with human capital development could provide a take-off for economic growth across the continent. It is, however, a take-off that could then only be sustained by good governance.[2]

This is a story about breaking the confines of one's circumstances, not only for Africa but for individuals the world over. It is an account of failures and successes, compromise and resoluteness, fear and humour.

This book has been informed by access to Sam Jonah himself, his private letters, Ashanti Goldfields's archive material, board minutes and other internal documents, as well as by nearly a hundred interviews – with Jonah, his family, friends, industry associates, rivals, international bankers and politicians. I also made extensive use of publicly available reports, newspaper articles as well as court and parliamentary records. The former president of Ghana, Jerry John ('JJ') Rawlings, and his wife, Nana Konadu, declined the opportunity to put their views across to me.

I make no claim to have produced a definitive biography, if such an entity even exists. The focus of this book is on Sam Jonah the businessman, and there are aspects of his life such as his extensive philanthropic work, which I do not even attempt to explore here.

In order to assist those readers who might not be familiar with Ghanaian terms and/or mining and financial terms I have compiled a select Glossary that starts on page 263. I wanted the text to have a Ghanaian flavour, which is why all of the chapter titles are English translations of Asante proverbs.[3] Many of these proverbs are well known and can be found online, with slight variations.

All of the travelling, research and writing expenses incurred in the course of this project were personally borne or indirectly met through the United Kingdom Economic and Social Research Council's sponsorship of my doctorate research. Within the limits of my ability I present my account of events and my own opinions.

My sincere thanks go to all those individuals who contributed in various ways to this book. Unless anonymity was requested, each person is named in the Acknowledgements on page 269. I must, however, particularly mention Sam Jonah, Rosaline Nutsugah, Baroness Lynda

Chalker, Andrea Nattrass, Christopher Paterson, Dusanka Stojakovic, Terry Morris, Robin Wade, Gareth Austin and Tim Leunig. Last but not least, my thanks to Ross Taylor for his endless humour and support over the eighteen months of this project.

'You must eat an elephant one bite at a time'

Sam Jonah is in the gold business. It is difficult to exaggerate the importance of this mineral in times of political and financial uncertainty, which is why an estimated four hundred billion dollars worth of bullion is held by the world's central banks.[1] Africa is one of the largest sources of gold: dominated by South Africa, the continent has produced nearly two-thirds of the world's gold since 1850.[2] Although its market share has declined in the last two decades with discoveries made elsewhere, the African continent still leads world production.[3] Surprisingly, for an industry so dependent on African countries and African workers underground, very few blacks have made it to positions of any authority overground.[4] Sam Jonah stood out in this regard. In September 1986 after almost one hundred years of operations in West Africa, the Ashanti Goldfields Corporation (AGC) appointed Jonah as the firm's first black African managing director.

AGC was incorporated in London in 1897 and listed on the London Stock Exchange soon afterwards. The location of the company's principal mine at Obuasi, in the Ashanti region of present-day Ghana, had been mined for centuries by local artisans using traditional methods before an astute Englishman, Edwin Arthur Cade, acquired a mining concession there in 1895.[5] Short and wiry with red hair, Cade worked as a London merchant specialising in West African trade.[6] He exported British-manufactured goods to one of his clients, an African trader named Joseph Biney,[7] who was based in Cape Coast, then the principal trading post in the British Gold Coast Colony. The colony's name derived from centuries of trade with Europeans, initially dominated by the

1

supply of gold dust and nuggets, but later slaves. In fact, gold mining and trading from the region pre-dated the arrival of the Portuguese in 1471, with an overland Saharan trade between Africans and Moors and Phoenicians.[8] Prior to the Witwatersrand discoveries in 1886, it is estimated that a third of the world's gold came from this area of West Africa where the Atlantic bends eastwards.[9] The stretch of ocean known as the Gulf of Guinea gave its name to the gold exported from here to mint guineas.[10]

Between 1877 and 1885 a rush of Europeans attempted to secure gold mining concessions in the south-west of the Gold Coast Colony.[11] Biney, along with two African friends, Joseph Ellis and Joseph Brown, responded to the financial opportunity by deciding to seek their own mining lease. None of the European gold hunters had gone beyond the borders of British protection in the colony into Ashanti territory. The three entrepreneurs – Biney, Ellis and Brown – despite the state-level rivalry between their tribe,[12] the Fante, who had joined forces with the British against their rivals the Asante, boldly used their language advantages over Europeans to locate the gold-rich Obuasi area under Asante suzerainty.[13] Obuasi had been deliberately kept secret from Europeans.[14]

Obuasi translates as 'under the rock' – a direct reference to the gold, which is found in a predominantly quartz geological formation. The three Fante entrepreneurs negotiated a hundred-year mine lease with the Bekwaihene (Bekwai king), an underlord of the Asantehene (Asante king). Although the Bekwaihene had taken control of the Obuasi area, the land did not belong to him. The rightful owners, the Adansi, had been chased away because they betrayed the Asante confederacy by requesting British protection.[15] Biney, Ellis and Brown and, at a later juncture, Cade took advantage of Asante's newly weakened political power. It had not always been this way.

The might and political sophistication of the Asante kingdom have long impressed historians.[16] The kingdom was founded in the seventeenth century by the unification of several clans led by the Oyoko. Its first king, Osei Tutu I, began geographic expansion through military action. The name Asante may derive from the words 'osa nti' (for the sake of war) applied to the Oyoko by their adversaries.[17] The kingdom radiated from Kumasi, the capital and home of the Golden Stool, with five core polities surrounded by outer subject territories. In English, the Golden Stool is sometimes inaccurately understood as the Asantehene's throne, but it is much more than a physical object. It was moulded in the early days of the kingdom to shape the ideology of the Oyoko rulers and their subjects. The Golden Stool symbolised the Asantehene's superordination – all other stools, representing chiefdoms, were by law to be made of inferior materials to reflect their subordination. The Asantehene's divine selection and powers, the kingdom's political sovereignty and the soul of the nation rested in the Golden Stool.[18]

The centralisation of power in Kumasi, effective tax collection, diplomacy, and the brutal treatment of enemies enabled a high level of control over the disparate ethnic groups under Asante power. At its peak in the early nineteenth century the kingdom covered most of what is Ghana today. The Asante fought off British control for nearly a century, finally succumbing in 1896. In 1902, after a final rebellion was quashed, Asante territory was declared a Crown colony. It was a kingdom whose strength had been tied to its gold wealth – not unlike today's modern economies. The Asantehene and his confederation of paramount chiefs had controlled gold production, as well as its northward movement for the Saharan trade and southward for coastal trade. The beginning of Asante's demise was marked by a progressive loss of sovereignty over the strategically important coastal fringe to the British, aligned with the Fante.

Biney used his trade contact with Cade to import small items of mining machinery from London. Ellis took charge of production. Unfortunately, their attempt to use modern technology to extract gold from the numerous artisanal pits scattered in the Obuasi area proved difficult.[19] In the first five years of operations most of their income came from the traditional miners who remained on the land and paid them a third of their output as rent.[20]

Disappointed with their modern mining experiment, Biney sent his English agent a few gold samples with the invitation to 'come and see!'[21] The men hoped to sell the lease on. Edwin Cade had the gold assayed by Johnson Matthey in London and its high gold content motivated him to rush to Obuasi. He set off from Liverpool in June 1895.[22] After a two-week sea voyage he arrived in Cape Coast. It took a further twelve days of travelling in a hammock carried by men on foot to reach Obuasi. The first part of the journey followed an old military road cut by the British during the Asante wars of 1872–74. The route then turned north-westerly and the going became much harder, switchbacking over endless thicket-covered hills, and through knee-deep swamps and streams. At Obuasi, Cade was immediately impressed by the indigenous mining skills and he collected random ore samples from a variety of locations on the property. The land was 'pregnant with gold' he wrote excitedly to his financial backers.[23]

There and then, Cade drew up a lease sale agreement. Scarcely believing his luck, he exploited the absence of any official maps to include two mines belonging to the Bekwaihene within the boundaries of his concession. Cade admitted: 'Whether or not he [the Bekwaihene] will think that I have overlapped him by my measurements later on, I do not here discuss. The deed is fully accepted, and what is now therein must remain.'[24] The vendors received a £200 deposit straight away.[25] The subjugation of Asante, which occurred in January 1896 when the British invaded Kumasi, could not have proved more timely for Cade. The British Secretary of State for the Colonies, Joseph Chamberlain, with his expansionist views of Empire,[26] ratified Cade's agreement. After the incorporation of the Ashanti Goldfields Corporation in London in May 1897, Biney, Ellis and Brown received a further £2500 along with 2179 shares of £1 each.[27] The consideration was far short of the vendors' £250000 asking price.[28]

Chamberlain's instrument to legalise Cade's purchase was a new agreement dated 3 June 1897 between AGC and the governor of the Gold Coast Colony, William Edward Maxwell. This broadly scoped 1897 agreement would govern AGC's operations for 70 years. It exempted the firm from many regulations later imposed by the colonial administration on the Gold Coast's burgeoning mining industry, and it shielded AGC from corporate responsibilities. For example, the £133 and £66 annual land rent agreed by Cade in 1895 to be paid to the Bekwaihene and the exiled Adansihene respectively, remained unchanged for 70 years thanks to the 1897 document, despite legal challenges by the traditional chiefs for a fairer share of the firm's fortunes.[29]

The British firm and its investors did very well right from the start. AGC produced and sustained growth in gold ounces, profits and dividends from the third year of operations. This placed AGC apart from its expatriate competitors established at the turn of the century in a gold rush, dubbed the 'jungle boom'. Most of these companies went bust soon after milking unsuspecting investors.[30]

It was well after political independence had been won in Ghana in 1957 that attempts were made to rebalance the relationship between the needs of the firm and that of its host country. In 1968 the London and Rhodesia Mining and Land Company (Lonrho) bought AGC and took the firm private. Lonrho offered the Ghana government 20 per cent equity ownership in exchange for support for a Lonrho takeover and an extension to the mine's lease. The government acceded. Following a military coup in 1972, the second since independence, more drastic measures were taken to redistribute Ashanti's earnings. A government decree gave the state 55 per cent ownership of the firm. Thereafter, through various taxes, royalties and dividends, the government's direct benefits from Ashanti's operations rose to 56 per cent of gross revenue.[31]

As a consequence of this once again unbalanced situation, new investment in capital dried up at the mine. Combined with the economic consequences of nine changes in government, mostly through coups d'état, in the space of 25 years following independence, Ashanti's output and profitability dwindled. In 1982 the company reported its first operating loss since 1898, and this in the face of buoyant gold prices.

In 1982 the Ghanaian economy was on the brink of total collapse. Inflation raged in triple figures, real gross domestic product (GDP) per capita had declined by 22 per cent between 1957 and 1982, and over the same period the ratio of investment to GDP fell 70 per cent.[32] Gold production at AGC, which had been falling dramatically since 1972, reached an all-time low in 1986.

It was at this nadir that Tiny Rowland, Lonrho's controversial managing director, promoted Sam Jonah, a career miner raised in Obuasi, to take control of the mine's management.

'The day a black man runs that company is the day I leave town,' Sam's father, Thomas, used to say in complete disgust at the atrophy of development since independence.

5

'It's time for you to leave town, Thomas,' his son proudly announced, breaking into a smile before spilling his news late in September 1986.

Thomas grunted. The expectation of failure was not just from his sceptical father. As Jonah was introduced into the white, male world that dominated the gold industry, the heat of the men's doubts about him burned into Jonah's resolve. He felt the weight of his colour, of his entire race, on his shoulders. Fortunately, his unique set of multiple 'identities' created a phenomenal opportunity to awaken the gold giant that he knew Ashanti could be. Not only was Jonah a Ghanaian, he was also a local boy brought up in Obuasi; not only had he worked at the mine since the age of nineteen, he was also superbly qualified technically. After Jonah's appointment as managing director he became a Lonrho employee, and at the same time he was a personal friend of prominent members of the ruling administration, Jerry John Rawlings's Provisional National Defence Council (PNDC). This combination of characteristics could potentially achieve a better balance in the relationship between the firm and the state while restoring the firm's fortunes.

Jonah was determined to build a 'First' World company, to dispel the unspoken belief that coming from the 'Third' World implied that he would be a third-rate businessman. However, as Jonah and Ashanti grew in international stature he would discover that the road to success was strewn with bridgeless chasms and near-vertical climbs.

CHAPTER I

'Money is sharper than a sword'

September–October 1999

No one saw it coming. 'I should imagine there would be a few fund managers being got out of bed in New York at the moment,' declared the chief executive of a major Australian gold mining group.[1] 'This is a very, very big surprise,' a leading analyst remarked.[2] It's 'incredible,' said another, 'I just keep shaking my head.'[3] The speed and heights of the gold price surge between Monday 27 September and Tuesday 5 October 1999 was nothing short of modern-day gold fever.

On Monday, New York's gold price closed at $281.90 – an increase of $13.50 on the previous trading day, the largest one-day rise in thirteen years. More records would be broken. Hectic trading on Tuesday hit $327.30 before cooling to $307.90 – still a massive 9.2 per cent jump on Monday's close. And the price would rocket further. By close of play a week later the spot price had reached $324. At the height of the fever closing prices had gained $56 in seven trading days; over the same period intraday spikes of nearly $90 were seen. The bullion market was thunderstruck.

The downward march of gold

From an all-time high of $875 an ounce in January 1980 gold had declined steadily to reach a low of $253.20 in July 1999. While technology and productivity gains in mining and lacklustre retail demand for jewellery brought prices down, the main reason for the decline was the behaviour of gold producers and central banks. An active forward selling market helped to dampen spot prices and falling inflation diminished the use of gold as a store of value. This partly motivated central banks, holding about a quarter of the world's out-of-the-ground gold stocks, estimated at 120 000 tonnes,[4] to offload their gold reserves. An announcement in May 1999 by the Old Lady of Threadneedle Street (the Bank of England), a former bastion for bullion, to auction 415 tonnes of gold deepened negative sentiment. The impact on the gold market belied the relatively small quantities involved because of the identity of the seller and the unwelcome signal this gave about the benefit of holding gold. The first Bank of England auction proceeded on 20 July and caused the gold price to sink to a twenty-year low.

To raise $2.3bn towards relieving the debt of the world's poorest countries, the International Monetary Fund (IMF) announced plans to liquidate 10 per cent of its gold reserves, totalling 310 tonnes. If producers and dealers were thinking that things could not possibly get any more bleak, they were wrong. The Central Bank of Switzerland followed with grander intentions of cashing in 1 300 tonnes of bullion, which was half its holdings.

In an effort to counter these developments, the World Gold Council (WGC), representing the gold industry, urgently lobbied the central banks against further sales. The WGC broadcast television adverts preying on individuals' turn of the millennium (Y2K) fears and the imminent pop of the dotcom bubble to promote gold's superiority as an investment. Thousands of citizens signed a WGC petition to voice their discontent at the central banks' sell-offs.[5] Gold producers lent their verbal support but simultaneously sold significant and rising proportions of their future production at the current low prices, fettering any upward price movement in the short term. Producers were hurting. Many mines wound down operations to a care-and-maintenance basis or quit altogether because production costs exceeded revenues.[6] Tens of thousands of miners worldwide faced redundancy.

The horizon appeared so gloomy that even when the IMF rejigged its plans to avoid dumping gold on the market by selling it privately to central banks instead, the move did little to restore confidence. What good would more unwanted bullion be in the hands of central banks? It did nothing to reverse the declining role of gold as a reserve asset. The Australian government's chief commodities' forecaster predicted, along with many analysts, a continued downward movement of gold prices.[7] With the adoption of the euro as an official currency in January 1999, the fate of the European members' 12 000 tonnes of gold reserves remained a particularly large cloud in the dark skies.

Since the central banks held more gold than they desired, some of this could be lent to bullion dealers and gold producers with interest. This interest rate, called the gold lease rate, was relatively cheap while the supply of gold was abundant. For example, monthly lease rates of 1 per cent early in 1999 compared to interbank money lending rates of 5 per cent. Speculators and gold producers could borrow gold at 1 per cent, sell it at today's price and lend on the proceeds or invest them in other securities at, for example, 5 per cent. With the gold price on a declining trend, gold could be bought back at a cheaper price in the future to return to the bullion lenders and make a sure profit – that is, as long as the gold price continued to fall and the lease rates remained low. By September 1999, the amount of gold on loan from central banks was estimated at more than 4 500 tonnes, about double what it had been five years earlier.[8] Borrowing an asset, in this case, gold, with a view to selling it in anticipation of a price fall to allow you to buy it back at a cheaper price is known as 'shorting' in trading jargon.

Parallel and related to the gold leasing phenomenon was the sharp growth of the gold derivatives market. Although a latecomer to derivatives, by the early 1990s the gold sector scintillated with dynamism and creativity in these instruments. Central banks themselves held significant gold futures and options positions.

By the end of the 1990s the bullion market was notable for the high levels of lending, high levels of shorting and high levels of derivatives trading. All three characteristics were interrelated. Then came the shock.

Gold fever strikes

On Sunday 26 September 1999, finance ministers and central bankers convened in Washington to discuss the IMF's revised debt relief plans. Media attention focused on this poverty agenda. Then, unexpectedly, fifteen European central bankers released a press statement. Firstly, they had agreed to limit bullion sales to 400 tonnes a year for the next five years, an amount that included the Bank of England's and Swiss Central Bank's already announced sales of 415 and 1 300 tonnes respectively. Secondly, the banks would not expand their gold leasing or futures and options positions. Thirdly, they stressed that 'gold will remain an important element of global monetary reserves'.[9] The restoration of gold as a reserve asset, the strategic unity and, above all, the certainty for the next five years set the market ablaze.

Investors who had fled bullion returned, attracted by the rising gold price. As 1999 drew to a close dotcom euphoria was turning green; nobody knew what blow-out to expect from the millennium bug; the Dow jittered towards the 10 000 level and the FTSE 100 threatened to dip below 6 000. All of a sudden gold seemed a safer bet than shares. But new investors played only a small part in the unprecedented gold price acceleration. In the opinion of many analysts, the price of gold was driven well above what could be expected from the confidence-boosting central bank decision, and way above the industry's supply and demand fundamentals.

The principal factor in the dynamic that made shorting profitable – falling spot prices – had literally and fantastically reversed overnight. Producers, hedge funds and speculators who had sold gold they didn't own were caught short. Those who could afford to, frantically bought gold to repay borrowings, propelling the price even higher. People were buying because they had to. In the preceding three years, shorting gold had also been successful because of the low gold lease rates. But now, with the central banks refusing to expand lending, the lease rate soared from 1 per cent earlier in the year to 9.93 per cent on 29 September.[10] Short sellers were being squeezed at both ends – by the price and the lease rate hikes.

The exact extent of short positions, and hence the potential zenith of the rally, was unknown. This is because gold is mostly traded over-the-counter (OTC), that is, directly between private parties rather than through a transparent exchange. Only the parties to OTC contracts know their exact trading position. Estimates of the amount of shorting ranged between 4 000 and 8 000 tonnes, about two to four times the annual production of new gold. If the upper estimate was to be believed, forced buying to honour bullion liabilities could rocket the gold price to $500 an ounce.[11]

There were grave implications for gold derivatives positions. The value of these instruments related directly to the higher spot price, the surge in price volatility and the lease rate hikes. On COMEX (New York's commodity exchange) and TOCOM (Tokyo's commodity exchange) it was estimated that gold futures contracts exceeded warehouse stocks by twenty times.[12] With the futures exchanges' set delivery dates in December, a continued rise in the gold price created the potential for a massive crunch when options well in the money could forseeably demand physical delivery of gold instead of the usual contract rollovers. There simply would not be the bullion to meet these commitments.

Gold, unlike pork or wheat, is more than merely a commodity. Gold is natural money. In fact, paper or coin money can be seen as the first derivative instrument of gold.[13] When currencies were backed by gold, the paper and coins merely represented the underlying asset.[14] Yet gold had assumed commodity status rather than money status. The difference is not that academic if you compare the consequences of a worldwide shortage of pork or the global ruin of pork producers to the demise of gold traders and producers. Astute analysts immediately appreciated the risk of a global financial meltdown. Should the gold market collapse, it could impact on the value of central bank reserves, credit supply and therefore interest rates; it could induce recessions in one country after another; not to mention the domino effect that failed bullion banks could have on other international financial institutions and markets.

For the shareholders of gold companies, the immediate interpretation of the gold price surge was positive. Gold producers' share prices jumped as much as 30 per cent in the two days following the central banks' strategic about-turn. The economy of South Africa, the world's largest gold producer, stood to benefit – the rally improved the share price of dominant gold firms, contributed to a strengthening of South Africa's currency, the rand, and reprieved miners facing redundancy. But there was no cheer at Ashanti Goldfields. Rumours flew between bankers and financial journalists that the increase in gold prices was about to sink the pan-African gold producer.

Ashanti Goldfields Corporation (AGC), the flagship Ghanaian mining company and the country's biggest private sector employer, was in many respects the stuff of legend. Its principal mine at Obuasi had been in operation for over a hundred years producing unusually high-yielding ore. Under the leadership of an African, Sam Jonah, the company had evolved from a single mine to an African multinational, managed at all levels by Africans with only a smattering of expatriates. Ashanti was the only over-a-million-ounces gold producer (known in the industry as a senior producer) not domiciled in the United States of America, Canada, Australia or South Africa. Mine peers, aware of the huge geological, technical and financial challenges peculiar to gold mining respected Jonah's operational achievements. His recent acquisition of gold mines across the African continent had catapulted Ashanti into an elite league of producers. In recognition of Jonah's outstanding performance in the industry, COMEX had planned to honour the chief executive with its CEO of the Year Award for 1999,[15] but, given all the talk about impending financial disaster, it was mutually agreed not to proceed. For the foreseeable future Ashanti's achievements would be buried by financial woes.

Trouble at Ashanti

If physical attributes alone were to determine leadership skills, then Sam Jonah's mere presence would give him an advantage. Big and black with a broad, quick-to-smile face, he is hard to miss – particularly in a global industry in which the upper echelons, due primarily to the capital-intensive nature of gold mining, are distinctly white. In contrast to Jonah, Mark Keatley, Ashanti's chief financial officer (CFO) at the time of the September 1999 gold rally, is an unobtrusive character. His remarkably youthful appearance may be envied in many walks of life, but is possibly a hindrance in the sphere of international business. What Keatley might lack in physical presence, however, is more than compensated for by his sharp mind, impressive memory and ability to work 24 hours a day if needed, often delivering results ahead of deadlines. The provenance of his accent is momentarily distracting. Years spent in Anglophone West Africa account for his slower, more enunciated speech.

On Wednesday 22 September, the day after the Bank of England's second gold auction Keatley knocked on the door to Jonah's office on the second floor of Gold House. Ashanti's modest headquarters are located near the Kotoka International Airport in Accra, off an arterial dual carriageway that links the north and south of the equatorial city. On entering Gold House a visitor's first sensation is one of relief to escape the blistering sun into an air-conditioned foyer. There is nothing impressive about the surroundings. A security officer sits behind an old, rather tall, dark wooden desk. As you walk up the stairs you pass an en-larged colour print of a gold-laden Asante chair and another of miners at work. The wooden furniture in the offices is tasteful, but the edges of the tables and the arms of the chairs reveal that they are old. Thanks to the dual-aspect windows, the second floor is lighter than the offices below. Jonah's office doubles as a conference room. A conference table seating twelve takes up most of the space. Parallel to this stands a large desk in front of a bay window. A comfortable three-piece lounge suite sits against the wall to the right of the door. Bold, contemporary African artworks decorate the walls.

Keatley and Jonah discussed the previous day's events. The market had expected the second Bank of England auction to portend a further plunge in gold prices, as it had on 20 July. But South African gold pro-ducers had unexpectedly buoyed the price by offering about 2 per cent above the pre-auction market rate.[16] On the back of this, the two men, as much like father and son as boss and subordinate, assessed the prob-ability and implications of a moderate gold price rise on the AGC hedge portfolio. Keatley reiterated his opinion that the factors depressing gold in the short and medium term had not changed; he felt that the South African auction manoeuvres were a transient blip and that gold had not yet bottomed.

Keatley had been appointed as Ashanti's CFO in October 1994. He had first encountered Jonah and Ashanti when he worked on African projects with the International Finance Corporation (IFC), a commer-cial arm of the World Bank. It had been a recommendation from IFC managers who were impressed by Jonah's technical knowledge and growth vision as the deputy managing director of the Obuasi mine that had prompted Tiny Rowland to appoint Jonah as the managing director (MD) of Ashanti in 1986. Under Jonah's helm, Ashanti worked closely with the IFC whose credibility paved the way for hitherto unheard of injections of capital. To lend to a part-private, part-state-owned company in a non-democratic African country plagued by military coups was a hefty ask. But the IFC managed to lead syndicates of international commercial banks to lend Ashanti a total of $245m to rehabilitate and expand Obuasi. It was during these IFC days that Ashanti made its first forays, initiated by Jonah, into hedging.

A gold denominated loan was concluded in March 1990 – gold was borrowed from bullion banks and sold for $40m cash to be repaid either in gold or cash, depending on movements in the gold price, lease rates and interest rates. The first put options (contracts giving Ashanti the right, without obligation, to sell gold at a fixed price at a future date) were bought in the second quarter of 1990: 29 424 contracts from Degussa, Ashanti's gold refiner.[17]

From 1996 a declining gold price had changed the economics of mining. In the face of falling prices, a mine will take a number of steps to remain profitable. It will drive down costs as much as possible, but, with a large proportion of fixed costs, mainly from capital equipment, it will try to expand production year-on-year with the same cost base. Ashanti attempted to do this. In addition, motivated by the downward trend in gold prices, the hedge book grew in size and complexity from the early IFC arrangements.

Newspapers reported Ashanti's use of exotic or complex derivatives as evidence that the hedge book was not used for hedging at all but for speculative profit.[18] Others insinuated that Jonah and his management team had been blinded by Wall Street gurus into buying products that they simply did not understand.[19] Mistakes were made, but these criticisms were either simplistic or plain wrong. Here are the facts.

The nature of Ashanti's hedge book

Ashanti, calculating that the price of gold would continue to trade in the $250–$270 region, designed its hedge book to realise an average price of at least $355. This would cover the cost of production as well as the company's financing and capital expenditure needs.[20] To achieve this, straightforward downside protection was obtained through forward

14

sales (contracts to deliver gold some time in the future at a price specified today) and the purchase of put options. Out of 22.6 million ounces
of reserves, 36 per cent (8 million ounces) were protected over the next
fourteen years through forward sales and puts. Buying puts provides
excellent price protection but they are expensive. To help finance the
cost of this downside protection 3.5 million ounces of gold were committed to selling call options. These are contracts obliging Ashanti to sell
gold at a specified price if the holder of the call chooses to exercise its
right to buy. On average, the premium earned on the sale of two calls
would cover the cost of purchase of one put contract.

Ashanti's hedge book also committed a further 7.6 million ounces
(ultimately of its own but initially borrowed from bullion dealers) to
lease rate swaps. The purpose of these instruments was to increase cash
flows into treasury to increase the average realised gold price of the
hedge book. Under these swap agreements Ashanti committed varying
amounts of ounces that converted into dollars either at the spot gold
price or at a set gold price. Ashanti would pay a floating lease rate on
these dollar amounts (on a monthly, quarterly or semi-annual basis) in
exchange for receiving fixed lease rate income. These fixed amounts
ranged between 0 per cent and 2.25 per cent.

So, at the time of the gold price surge Ashanti had 85 per cent of
reserves committed in one form or another. And out of the total amount
of ounces contained in the hedge book, 36 per cent could be described
as pure protected ounces.[21]

In June 1999, with the gold price fairly stable and below $265, and
with lease rates under 1.4 per cent, the value of Ashanti's hedge portfolio was a positive $290m. In the wake of the central banks' moratorium
at the end of September every dollar increase in the gold price knocked
approximately $10m off the value of Ashanti's hedge portfolio. But what
really sank the hedge book was the hike in gold lease rates. The design
of the hedge book aimed to protect an Ashanti ounce at around $355.
But every 1 per cent increase above 2 per cent in the gold lease rate
knocked $20 off that realisable price (through the cash outflow effects
of the lease rate swaps). Lease rates hit 9.9 per cent on 29 September and
remained above 5 per cent until mid-October. It was the combination
of the volatility and heights of the gold price as well as the gold lease

rate that pulled the book underwater to the tune of negative $570m.

This paper loss represented how much it would cost Ashanti to honour all of its hedge contracts immediately. Each type of instrument in the hedge book, from the vanilla to the more exotic structures, took a dive in value. But the lease rate swaps were disproportionately responsible for much of the depreciation, followed by the call options sold.

Stress-testing a hedge book should include extreme scenarios and indeed Ashanti did consider the effects of a sudden $50–$70 rise in the gold price. At an analysts' teleconference the CFO remarked in April 1999: 'Well, John, at 325 the book would be broadly neutral.'[22] The statement was true, assuming no change in lease rates. The subsequent ten-fold increase in lease rates, accompanied by a shooting gold price, far from producing a neutral portfolio burnt a hole right through it.

From glory to infamy

The hedge book that was now severely censured by the press followed the same management policy that had earned Jonah and his team global praise in the preceding years.[23] Just months before the crisis Keatley as CFO and his treasurer, Mona Caesar-Addo, were profiled in Corporate Finance magazine as 'Dealmakers of the Month'.[24] Jonah was proud of Ashanti's sophistication and reputation in this area. Hedging had been introduced under his watch, and it had become inextricably meshed with production.

Until the end of September 1999 Ashanti's hedging strategy had worked beautifully. Hedged income was less volatile than the unhedged income flows, and Ashanti always realised a price above spot for its gold. In fact, from the last quarter of 1996 income earned from the hedge book consistently exceeded operating profit. This hedging income was no secret; it was plainly and properly disclosed in Ashanti's annual reports and regulatory filings. Hedging enhanced Ashanti's ability to borrow by giving lenders confidence in income streams. After price protection, Ashanti's stated objective in its hedging strategy was 'to raise cash in order to pay back debt or to finance capital expenditure or acquisitions'.[25] These are, as Barrick (North America's largest gold producer) and other industry giants would argue, legitimate, shareholder

16

value-enhancing objectives, which can outweigh the risks of hedging.[26] Obviously, when Ashanti's hedge book lead-balled in value to a negative $570m it shattered shareholder value. So what had gone wrong if its hedging policy had worked well until then?

What went wrong?

Two things went wrong. The first factor was out of Ashanti's control and if history could be played back Jonah likely would not have changed his actions — even with the benefit of hindsight. The second factor should have and could have been better managed or even avoided.

In the first place, Jonah made a judgement call — shared by the majority of the bullion market — that gold prices would continue to fall,[27] and the design and profitability of the Ashanti hedge book reflected this. With the market information available from 1996 until 26 September 1999, particularly the actions of central banks oversupplying the market with leased gold and the aggressive and growing hedging activities of producers, it was reasonable to take a position that gold prices would continue to fall. The odd contrary voice proselytised that the gold market had already bottomed, for example, John Hathaway's respected but minority view prior to the European central banks' shock decision.[28] Jonah made a judgement call that a rapid hike in the gold price was remote. The bombshelled bullion market and press coverage following the banks' famous announcement reflected the unlikelihood of such an event. Consequently, it is fair to say that Jonah's assessment of a downward trend in gold prices and Ashanti's design of a hedge book to fit this expectation would not have changed even with hindsight.

While conscious of liquidity risk and addressing it by negotiating as generous credit limits as possible with each hedge counterparty, it transpired that Ashanti did not have the in-house capability to *accurately* assess its liquidity risk exposure. It only had the technological and personnel know-how to *roughly* value the more complex derivatives to changes in the gold price and lease rate. For the non-standard elements in the hedge book Ashanti relied on hedge counterparties to supply it with individual valuations that were then summed up on an Excel spreadsheet. But the sum of the bilateral positions did not give a complete picture of Ashanti's total liabilities. With knock-outs, knock-ins, gamma, delta, kappa, lambda and rho considerations, precisely calculating the changing value of the entire portfolio did not only sound like Greek. In fact, only two or three brains on planet Earth had the capability to do so. Ashanti's inability to value the more complicated instruments in the hedge book independently and accurately should have triggered internal control warning lights. Had Ashanti abided by the old derivatives adage: 'Don't trade what you can't value',[29] then the hedge book would have been far simpler, less profitable but also less vulnerable to huge value wipe-outs. This was a lesson learnt.

When you promise to deliver gold at a future date the counterparty to the OTC deal is exposed to the possibility that you will fail to honour the contract. Depending on your circumstances the counterparty may demand collateral to offset any such credit risk. Ashanti operated in a country where governments (past and present) had meddled in private business. Lonrho's mining lease had itself been cancelled by fiat in 1972.[30] In 1992, the lease of Vacuum Salt Products Limited met a similar fate.[31] With such country-specific political risks, hedge counterparties understandably set collateral requirements for Ashanti's hedging contracts. Ashanti traded with nineteen hedge banks but two of them, N.M. Rothschild and Engelhard, did not impose any credit limits; the remaining seventeen hedge counterparties had varying kick-in points before security, or margin, would be demanded. In aggregate, the banks allowed Ashanti to be in the red by $300m before having to post margin. One econometrician calculated that had Ashanti's book comprised solely vanilla-type contracts then the impact of the gold rush would have been a loss of −$277m. This would have been within Ashanti's $300m margin-free trading limit, so avoiding margin calls.[32] But with a book loss of −$570m the hedge counterparties requested $270m from Ashanti to reassure them of the company's continued ability to meet its commitments. The trouble was that Ashanti only had $70m ready cash.

The proverbial hits the fan

Ashanti was not the only gold producer to find itself caught with a hedge book designed for more pessimistic times: Sons of Gwalia,

Emperor, Cambior, even Barrick, faced a similar predicament. But, unlike Ashanti, other senior world producers had cash in the bank to meet their margin requirements, which were generally less onerous, or they could afford to repurchase their hedge positions. Ashanti's recent acquisitions drive, an industrial strike at Obuasi in May 1999, weather-related production problems at its mine in Guinea and the cost of developing a lucrative concession in Geita, Tanzania, had sapped cash.

The first margin call came on Tuesday 28 September. It was only a matter of time before others followed. Shock and disbelief charged through Jonah as the markets played out his most remote fears. Just days earlier a rapid $50 jump in the gold price had seemed improbable, and a rapid $50 jump with a simultaneous 1 000 per cent catapult of lease rates, impossible. He telephoned Ghana's minister of finance and Ashanti's chairman, Richard Kwame Peprah, who was attending a conference in Bermuda: 'The shit has hit the fan.'

The firm's inability to meet the hedge collateral demands constituted a breach of other loan terms and conditions. In addition to the seventeen hedge counterparties there were twenty-three revolving credit facility banks, three project finance lenders and numerous bondholders. Many bank institutions found themselves in all these categories. The hedge parties were in a position to declare Ashanti insolvent, which would draw in the other creditors to scramble over the company's diminished assets. With a balance sheet debt of $400m, the banks' total credit exposure to Ashanti, including the hedge losses, touched $1bn as the gold price continued its ascent.

The newspapers had a field day: 'Gold Giant Digs itself into a Hole';[33] 'Ashanti Glisters but may not be Gold';[34] 'Ashanti in Meltdown as Gold Spike Exposes Hedging Loss';[35] Empire building goes horribly awry for Jonah, the would-be African Tiny Rowland.[36] Between 27 September and 6 October 1999 Ashanti's share price collapsed from $9 to $4.

Thirty-two thousand Ghanaian shareholders, mostly owners of single shares, joined by eighteen million compatriots who saw themselves as 'honorary shareholders', attacked Jonah on radio, television and through the country's burgeoning private press. How could a company lose money when the price of its product had gone up? People concluded that only gross mismanagement and corruption could account for such a paradox and Jonah was judged guilty of ruining the nation's prime asset. The crisis appeared to confirm President Rawlings's public declarations that Jonah was a common criminal.

A rack of missiles released by hedge counterparties, bankers, shareholders and the international press fell towards Jonah and Ashanti. In the pause before they detonated, the beleaguered chief executive prepared to lose the job and career he had planned and painstakingly forged from the age of nineteen. It was one thing to lose his job, but a spectacular and public rift between Jonah and Ghana's President Rawlings threatened worse. One way or another many of Rawlings's enemies eventually lost their dignity or wealth, and in several prominent cases their lives.[37] Jonah pictured Rawlings's smile as the president contemplated his luck: events had placed Jonah's neck neatly between his hands.

CHAPTER 2

'Do not follow the path. Go where there is no path to begin the trail'

1949–69

Samuel Esson Jonah was born on 19 November 1949 in Kibi, a military base in the eastern part of the Gold Coast Colony. This was a politically explosive time. Changes precipitating the Gold Coast's independence in 1957 started in the aftermath of riots in Accra in 1948. On Saturday 28 February 1948 a peaceful rally of war veterans protesting over their pensions was violently disrupted when a policeman, fearing the unarmed men were heading for the governor's residence, shot into the crowd. Several days of rioting ensued with European stores looted and vandalised. By the end of the disturbances 29 Africans were dead and hundreds injured.[1]

Austere economic conditions had been endured during the Second World War as the colony directed funds to the extraction of valuable materials such as bauxite, manganese and industrial diamonds, for the British war effort. Immediately after the war, further hardships arose from inflation and shortages of consumer goods.

An array of nationalist political parties capitalised on the economic situation to crystallise anti-colonial feelings. The United Gold Coast Convention (UGCC), established in 1947, emerged as the most prominent party. Its executive council comprised Gold Coasters who had been educated abroad, notably its leader, J.B. Danquah, and secretary, Kwame Nkrumah. The entire UGCC leadership was wrongly held responsible for instigating the riots and was swiftly imprisoned. This only raised the party's political prestige and galvanised national support. When an independent commission cleared the six men of any involvement in the riots, and fearing further political unrest from one of its most economically important colonies, the British government was forced to fast-forward its plans to devolve political power on the Gold Coast.[2]

A new constitution was formulated that permitted an indirectly elected Legislative Assembly with an African majority. Before this had been effected Nkrumah split from the UGCC. He accused Danquah of conservatism and formed his own, more radical, Convention People's Party (CPP). At the risk of oversimplification, the newly created CPP broadly won the support of the youth, farmers and trade unions. This left the UGCC's natural constituency as the indigenous elite: mercantilists, professionals and chiefs. This broad-brush distinction would permeate Ghana's post-colonial politics.

Demanding 'Self-government *now!*' Nkrumah launched his Direct Action campaign to physically frustrate European-controlled enterprises and the colonial administration. This led to a second spell in prison for Nkrumah, but his CPP won the first Legislative Assembly elections in 1951. In a dramatic reversal of roles, Nkrumah was released as a prisoner to become the head of government business. Although Governor Charles Arden-Clarke maintained veto powers, these were in practice politically redundant.

With an African in charge of the budget, in the first step towards complete political devolution, Nkrumah placed new emphasis on visible development projects such as infrastructure, schools and hospitals. For the Jonah family, the arrival of a seventh child (hence Sam's middle name, Esson, meaning seven) coincided with these momentous times.

The Jonah household

Sam was the fifth child to survive; two babies had died before their first birthdays. Soon after his birth, Sam's father, Thomas, left the army. He had reached the rank of sergeant major and had served during the Second World War as part of the Royal West African Frontier Force. Thomas decided to set up his own construction company. This decision may have been influenced by the treatment of the ex-serviceman in 1948. However, along with a significant minority whose collective voice has been largely silenced in the historical record, Thomas did not support the anti-colonial element of the Accra riots. His motive for entering private enterprise was more likely an appreciation of the business opportunities that the colony's development agenda created for those who had construction skills. The number of construction companies in the Gold Coast jumped from 27 in 1949 to 89 between 1950–59.[3]

Thomas moved his wife, Beatrice Sampson, and their five children to Obuasi in 1950. Three daughters were born after the move. The British mining firm, the Ashanti Goldfields Corporation (AGC), dominated Obuasi's employment opportunities and Thomas could readily obtain subcontractor work there. In addition, Beatrice's home town of Assin Kushea was only 35 miles south of Obuasi, which would have allowed better access to the practical benefits of the extended family, had Thomas permitted it.

Beatrice was an Assin. The Assin are a subgroup of the Fante, who in turn are a subgroup of the Akan. The Akan include the majority Twi-speaking Asante population in Ghana. The Twi and Fante languages are similar; someone speaking the one can understand a person speaking the other. Thomas was also a Fante, originating from the Cape Coast area. The children were strictly Assin, since the Akan practise matrilineal heritage. Beatrice belonged to the royal family of Assin Kushea, which could reliably trace its origins to the late seventeenth century when a King Agyensem of Kushea was recorded as a prominent visitor to Kumasi.[4] The chieftaincy was a lucrative one. Thanks to timber and other natural resources in the area the Agyensems were able to build palaces in Kumasi and Cape Coast as well as in Kushea. Thomas did not want his children to get puffed up with the idea of being little princes and princesses. Consequently, he forbade visits to Kushea where he knew that the children's relative, the Queen Mother, would spoil them. Nevertheless, the children often spent time with their uncle, Nana Prah Agyensem V in his Kumasi residence.

In 1950, Obuasi was the fifth-largest town in the Gold Coast Colony, with a population of about 16 000.[5] Like most mining towns, Obuasi was, and still is, drab and shabby. The land belonged to the mine, which, out of fear of subsidence affecting underground workings, did not grant permits for multiple-storey buildings. Until recently the inhabitants of the town were afraid to make any ostentatious improvements to their

properties for fear of being of accused of gold theft. Most of the buildings are single-storey, tin-roofed and covered in red-brown dust. A saggy
network of self-connected electricity and telephone lines and crooked
television aerials hover above the houses, adding to the disorderly feel.
The odd whitewashed house or two-storey building are new developments. Forested, undulating hills silhouette the skyline. This is another
relatively recent change. Residents will tell you that twenty years ago
the hills around the mine were bare due to the arsenic compounds released into the air from the old ways of producing gold.

Sam Jonah grew up in one of the nondescript houses on the main
road. At the time his father built it in 1950 it was one of the best houses
in town. Thomas inscribed on it, '*Wobisa wo din enye wo sika*' (literally,
they ask about your name, not your money), meaning that who you are
is always more important than what you have. Although you could enter
the house from the main road, everyone used the stepped entrance at
the back on the parallel dirt road. All the rooms opened onto a central
courtyard. There were two storage rooms, a living room, the parents'
bedroom, one bedroom for all the girls and another for all the boys.

In order of descending seniority the children were Margaret (named
after Thomas's mother), Nathaniel, Ernest, Victor, Samuel, Vida, a second
Margaret (this one named after Thomas's sister) and Hetty. At home, the
children were called by their day names. Since both Victor and Sam
were born on a Sunday, Victor was called Kwesi Panyin (literally, Kwesi
the elder) and Sam, Kwesi Kakraba (the younger) or alternatively, Kwesi
Ketewa (little Kwesi). This was ironic as Sam was bigger and taller than
Victor. When one of Beatrice's sisters, Hetty, died suddenly, her two
children, Garnet and Mavis, were raised as the family's own. Besides
these cousins, other relatives were constantly staying for varying periods
of time. At meal times, in particular, the number of people in the courtyard would swell to enjoy Beatrice's renowned hospitality.

It was often said that Thomas had forgotten that he had left the army
as he ran his home on military lines. The children would get up at 4.30
a.m. to fetch water from the communal pipe, which was located near the
house because of Thomas's status in the town. Without running water in
the building there was no toilet at home until 1969 when the house was
modernised. Before that everyone used the public latrine about a hundred

yards away, near the Anglican school. Water had to be fetched every morning for bathing and cooking. Sam was nominated by his father to fetch water for elderly or respected people who lived nearby. This group included Julius Opara, an AGC employee who everyone believed to be very important at the mine. Years later Sam would discover that Julius was a clerk in the transport department. But with the limited scope of opportunities for Africans at the time this was not to be decried.

Childhood adventures

Victor, Garnet and Sam were each separated by a year in age. The three were always together and their world was one of constant adventure. Despite the strong culture of seniority, which would have designated Victor as the natural leader among them, the initiative for different escapades varied among the boys. Although they quarrelled and at times a duumvirate condemned one to isolation, this never lasted long. The affection between them was too strong. For example, when eating fufu (pounded yam and plantain) and soup in a communal bowl, Kwesi Panyin would hide some meat under the fufu nearest to Kwesi Ketewa, just to make sure that he was not deprived by the large number of visitors' hands.

One day when Sam and Garnet were four and five years old respectively, they plotted to accost two white men. They confidently strode up to two golfers and blurted in made-up English, 'Ano-we, ano-wa, ano-golfman!' Amused by their antics, or perhaps in condescension, one of the men dropped a coin towards them. The boys grabbed it off the turf and ran home elated that they had been rewarded for speaking such impressive English.

Sometimes the threesome explored barefooted in the forest, eating wild oranges despite adult warnings that they would fall sick if they did. Days were spent chasing birds, setting traps and fishing in nearby streams with improvised rods. They avoided a part of the town where the water, polluted by the mine, was black – nobody ventured there. With other children they played football in an area that everyone called Senet Park. Unknown to them, Senet was an adulteration in the pronunciation of cyanide. The concrete-like surface was the dried-out, contaminated residue from the mine's treatment plant, but it made an excellent football ground.

The boys loved football. The town buzzed whenever visiting clubs came to play the local mining side. Sometimes a reserve team from Kumasi's famous Kotoka club would come to Obuasi. Unable to pay the gate fee the three burrowed under the corrugated iron wall of the makeshift Horsey Park ground to get inside. If they were unlucky a boot or two would kick their hands and heads away, but that never stopped them from trying.

Once a week Beatrice sent the trio to nearby villages and markets to sell her home-made articles – sometimes underwear, sometimes bofroat (tasty fried doughnuts). One of the boys would ring the small handbell used by traders to announce their presence; another would shout whatever it was that they were selling that day; and the third would carry the goods. They took turns in these roles. 'Cling-cling! Cling-cling!' 'Bofroat-o! Bofroat-o!'

On other occasions the boys roamed onto mine property. They retrieved out-of-date cans thrown out by the mine's trading store and hid nearby to eat the contents. They wondered why the Europeans were so wasteful. But they did like some things about them. Their cemetery was a great playground; it was like a garden, unlike the overgrown, ghost-like African one, which they dared each other to enter.

One day the boys decided to try to make some money by selling their dog's beautiful puppies. They carried them in a cardboard box to the European mine bungalows. At one house, a man opened the door. He looked from their beaming faces to the box and back at them, and then, leaving the door ajar, he disappeared inside. The happy thought that he would return with money lasted just a few seconds before a large guard dog leapt from the interior darkness. The puppies were knocked into the air. As the boys scrambled over the nearest wall they turned to see the puppies being mauled into shreds. Hot tears streamed down Sam's face. The colour of the man was of no relevance to the boys. As far as they were concerned, their misfortune was as a result of them being where they were not supposed to be. Sam wanted to blurt the details to his mother, but his fear of a beating suppressed the urge.

Thomas and Beatrice

Both Thomas and Beatrice would mete out corporal punishment to their children. Most of the time the beatings related to a specific transgression and you knew when you had earned one. One Saturday, however, the threesome had completed their house chores and homework and so went to play football. At the age of eight Sam had set up a football team, the 'Simple Winners', and equipped them with matching football shirts that his father had obtained from Nigeria. On this particular Saturday they were enjoying a game with local boys when Thomas suddenly appeared in the distance. He clapped his hands, and from the tone of his voice as he shouted their names the boys spontaneously burst into tears. They racked their brains for sins of omission and commission as they crossed the football pitch towards home. The beating for idleness that ensued was harsh and Beatrice eventually interceded on the boys' behalf. Their mother was no soft touch herself. As the boys grew bigger and she could not dominate them physically she would postpone their comeuppance for misbehaviour until dawn, when they were still in bed sleeping and unable to retaliate. After locking the door to prevent the next-door neighbours from intervening she would pour a bucket of icy water over the culprit followed by a thrashing with a cane or a belt. That said, her punishments were more predictable.

Fortunately, from the boys' perspective, Thomas's construction work kept him away from home for weeks at a time. The disadvantage was that his return dates were unknown, so there was never any permanent sense of relaxation. Since their father's favourite saying was 'a boy's best friend is his book', the children routinely posted someone as a sentry and each child kept a book at hand to feign studying when Thomas's approach was signalled.

Their father was an enigma to the young boys. He was both authoritarian and liberal. He wouldn't hesitate to remove his sandal to beat his children, but he insisted that they call him by his first name, Thomas, which was unheard of at the time, and was interpreted by other parents as an encouragement of disrespect for elders. Thomas also forbade the younger children from addressing their elder siblings with the prefix, 'Sister ' or 'Brother', for example, 'Sister Margaret' or 'Brother Nat'. The practice was, and still is, common in many Ghanaian families as a sign of respect in the age-biased society, but Thomas hated the notion that age alone merited respect or superiority. Respect had to be earned and everyone was equal. He distributed household chores according to ability, not seniority. He was both folksy and frightening. He could be very charming: women loved him; his older children and adults in general admired his sharp wit; and although the young boys often associated him with fear he could also make them laugh.

Occasionally he would march them all with baskets into the forest to look for snails. Their initial moaning about the task soon gave way to a fun, competitive search. Thomas would collect his own and when satisfied with their efforts they would march back home. On their return their father divided the snails into parcels and sent each child to deliver one to an individual in the town. In a practical way he was teaching them to be generous. Sometimes he would give all the snails away. On other occasions he would keep a handful to make his special dish, snail soup. When the children returned from their errands they would all tuck in, enjoying the treat and laughing at Thomas's boasts to Beatrice of his culinary excellence.

Beatrice's social life centred on the Anglican Church. She took it upon herself to make the choristers' and priests' vestments, and arrived at church early to arrange things needed for the service. Although a Salvation Armyist, Thomas did not discourage his wife and children from going to the Anglican Church. In fact, he built a mission house for the Anglicans and sent Sam to live there for a while with the young Anglican priest, Edmund Yeboah. During this time Sam developed a childlike affection for the church and genuinely contemplated fulfilling his father's desire for him to become a priest. Thomas had specific career goals for each of his sons. He wanted Nathaniel to be a lawyer, Ernest a prison officer – since his great friend was the country's first Ghanaian director of prisons – Victor to be a sea captain, and Sam to be a priest. The absence of career goals for his daughters is perhaps noticeable to us in the twenty-first century, but it was not so strange in the 1950s.

The children enjoyed a childhood without want as Thomas's business thrived and he was soon involved with road construction across the colony. The 1950s were prosperous years for the Gold Coast. Further constitutional changes permitted a general election in June 1954, which Nkrumah's CPP won. An exclusively African cabinet was subsequently formed. In August 1954, J.B. Danquah headed a new opposition party, the National Liberation Movement (NLM), assisted in its overseas fund-raising efforts by Dr Kofi Busia. Although the NLM was accused of tribalism because of its strong support base in the Ashanti region, the party incorporated Northern and Ewe opposition parties. The NLM lobbied for a federalist system of government that delayed independence by necessitating another general election in 1956. CPP victory ended the federalist movement and independence quickly followed at the stroke of midnight on Tuesday 5 March 1957, when the new nation took on a new name, Ghana.

Families tuned into the radio to hear Nkrumah's independence speech. Ghana, the first black African country to gain its independence was blazing a trail, which Nkrumah intended to extend across the continent: 'We again rededicate ourselves in the struggle to emancipate other countries in Africa; for our independence is meaningless unless it is linked up with the total liberation of the African continent.'[6] Celebrations lasted for days. Beatrice chastised Thomas for blackening the joyous occasion with his pessimistic predictions for the country in the hands of Africans. His minority view was based on simple observations between the way the whites did things and the way the Africans did – the state of the local cemeteries being a favourite case in point. Although Thomas's superficial reasoning was erroneous, his omens would sadly come true, but for more complicated reasons.

Elementary school

Beatrice's first cousin, Master Aitkens, was the head teacher at Obuasi Anglican Elementary School. The boys frequently found themselves pulling their shirts on as they ran barefooted as fast as they could to arrive before the school bell stopped tolling. Regular bouts of stomach illness (later identified as a duodenal ulcer and operated on), frequently kept Sam away from school for days at a stretch. Yet still, he always topped his class tests and was the class prefect each year. His father displayed each child's academic report on a wall at home. Stragglers were shamed or caned to encourage them to imitate the high achievers. However, there was no jealousy between Victor, Garnet and Sam. They admired Sam's abilities; he was a sweet, clever boy. And Sam himself, while proud of his achievements, did not laud them over his siblings and cousins.

The Common Entrance Exam was taken any time after the age of eleven. The few who passed would go on to secondary school. Those who passed extremely well hoped to continue their education in Cape Coast, the home of long-established, missionary-founded grammar schools. Sam beat everyone else at the school and passed well enough to continue to Adisadel College, the Anglican boys' grammar school in Cape Coast. Victor and Garnet went in the same year to less prestigious schools in the harbour town of Takoradi. One of Sam's elementary school friends, Richard Kwame Peprah, also did well. Richard had only been in Obuasi for a year as his father's job as a police commissioner moved the family around the country. He decided to go to Achimota College, a co-educational grammar school in Accra. Despite the short time that they spent together, Richard and Sam became good friends. Their paths would cross again as adults.

Secondary school

The experience of going away to boarding school provoked a mixture of fear and excitement in Sam. While he was a second-generation liter-ate, many of the children of his generation were the first in their families to go to secondary school and they left home with the hopes and missed opportunities of their parents and relatives on their shoulders. It is hard to describe the culture shock that some boys from rural areas and small towns experienced when they arrived at these esteemed educational institutions. Some had never worn shoes before, had not eaten with cutlery and had not enjoyed three meals a day. Those who had been the stars of their provincial schools now met with students who were more clever and sophisticated. As Adisadel was an all-boys school, these awk-ward awakenings were endured without the judgemental eyes of girls. Some boys who went to the co-educational Achimota College never redeemed themselves before the fairer sex for carrying their shoes in their hands and walking barefoot – not realising that the expensive shoes required on the uniform list were supposed to be worn at all times.

State transport buses picked up students on their way to Cape Coast. Trunks filled with the prescribed uniform, and tuck boxes for snacks and provisions, popularly called 'chop boxes', were loaded on top. Most students looked forward to these journeys and the opportunity to make friends with students from other schools. While boarding a Cape Coast bus at the Kumasi central station, John Otoo, a manly-looking student on his way to Adisadel for the first time, dropped his chop box; it flew wide open as it hit the dust. Unable to afford provisions, Otoo's family had only managed to send him off with a chop box to hold both his uniform and the few tins of sardines that they had scrimped to buy. The laughter from other first form students – initially at his seeming ignorance that a chop box was not meant for clothes, and then at the realisation that he was too poor to fill it with food – cut him to pieces. On a one-to-one basis he would have silenced those laughing with his superior strength, but on this occasion Otoo's fists were impotent.

Adisadel College (commuted to Adisco by the students) started as the Society for the Propagation of the Gospel Grammar School located near Cape Coast Castle in 1910.[7] In 1924 the Anglican Mission changed the school name to St Nicholas Grammar School. With increasing demand for places, the school moved in 1929 to larger premises on a hilltop on the outskirts of Cape Coast and it gradually assumed the name of the nearby village, Adisadel. The spirit of the school is captured in the words of Reverend Alan John Knight, the English headmaster who established the school in its new location: 'We specialise in the wholly impossible.'[8] These were not empty words; Knight firmly believed in them. When the contractor employed to build the new school failed to make sufficient progress, Knight organised the boys and with the help of a local foreman the majority of the construction work was completed by the students themselves. When there were no universities in the colony, Adisadel students were encouraged to complete University of London overseas graduate programmes through correspondence. Knight's self-help attitude and his refusal to acknowledge obstacles left a strong legacy.

Character-building and academic achievement were the core educational philosophies of the school's founders, as well as the Gold Coast colonial administration. This replicated the educational experience and values of these Eton–Marlborough and Oxford–Cambridge men. Their enthusiasm and energies cannot be criticised. However, the appropriateness of a curriculum that, for example, prided itself on performing *Antigone, Agamemnon* and *Acestes* in the original Greek, without consideration for the colony's economic development needs was regrettable. Even after independence in 1957, the elitist approach to secondary school education and contempt for vocational skills, particularly those agricultural in nature, continued. Peripheral changes were made to the content of particular subjects, such as the substitution of Ghanaian and African history for British Empire, European and ancient history, but the central ethos remained unchanged.

In 1961, Nkrumah instigated a scientific drive and established the University of Science and Technology in Kumasi. At Adisadel, the headmaster, T.J. Drury, responded by removing Greek from the curriculum and creating a new science department. Traces of the school's classical tradition remained in the use of Greek and Latin words in everyday school-life: the headmaster's house was known as the Acropolis; a class prefect was referred to as the Dux; toilets were called torpors; each house had a Latin motto and the school motto itself was '*Vel primus vel cum primis*' (either the first or with the first).

When they arrived for the first time in September 1962, Sam, John Otoo and the ninety or so other first formers absorbed the school's formidable grounds. The gated drive, bordered by royal palms, led to a gravel forecourt dominated by an intricate water fountain. The first building to come into sight was the chapel on the left. Then, immediately in front, stood a long, whitewashed building with arched verandas where the headmaster's office and administration were located. Continuing in line with the administration block and in the same architectural style were two-storey classroom buildings and the assembly hall, Canterbury Hall. Parallel to the classrooms and Canterbury Hall were four dormitory blocks: Hamlyn, Elliot, Canterbury and Knight (all named after important figures in the school's and the Anglican Church's histories). A neat lawn, with a clock tower at its centre, separated the two rows of buildings. The dining hall, at the top of the lawn, formed a

U-shape with the other blocks. Standing beneath the 'Manners Maketh Man' inscription above the dining hall doors and looking straight ahead, the clock tower and fountain were perfectly aligned. Behind the classroom block was a pathway known as Appian Way. From here 89 steps descended the hill to the school's sports fields and the newer dormitory blocks: Jubilee, Quaque and Aglionby. Each house had a common room, library and refectory where chop box food could be eaten. Sparked by the Congo war in 1961, the students took to calling the old school compound at the top of the hill, Leopoldville, and the newer buildings in the valley Katanga, representing the secessionists in the crisis. Looking southwards from Leopoldville the palm-fringed sea and lagoons of Cape Coast filled the horizon.

The first formers arrived at Adisadel a week earlier than the rest of the students. They ranged in age from twelve to seventeen. This first week was devoted to orientation and induction. The school prefects arrived early to take on this responsibility. The 'homos' as the newcomers were termed, were imbibed with the school's traditions and rules. On a practical level, they were shown how to use a knife and fork and even personal hygiene issues were discussed for the benefit of all. The homos were prepared by the prefects for a week of bullying, an initiation tradition that would start with the arrival of the other students and end on the second Saturday of term with 'homos night'. On that Saturday the homos dressed up like fetishes, draped in white bedsheets with powdered white faces; only wearing one shoe they paraded about the school singing to the tune of *Holy Holy Holy*, 'Homos homos homos; We are very foolish, we've come to Adisco to be sensible'. After supper they displayed hidden talents in Canterbury Hall in a concert that culminated in singing the school song and receiving 'the blessing' as official Santa Clausians – a name derived from the patron saint of the school, St Nicholas.

Sam was proud of himself when the initiation week came to an end. He had endured his fair share of humiliations during the week. A second former had found it very amusing to draw a clock showing 2.00 p.m. on a piece of paper; he pinned this to the wall and ordered Sam to kneel on the hard concrete floor of his dormitory until five minutes past two. Sam obeyed, laughing at the ingenuity, but numbness and pain soon set in. He was only released after a couple of hours when the senior gave in to his pleas for relief. Sam only cried once during the week. His parents had assured him that a fifth former, the son of the Obuasi railway station manager, would look after him on his arrival. On the afternoon of the 'day of blessing', on the last day of homos week, this fifth former took Sam to the cricket green and boxed him in the face. As he was seeing stars he heard the senior explain, 'That's to make you respect me; if I don't bully you, you won't respect me.' Sam thought that this was an odd way to gain respect; if anything, the boy's unnecessary cruelty had the opposite effect. In addition to the physical pain Sam felt, his feelings were hurt because he had trusted the boy. On homos night Sam recited a poem, 'People will talk about you', which received humorous applause. All in all he had come out of the week respectably and walked about with a more confident gait than many of his peers.

Initially, new boys made friends with other first formers who shared the same class and house. Sam was in Hamlyn House whose motto was '*Una Mente*' (one mind). The dormitories were arranged on two floors with the juniors, Forms 1 to 3, on the top floor and the seniors on the ground floor. Each compartment comprised two bunk beds separated by a large desk seating four with cabinets beneath for toiletries and drawers for books. John Otoo, Sam and a Cape Coast boy, Tim Brew, quickly struck up a friendship as they were all in Hamlyn and Form 1B.

The morning bell rang at 5.00 a.m. allowing a period for exercise and dormitory cleaning duties before bathing. Morning assembly was held in Canterbury Hall at 7.30 a.m. with the headmaster and teachers in their graduation gowns. Two periods of classes were followed by breakfast. Then there were six more classes, interrupted by a short twenty-minute break. The school day ended at 1.30 p.m. for lunch. After lunch the boys returned to their dormitories for a one-hour siesta. The afternoons were free for them to indulge in the impressive variety of clubs and hobbies on offer. There was a jazz club, a photographic society fully equipped with its own darkroom and filming unit, pottery, woodwork, various sports clubs – cricket, hockey, football, tennis and athletics – and the usual array of academic-related societies: drama, history, French, maths, science and so forth. After bathing the boys would dress for dinner in white shirts and khaki shorts instead of the blue shirts worn during the day. They proceeded to their classrooms for prep between

6.30 p.m. and 9.00 p.m. 'Lights out' was at 9.30 p.m.

For the majority of students school meals were sumptuous. The variety and portions endeared the boys to the domestic bursar, the motherly Rachel Lokko. With ample dining hall food, it was mostly at the weekends when the gap between breakfast and lunch felt extraordinarily long that the boys would make use of their chop boxes. The first time that Sam saw Otoo's nearly bare chop box, he gave him a key to his own well-stocked chop box and told him to help himself whenever he wanted.

The first term in the classroom was spent jostling for positions. Everyone there had been the best or one of the best from their own schools and the competition was fierce. The students appreciated the opportunity they had to come to this elite school, the school fees that were being paid, and the expectation from parents and teachers that they were being groomed for leadership. The majority of teachers at this time were expatriates – mostly British but also a significant Russian contingency thanks to Nkrumah's strengthening ties with the Eastern bloc. From 1963 the first, permanent Ghanaian headmaster, the ebullient Robert Orleans-Pobee, took the helm at the school.

The syllabuses taught followed the University of London Overseas O and A levels. No teacher could have hoped for more studious children keen to apply themselves, and disciplinary problems were rare. But it was a real challenge of devotion to adapt a culturally alien syllabus in a way that would connect with the boys on a deeper than mechanical, or learning by rote, level. The importance of this struck the physics and maths teacher, Vince Harris, very soon after his appointment, not long after graduating himself from university in the United Kingdom. He was rattling on about the physics of a lever to first formers hoping that the more he talked, the quicker their blank expressions would vanish. After an hour or so one boy asked, 'What is a lever?' It dawned on Harris that it was not the mathematical rules that they were grappling with but the fundamental concepts themselves. He had taken for granted how his English childhood experiences of fixing electrical appliances at home with his father and meddling with gadgets had exposed him naturally to scientific principles. Harris procured several Meccano sets from England. These greatly helped to introduce visually and tangibly basic physics concepts to the first formers.

Other cultural differences affected teaching methods. The Ghanaian tradition of seniority according to which children were constantly reminded to respect their elders had obvious discipline benefits, but it also distanced the teachers from the students. Attempts to be 'matey' with them fell flat, since the children would not dream of being matey with their parents at home. In situations such as these Sam was different from the other boys. As he was on first-name terms with his father and was used to socialising with his elder brothers and Father Yeboah he knew that informality with those older than you or those in positions of authority did not equate to disrespect.

Half-term was an extended weekend when all boys had permission to leave school. Most would stay on campus since travelling home was too far. Others would venture into the bustling, colourful town of Cape Coast or visit friends and relatives in nearby schools. Sam had several 'aunties' in Cape Coast and he took Otoo and others to visit them; they would eat magnificently and stock up their chop boxes.

Test results at the end of the first term provided real proof of your class position. Jonah was tenth out of a class of thirty-three. 'How did you do, Kusi?' he asked the small boy from Kumasi who sat behind him in Form 1B. Kusi's parents could neither read nor write; his father was a kente weaver by trade but spent most of his time subsistence farming. The opportunity to study at Adisadel was afforded by a Cocoa Marketing Board scholarship allocated to his primary school. At his reply, 'I was sixth', Jonah exclaimed, 'So even *you* beat me!' and he gave Kusi a knock on the head.

Apart from playing football, which he loved, but where he was outshone by others, and his obligatory participation in house sports, Sam spent most of his afternoons studying. He and Otoo were banned from the hockey club because of their instinctive urge to go for the man even if they missed the ball. He fell into the group of students who were labelled 'waste pipes' because they did not care much for extracurricular activities. Not overly perturbed, Jonah vowed to study harder. It was a fair start, and he was not ashamed to deliver his report to his father. Senior Kumasi boys organised a truck home at the end of term, which would stop in Obuasi. Unlike the state transport buses this was a 'boneshaker' but the journey home was very enjoyable. They sang profane songs, mocked passers-by and burst into their school song every time they passed another Cape Coast school bus.

Holidays at home

When he was at home during the children's vacation, Thomas's unique methods of instilling lessons into them continued. As much as the children loved eating fufu, it was a long and laborious outdoor process to make it and Beatrice would often ask a migrant mine labourer to pound the fufu for her in exchange for a bowlful with soup afterwards. One day during a school holiday, Thomas pounded the fufu himself. Cars slowed down as the drivers did a double-take at what they were seeing. Thomas called over his eldest sons, Nat and Ernest, to take it in turns to pound the fufu. Passing the heavy stamping rod to them he commented rhetorically, 'Am I no longer Master Jonah because I pounded this fufu?' They were gobsmacked to be asked to do such a menial task, and in full view of the girls passing by on the street. Unable to object, they pounded away, shedding tears. Later, when the fufu was being enjoyed by the family Thomas remarked, 'If you are good enough to eat it remember you're good enough to pound it.' It was a lesson in humility that stuck with Sam.

As the young boys reached their teens Thomas repeatedly warned them that if they got a girl pregnant they would stop school and be sent down the mines to work to support the child and mother – the worst possible job he could think of. Although the family had little direct contact with the mine thanks to Thomas's construction business, the children knew that underground life was wretched because of the living conditions of the migrant miners around them. Thomas's exhortations may seem hypocritical in view of the fact that he had mistresses and children outside his marriage – these were the 'aunties' in Cape Coast – but in terms of Ghanaian culture, a wealthy man, however Christian, is rarely condemned for extramarital affairs. With four sons in a mining town with few distractions Thomas was more concerned about the academic and economic consequences of unplanned pregnancies than with any moral judgement.

There wasn't much to do in Obuasi. The bars were frequented by black and white miners. Witnessing the dissolute behaviour of white men brought home a crucial reality to Sam: people were people. Just because some were white didn't mean they were angels. There were good and bad whites, as there were good and bad blacks. This was an important revelation for the youngster since many of Sam's contemporaries only ever saw white men in positions of respectable authority. That whites could be friends and not just superiors in the roles of teachers or bosses was learned from Thomas's European business associates. Some Italian contractors, in particular, often visited the Jonah family at home. They would stay for meals and Beatrice would indulge their requests for groundnut soup with chicken. On other occasions the Italians just shared a beer with Thomas or played with the children.

To occupy himself during school vacations Sam joined the local Students' Union (SU), as an alternative to Nkrumah's Young Pioneers, which Thomas despised for its political connections. Sam was elected to the SU executive. It was mostly an opportunity for boys and girls to fraternise, to relate school stories and occasionally to organise dances. The younger members found Sam quite strict; for example, he would bar them from coming into the meetings if they arrived late.

Back at school

It would be true to say that most students looked forward to the start of the new school term. Adisadel transported them to another world. The warmth of the camaraderie, the fatherliness of Orleans-Pobee and the strength of the school's traditions filled Santa Clausians with pride. They took to heart the words from the school song, 'Others have laboured; and we share their glory. Ours to do exploits and add to their gain.'

The boys returned with imagined and exaggerated stories about girls. Otoo listened to Jonah's tales, but reckoned that they existed only in his vivid imagination. Sometimes they would visit the common room at Aglionby House where one wall was plastered with photographs of girlfriends. Every term a prize would be awarded to the boy who was judged to have the most beautiful girlfriend. It was only later that some of these beauties were discovered to be the winners' sisters.

Sam was known to devour the newspapers in the library, a habit picked up from his father. Despite Nkrumah's growing censorship of the press Sam learnt a lot from the news about national and international issues such as apartheid, which most of his classmates did not know how to pronounce, let alone understand. His consciousness of racism may have stemmed from his coming from a mining town where he was exposed to foreigners. His love of current affairs brought him to the notice of his seniors. One of them nicknamed him Tula, after Malam Tula, the would-be assassin of Kwame Nkrumah, whose name was all over the Ghanaian news pages in 1963 during his trial. Sixth formers in Hamlyn House often asked Jonah to read the papers to them. He was at ease in the company of older boys and this elevated him in the eyes of his classmates.

Nicknames, or 'guy names' as the boys called them, were common. Some were transitory but others lasted into adulthood – a few old boys would only be identifiable today by their guy names, their real names having long passed into disuse. In Hamlyn House there were Oliver Twist, Unlawful, Spider, and Premature, amongst others, each with an interesting and creative origin. For no particular reason Sam chose to call himself Teddy. This became Teddy Tula. Tula was a notorious tag, but not derisory. When he was in Form 3 some students ridiculed Jonah's plump backside and tried to match a name for it; he repeatedly knocked them on the head and eventually they gave up.

Jonah was pugnacious but not a serious bully, unlike his close friend Otoo, who found it hard to restrain his fists even against his seniors. Others' fear of Otoo benefited Jonah vicariously. Orleans-Pobee encouraged Otoo to box for the school, which helped to temper his aggression; a less assured and understanding head teacher would have had a good and easy excuse to expel him from the school. While Otoo readily took offence, Jonah was rather self-deprecating. One day when an English master had to teach without a blackboard, Jonah lifted his shirt, revealed his back and joked, 'Use this instead, it's big and black enough!' He was not ashamed in Nkrumah's increasingly anti-religious and communist political climate to volunteer for chapel service duties.

Academic competition stepped up at the end of Form 3 when the year-end exams would be used to split students into three streams that would ultimately determine their career paths, namely, 4A for arts, 4B for additional maths and science, and 4C for science. The most prestigious stream was 4B and the brightest boys aimed to do well enough to be picked for this class. Sam studied furiously. He acquired the nickname, 'Backhouse' after the author of the additional maths textbook that he was perpetually buried in. Sam made it into 4B and it was here that he struck up a close but competitive relationship with Reindorf Perbi. The two enjoyed studying intensely, shared notes, and even assisted fifth and sixth formers with their maths exercises.

Political developments

In 1964 Nkrumah declared himself president for life and all political parties apart from the CPP were made illegal. Economic stagnation paralleled the political deterioration. The economic problems were rooted in the fact that from the late 1950s the terms of trade for primary product exporters turned unfavourable, but the pace of Ghanaian expenditure on necessary development work as well as on less defensible white elephants continued unabated. A typical case of a white elephant was a fruit canning complex in Wenchi, in the Brong Ahafo region. An area of 1 400 acres was set aside to grow mangoes and a factory was built concurrently to be supplied with 7 000 tonnes of mangoes a year. The problem was that the region only had scattered mango trees, and the planners overlooked the fact that it would take five to seven years for newly planted mango trees to bear fruit. Meanwhile the factory stood idle.[9] The country's debt rocketed as it turned to supplier credit because government reserves were fast disappearing. Foreign suppliers flocked to sell anything and everything at excessive prices to the Ghanaian government. At the same time, Western governments, anxious over Nkrumah's liaisons with Russia and China, worked to block any financial aid to him.[10] This combined with low primary export prices, poor feasibility planning, mismanagement, systemic sycophancy and corruption to cause economic retardation.

The last two factors were responsible for the demise of Thomas's construction business. From 1964 all types of government contracts were exclusively awarded to CPP supporters.[11] Thomas's contracts dried up because he refused to sign up as a CPP member and did not allow his children to join Nkrumah's Young Pioneers.

The economic situation started to affect Adisadel's resources. Thanks to Orleans-Pobee's good relationship with government ministers and parents, the school fared better than most in procuring books and food. An adjoining 50-acre plot of land was acquired from the Cape Coast Ebiradze clan to maintain a sizeable school farm. The domestic bursar replaced formerly imported foodstuffs with local and often school-grown items. Wealthy parents were encouraged to donate sheep and cows, which would be seen tethered near the dining hall and provided protein for the boys. The severity of the economic hardship was apparent from the empty shelves in the trading stores in Cape Coast by 1965. You could not even buy a box of matches; they were only available for sale by the stick.[12]

The government's moral bankruptcy, evidenced in human rights abuses of political opponents that the international press had repeatedly reported on,[13] finally met with economic bankruptcy, precipitated by Western design.[14] On 24 February 1966 while Nkrumah was on a visit to China, his government was deposed in a military coup. This action set a regrettable precedent for Ghanaian politics.

Sam's final years at school

The coup was greeted with jubilation at Adisadel College, partly because a Santa Clausian, Colonel A.A. Afrifa, was instrumental in the overthrow of Nkrumah. A speedy exodus of Russian teachers ensued. The Ghana ministry of education advertised in *The Times* Education Supplement for British teachers to replace them. By Christmas 1966 there were signs of improvement and the teachers enjoyed their first and most refreshing taste of beer in months.

One of the greatest privileges for a Santa Clausian was to have his name engraved on one of the Honours Boards in the Canterbury Hall. Among them were the Hamlyn Greek Prize, Hare's Classics Prize, Dyce-Sharper Essay Prize, the Victor Ludorum for the best sportsman, and the Fisher Mathematics Prize. Perbi and Jonah set their hearts on the Fisher, which was based on fifth form performance, but for some reason the prize was not awarded in 1967.

Jonah's other subjects were somewhat neglected because of his love of science. He loathed French and despite his pleas to drop it, the French master insisted that he was quite capable of passing the O level if he applied himself. During his O level French oral examination he relied on quick thinking to get through. He grilled those exiting the exam room to find out the topics discussed and flashed through his little-used, red and white *West Africa French-English Vocabulary* book to brush up on these topics. When it got to Sam's turn, after the usual familiarisation questions, the external examiner asked, '*Qu'est-ce que tu as mangé ce matin?*' He was thrown – nobody had mentioned food as a topic – the word for breakfast and all associated vocabulary escaped him. He remembered his father's observation that the lawyers he went to listen to in the district courthouse – one of his favourite pastimes – appeared credible just because of their confident speech. Thomas did not always understand their legal arguments, but he would take sides with the bench that spoke the most convincingly. Sam figured that what he needed to pass was fluency and confidence so he promptly replied, '*J'ai mangé des cocos*,' which was the only word relating to food he could think of. The examiner repeated the question and received the same response. The bizarre answer prompted him to put the question in English, to which Sam replied, 'I understood the question perfectly well in French, and I had coconuts for breakfast this morning!' He passed the exam.

The friendly rivalry with Perbi continued into sixth form. Seven students took pure maths, applied maths and physics A levels. In Lower Six, Mrs Mee, the maths teacher from the United Kingdom, awarded the maths prize to Perbi. The prize was normally determined by weekly test results from the first term and by these scores Sam was ahead of the rest of the class. So everyone was surprised that the prize had gone to Perbi. Sam embarked on a silent protest by refusing to participate in the classroom. Mrs Mee called him over to her bungalow to explain his change in behaviour. Perhaps failing to appreciate the importance of these prizes to the students, she thought nothing of the fact that instead of using test marks she had decided to award the prize according to class attitude and participation. Sam was furious at the unannounced change in the goalposts. 'In any case, who cares about maths?' he blurted. 'I'm off to Russia next year to train as a communist guerrilla to help my Mozambican brothers.' Sam had no communist sympathies whatsoever, but he wanted to get one back on Mrs Mee for – in his opinion – awarding the prize unfairly. With the Cold War at the forefront of everybody's mind and Ghana's own communist relationships only severed in the very recent past, Mrs Mee felt terribly guilty for encouraging this unfavourable decision. She launched into a passionate speech about the disadvantages of such a course, asking at one point, 'Do you have a girlfriend, Sam? I really think it would be a good idea to discuss these plans with her.' Sam let her finish and then barked, 'I've already made up my mind!' Turning abruptly he marched out. As soon as he was out in the warm evening air he burst into a satisfied laugh. Subsequently he congratulated Perbi on winning the prize adding, however, that it had been awarded unfairly.

During the second term of Lower Six, prefects were selected. There were no elections; all twelve positions – in order of prestige: head prefect, dining hall prefect, chapel prefect, sports prefect, entertainment, and seven house prefects – were appointed by the headmaster with the input of teachers and the outgoing prefects. Positions were based on behaviour as well as academic reputation, and competition was keen. Perbi's selection as head prefect surprised many, including Perbi himself, because he lacked physical presence and was not even Anglican. Sam was made chapel prefect. The prefects effectively controlled the boys' behaviour outside the classrooms. In the dining hall they sat on a high table; they enjoyed privileges such as private rooms and exeats and, most of all, the respect of the students and teachers.

Sunday evening's chapel service was a colourful affair. The boys wore their own cloths in the customary manner, five yards of patterned material wrapped around the body and thrown over one shoulder with traditional sandals. It was odd that the most visible aspect of their own culture should be displayed during Christian services – one of the strongest manifestations of colonial incursion.

One Sunday evening Jonah was busy working on his maths on a chalkboard he had installed in his room when he felt someone's presence. He turned to see the headmaster at his door watching him. 'What a fine example of a chapel prefect you are. While the whole school is waiting for you at the service, here you are in your room!' The rebuke came with a fatherly laugh; Orleans-Pobee could see from Jonah's

SAM JONAH AND THE REMAKING OF ASHANTI

expression that intense A level revision had blurred both time and day. The prefect rushed to his duties.

Considering career options

The physics master, Vince Harris, voluntarily took on the role of careers master. He organised visiting speakers from industry as well as various trips to employers. At one talk arranged in conjunction with female sixth formers from the neighbouring Wesley Girls' High School, a British speaker from the government education department discussed the scholarships available to study subjects abroad that were not currently available in Ghana's three universities.

Sam put up his hand and asked about mine engineering. His question was followed by a ripple of laughter. From the mocking look of the girl sitting next to him, he realised that he had blown any chance of chatting her up afterwards. It was considered as strange a question as the Wesley students asking about nursing careers when their school and peers expected them to become the brain surgeons of the future. The guest speaker himself remarked that in all the time he had delivered these scholarship talks Jonah's was the first question he had received about mine engineering. He had wondered why there was no appetite for this important national industry and had even spoken to the Ghanaian chief inspector of mines. The chief inspector explained that it took him a good ten years after graduating as a mine engineer abroad to find a wife in Ghana – nobody wanted to associate with someone in that line of work – such was the low appeal of the industry.

The speaker was so pleased at Sam's enthusiasm that he advised him to contact each of the mine companies, and if that failed to lead to a scholarship, he would ensure that Sam received a government one. His friends thought that it was odd to want to study mine engineering and even to go abroad when Ghana's universities had such an excellent reputation. Of the other six students in the maths–maths–physics A level group Perbi went on to become an accountant, two became professors, and the other three engineers.

A happy chapter in life comes to a close

The highlight of the school year was the Speech and Prize-giving Day and Founders Day, which were celebrated on the second Saturday and Sunday in March and steeped in ritual. The guest speaker at Speech Day would most likely be picked from the school's impressive alumni, many of whom continued the tradition to lead – in industry, commerce, medicine or politics. A sixth form classicist would deliver a Latin oration at Speech Day. The outgoing head prefect would pass on his staff, symbolising his authority, to the head prefect-elect at a ceremony on Founders Day. These were often tearful occasions for the upper sixth and fifth formers who prepared to leave the school. A Santa Clausian famously declared, 'Next to my wife and children, Adisadel comes first,' reflecting the indebtedness and love that the old boys feel towards their Alma Mater. Indeed, everybody left with the belief that they would go far in life, that great opportunities awaited them and that they had been fully equipped to exploit them.

Adisadel days were happy ones for Sam. The Santa Clausians who remember him saw him as studious and friendly, but not a sufferer of fools. Until he was chapel prefect many may not have noticed him at all since the most popular students were the athletes and the musicians. The school where he had spent seven formative years had prepared him for his career choice. Thomas's and Adisadel's discipline would make routine and hard work second nature. Sam's large family and his parents' open-home policy nurtured his sociability. His diverse encounters with non-Africans helped him to see the human before the race. The ease with which he mixed with students of varying ages and classes stemmed from a combination of humility and self-confidence in his abilities. To his self-confidence, Adisadel added aspiration: '*Vel primus vel cum primis*'.

CHAPTER 3

'When a ram is brave, it comes from its heart and not from its horns'

1969–70

'I'll even miss this boneshaker of a bus,' Sam admitted to himself on his last journey from Adisco to Obuasi. His excitement for the future was tempered by the loss of the familiarity and security that the last seven years had brought him. Sam thought about Brew, Perbi, Otoo, Kusi, and all the friends he had made since Form 1. The words of Proverbs 18, verse 24 came to mind, 'There exists a friend sticking closer than a brother.' He smiled, thinking that was true of each of his friends.

Opportunity and choice overwhelmed him. The country was in a similar state of optimism. Everyday life had improved to an extent under the eight-man military government, the National Liberation Council (NLC). Political prisoners and exiles returned home; people felt freer to speak their minds without fear of a CPP member reporting them for subversion. Basic goods such as milk, bread and sugar were more readily available. And now the chairman of the NLC was fulfilling his promise that the undemocratic removal of Nkrumah's despotic rule back in February 1966 had been an emergency measure only taken to restore democracy. Under a new constitution for Ghana's Second Republic a national assembly and a non-executive presidency were created. Elections would take place in August 1969. New political parties sprouted and criss-crossed the country with their campaigns, except for Nkrumah's now outlawed CPP. The NLC supported Danquah's legacy in the form of Kofi Busia and his Progress Party (PP), which went on to win the elections with a 59 per cent majority, although only 60 per cent of the electorate voted.[1]

The NLC, and later the PP, were pro-West and pro-capitalist. They welcomed IMF advice, which earned them a label as neo-colonialists, incited by Nkrumah's writings and radio broadcasts from his refuge in Conakry. The ideological battle for the minds of Ghanaians had yet to be won. The conservative, capitalist side accepted the world economic order and sought to balance the domestic economy despite the uneven playing field. The socialist, populist opponents railed against the periphery trade role that the core nations had forced them into. While they also were eager to right the economy, they believed it better to mismanage it in their own hands than have it prosper as a puppet of the West. In 1969 the country was at a crossroads and Sam too was faced with diverging paths.

What to do next?

It was not so much the thought of working in a mine that attracted Sam. Rather, his motivation for mine engineering occurred by default with the elimination of various alternatives. He did not want to do what was expected of every science student in Ghana: medicine, accounting, and civil, mechanical or electrical engineering. There was only one engineering school at the University of Science and Technology in Kumasi. Apart from the sheep-like feeling that these career choices stirred in him, he imagined the intense competition in his maths-maths-physics group magnified tenfold on a Ghanaian university course. He made the decision to study something less common and preferably outside Ghana. Aeronautical engineering flitted through his thoughts, but Ghana's flagship airline only had one aeroplane and there was no aeronautical industry to speak of.

He took a test as part of the African Scholarship Program of American Universities, which lured the best of Africa's science brains across the Atlantic, but failed to win any of these scholarships. Consequently, during Sam's final year at school he wrote scores of letters to tertiary institutions abroad. Several offers came back with study places but without scholarships. It was then that mine engineering grew in appeal. Mining was the most important sector of the Ghanaian economy after cocoa farming. There were gold, diamond, bauxite and manganese mines, state-owned mines and private ones. The career talk that Sam had attended stressed the dearth of qualified Ghanaians in this sector and so he decided to write to each of the gold mines to see what scholarships were available to study mine engineering abroad.

At this stage Sam had not thought much beyond gaining an appropriate degree qualification. He knew next to nothing about the actual workload of a mine engineer. Even though his home town centred on a gold mine he had had very limited contact with the Ashanti Goldfields Corporation (AGC) apart from a vacation job in 1967 as a clerk's assistant in the transport department with Julius Opara. There was nothing glamorous about this firm except the beautiful houses provided for senior white staff in the Lady Spears Estate, which spiralled up a hill, at the apex of which stood the elegant residence of AGC's chairman, Major General Sir Edward Spears. The thought had crossed Jonah's mind that it would be a lovely place to live. But there was very little company housing for the majority of black employees. Most were migrant workers from the Northern Region of Ghana. The mine periodically sent open-top trucks to recruitment stations in the north where men lined up to be selected according to their physique. It was a situation reminiscent of slave-trade days, except that economic coercion now substituted for physical coercion. The men left without their wives and families on short-term, renewable contracts. Workers also arrived at the mine from Nigeria, Mali, Burkina Faso and parts of the Ivory Coast. Crowded, makeshift homes in the ethnically defined ghettos, or zongos, of Obuasi town accommodated newcomers; as long as a sleeping mat could be squeezed in then a body would fill it.

Once at home Sam unpacked his chop box and trunk for the last time. His sisters were glad to have him back in Obuasi. The family was proud of him, and was even more impatient than he was to receive his A level results. The older boys had left home by now. Nat was working in Sussex, England, as a standards inspector after completing an engineering course there. Ernest was in Germany trying his hand at business. Victor had graduated from Nautical College and joined the state shipping line. His father was grateful for some male company and, in the absence of his brothers, Sam had grown closer to him during his sixth form years. In many ways – especially the speed of his wit and his luck with the ladies – he was more similar to Thomas than his brothers were.

Thomas was glad to see his son waiting in the courtyard as he stepped into the morning darkness for his usual 5:00 a.m. exercise. They walked for a good half-hour before Sam said a word. 'I've decided what I want to do at university,' he started, in English. 'I want to study mine engineering.'

'Mine engineering?' Thomas asked.

'Yes.'

'What, to work at AGC?'

'Yes. Or another mine.'

'But you don't need a degree to be a miner – you don't even need to go to school to be a miner.'

Sam tried to explain that a career as a mine engineer was more challenging and rewarding than a miner's work.

'But you have to go underground?'

'Yes.'

'So you want to be a miner.'

'Thomas, there's a need for Ghanaian science graduates in mining. It's very technical you know.' Knowing his father's views on black management, Sam teased, 'One day I could be the general manager of AGC!'

Without breaking his step Thomas retorted, 'And you know that will be the day I leave town! When a black man heads that company it will come to ruin. You mark my words.'

They returned home. Sam felt dejected. Was this the right thing to do? The only consolation was that his father's condemnation fell short of a prohibition. Sam decided to write to the mines anyway as he had planned. He needed a scholarship to ease the financial burden on his parents. Thomas's business had been destroyed as a result of his refusal to get involved with Nkrumah's CPP. He had started selling off his investments to finance his sons' education at home and abroad. If it came to it, Sam knew that Thomas would sell everything remaining to put him through university. Beatrice had worked harder and harder to grow her retail business. She had converted a room at the front of the house, facing the main road, into a general store. With the help of her daughters she was taking care of all the domestic expenses.

By the time Sam had washed and dressed after the morning's walk and talk, Thomas had spoken to his wife. Beatrice stormed into the bedroom that Sam now enjoyed to himself.

'Kwesi, what is this your father has told me?' Beatrice always spoke in Fante. 'You want to work in the mine? Have you known anybody in this family to have ever worked in that mine? You don't know how lucky you are that you've gone to school so that you do *not* have to work in such a place. How we've suffered to put you through school. And for what? So that you can work in the mine? Over my dead body. Don't you see those poor Northerners who work there? If they do not die underground, they die young from sickness. And for what? The pitiful wages that they earn! Here you have a comfortable home, but have you seen how they live? And you want to be a miner?'

'A mine *engineer*,' her son interjected in English.

'A mine inginair!' she parroted in English, quickly returning to Fante, 'A mine whatever! You want to go and work underground? You want to die young? What will become of you? Nothing will become of you! My son, you had better think again!'

Her rant escalated in speed and volume. She had sacrificed too much and built hopes too high to accept this career choice. It was not only the physical danger that worried her, it was also the shame she would feel when her friends and family knew. Ever the pragmatist, she had the further fear of Sam's inability as a miner to meet the financial responsibilities of a wife and children, not to mention an extended family.

His mother's anger hit him hard. 'Nothing will become of you! Nothing will become of you! Nothing will become of you!' looped in his head for minutes. Sam sensed that Beatrice's exit was a mere pause; the rave would be continued. The confrontation only put his back up. The desire to prove her wrong was the first positive and passionate motivation he had felt for his career choice. His determination swelled.

That day and for the next three months streams of emissaries arrived to dissuade the young man. There were uncles and aunts, Beatrice's friends, neighbours, and the Anglican, Catholic and Salvation Army clergymen. She even enlisted miners to relate the horrors of their job to her son. All their efforts were to no avail. Sam sent his first letter to the Consolidated African Selection Trust (Cast) diamond mine in Akwatia.

He expressed his eagerness to become a mine engineer and to enter any scholarship competitions offering overseas study.

Before Sam had sent his planned letter to AGC, the company had placed an advert in the national press offering several scholarship places to study technical areas of mining in the United Kingdom. Changes had been occurring at AGC since November 1968 when Lonrho had taken over the company. Lonrho's subsidiaries consisted of African businesses in a variety of sectors from agriculture and mining to manufacturing and hotels. It was Tiny Rowland, Lonrho's MD, who allegedly gave the NLC government the idea to end AGC's 90-year lease and replace it with a Lonrho lease of 50 years, in exchange for 20 per cent ownership of the new company and the option to buy a further 20 per cent for £1 a share.[2] Appealing to the Ghanaians' sense of ownership of their natural resources, Rowland offered four non-executive directorships to Ghanaians and requested that Lonrho be paid a management fee, in Ghanaian cedis and not in precious hard currency at that. Rowland wooed Minister of Mines Silvane Amagashi (who in 1969 became a salaried Lonrho consultant) and the four Ghanaians later appointed as non-executive directors by flying them to London and putting them up in the Dorchester.[3] When the takeover offer was made for AGC in October 1968, Amagashi's announcement that the existing lease would not be renewed did not leave AGC with much choice but to accept Rowland's bid.[4] Ashanti would become Lonrho's single largest asset. Rowland allowed the ageing Major General Spears who had served for a quarter of a century as AGC's chairman and MD to remain in the chairmanship role, but an end had come to the octogenarian's treatment of the mine as his personal fiefdom.

The Ghanaian government had changing expectations of the mine's new owners. Lonrho, at least on the surface, had a greater appreciation than the previous AGC board of its wider corporate responsibilities. With the presence of Africans on the board of directors for the first time, albeit in a non-executive capacity, some effort had to be shown towards the Africanisation of the senior workforce. It was inexcusable that after 72 years of operations there was just one technically senior Ghanaian in the mining department. The advert that Sam saw arose from this context. He applied quickly.

In the meantime an encouraging letter from Akwatia invited him to attend an interview. A very excited Ghanaian manager drove Jonah around the mine to show him the operations and verbally assured him of a position along with United Kingdom training. Cast was proud of the fact that, unlike AGC, the company had trained Ghanaians to senior technical staff positions since the mid-1950s.[5] When Thomas learnt that the diamond mines were surface pits it placated him a little – that was certainly preferable to underground work at AGC. But it made no difference to Beatrice. A miner was a miner, with about as much social respect as a night soil worker in Victorian England.

About a hundred people responded to AGC's advert. At the first round of interviews there was a general feeling of optimism since 'several' scholarships had been mentioned in the advert. When Jonah talked to the other candidates, it emerged that most of them had also applied to Ghanaian universities, so that if they were unsuccessful they would proceed in October to one of the three Ghanaian universities. In compliance with the rules Jonah had not done so. You were not allowed to make simultaneous higher education applications because the demand for Ghanaian universities was too high to allow students offered places to then turn them down because of an alternative acceptance. That would create empty spaces hindering someone else's opportunity for that year.

Within weeks Sam had received two letters offering training contracts to start with scholarships in the United Kingdom: one from Cast and the other from AGC. He decided to accept AGC's position because of the company's proximity to home. In July 1969 he started on an orientation programme with nine others who had made it through the interview process. Beatrice was heartbroken.

Two months into this training an AGC official told the young men that there would actually only be one scholarship on offer. No explanation was offered, but most likely the advert had partly served as a publicity stunt to convince the government of AGC's Africanisation efforts. Since he hadn't secured a Ghanaian university place as a fail-safe, Jonah felt lucky that he was the one eventually chosen to stay.

The bubble of joy from achieving this first step in his plan burst on receipt of news that the three-year scholarship for the Camborne School of Mines in Cornwall, England would only commence the following year, in October 1970. Sam's classmates would all be starting university soon, in October 1969, and now he would be a year behind. He felt deceived. If he had had a domestic university place he would have told AGC there and then what to do with its scholarship, but he did not have this option. AGC suggested some underground work experience on the Ayeinm mine as an 'official learner' – a euphemism for a labourer. This appealed to Sam more than sitting at home for a year.

Starting work underground

Ayeinm was one of several mines on the company's 100-square mile property. This mine was located about two miles south-west of the main Ashanti and Obuasi reefs that formed the core of AGC's operations. There was a mine surface train that took workers to Ayeinm, but the station was so far away that it was as much to walk from home straight to Ayeinm, a distance of about three miles. Sam would leave home by 5.30 a.m. at the latest for the start of the morning shift at 6.30 a.m.

The mine was organised along military lines. The general hands were grouped into production work gangs led by a blastman; the blastman reported to a foreman, who reported to a shift boss, who reported to a mine captain (the highest technical rank held by any Ghanaian in 1969). Above the mine captains were the underground managers, then the mine managers, and at the top of the pyramid sat the general mines manager (the General, or GM).

Jonah presented himself at Ayeinm. He was shown to the changing room for unranked miners; the shift bosses and other 'officers' used a separate changing room. As instructed, he had brought old clothes with him to wear underground. The company provided boots and a helmet with an electric lamp.

He followed the others out of the changing room, and reported to the foreman he had been assigned to work with, Victor Dagarti, a stout and muscular Northerner. Dagarti was not Victor's surname, but the name of his tribe; all the men from that tribe were surnamed Dagarti, reflecting management's general disregard for workers who were viewed as highly dispensable. Victor's crew marched to the top of the mineshaft.

They were all Dagarti apart from one Fante man and Jonah, who was also Fante. It was unusual for Fante and Asante men to work underground. They tended to be better educated and more disdainful of manual work and consequently occupied most of the surface jobs. Above the men towered the huge steel headgear, aerial ropeways and equipment that provided compressed air and ventilation underground. They filed into a rattley lift-cage. The lift operator stopped the cage at Level 14. Levels were approximately 100 feet apart vertically, so they were nearly a mile underground. They stepped out into the station, a large area surrounding the shaft access where equipment was kept. Sam was surprised at the size of the tunnels; electricity lit up the place. Victor's gang made its way in one direction. The breeze in the station area quickly disappeared; the air became thick and claustrophobic and the lighting less satisfactory. They arrived at a stope, a production area identified by geologists for its gold content and marked for ore removal. This was a particularly rich stope. Sam was put to work with the blastman.

The blastman's assistant's role was to make the place safe before explosives were used to break down the rock so that the ore could be evacuated. After testing the stability of the surrounding rock, the timber headman would be brought in to build a support structure. Then holes were drilled into the rock and cleared to receive the explosives. Sam was sent back to the station to collect explosives, which he carried back on his head. His next task was to make sure that everybody stood back while the blastman inserted the explosives, charged them and blasted the rock.

Instead of attacking the loose rock with shovels, Victor's men first hosed down the rubble to look for visible gold. They placed glittering chunks of rock in individual sacks and buried them in shallow holes. This was odd, Sam thought. Then they started shovelling the broken ore. At precisely 11.30 a.m. the shift boss, a Welshman called Shankland, did his inspection. The shift boss was responsible for Victor's working area as well as the level above. When on the upper level, Shankland shouted down the raise, a cut between two levels used to lower and raise equipment, 'Hello, hello, hello!' Victor and his men responded, 'Hello, hello, hello!'

'Is everything all right?' Shankland enquired.

'Yes, everything's all right.'

Minutes later Shankland arrived to inspect their stope. When he left Victor and his men really got to work. They placed their drills inside holes and left them running unmanned. Each man dug up his stashed ore and emptied the contents into wheelbarrows. They had welded pieces of pipe, which served as mortars to crush the stolen ore. Water was added. Then, using the fabric lining inside their helmets they sieved the solution to separate the free gold. Combining the free gold with smuggled mercury created an amalgam. They moulded this into roughly round pieces, wrapped them in plastic bags, smeared these with petroleum jelly and inserted them in their anuses. Jonah wondered whether the Vaseline and mercury had been transported in the same way. Despite patrolling security men, who were fooled by the sound of drilling, this illicit operation carried on until the end of the shift at 2.30 p.m. As the blastman's assistant Sam was unable to work without instruction, so he spent this time standing idle, watching the preoccupied crew.

This was the daily routine, preceded by a morning meal eaten at the station before moving to the production area. The workers brought their own food down the mine, which they ate communally. On Sam's third day Shankland came to the stope accompanied by Victor who had, unusually, met him at the station. Together they walked to a particular spot and called the timber headman. The shift boss ordered him to dig up the very spot where he had hidden his sack. 'I'm arresting you,' Shankland yelled. The timber headman started crying. He was instantly dismissed with the prospect of a stint in the local jail. He would never find employment on the mine again.

Shankland turned to warn Sam, 'Did you see what I did? Did you see him doing that?' 'Yes,' Sam replied, adding naively but in defence of justice, 'I'm surprised he's the only one you picked on, because everybody's buried theirs. I can show you.'

Before he had a chance to move Shankland erupted. 'Are you saying that I shouldn't arrest him? Are you telling me that I should let this guy go? You might be going to some big shot school and I am just a lowly miner trying to protect this company's assets and you're telling me that I should let this guy go? Come with me. We'll see what the mine captain has to say about this!'

It was in the Welshman's power to have him sacked. Sam panicked at the thought of his dreams coming to an unjust end as Shankland marched him into the cage. Fortunately for Sam the cage stopped at Level 12 and Kwesi Mensah, a Ghanaian mine captain, joined them. All the 'ranked' miners had been told about the 'official learner' and knew of his scholarship plans.

'Where are you going?' Mensah asked. Shankland explained that he'd caught a thief but this upstart had had the brass to tell him to overlook it, so he was taking him to his mine captain. 'He's clearly not cut out for this job,' he added. To Shankland's annoyance Mensah asked Sam in Fante what had happened. When Sam had explained the situation (also in Fante) Mensah turned to Shankland, 'He's only been here for three days; let him off.' Mensah was above Shankland in rank and, combined with his own guilt, but so as not to lose too much face, the shift boss ordered Sam to go home for the day.

The next morning, Victor was waiting for Sam. He launched into him in his pidgin English. 'You small boy, I dey try help you. De white people tell me to mek your life hell because one day you be big man over us. Bu' I no listen to dem. Bu' you, you go and report me dat dey for sack me. Yo'ng man, you no know wha' goes on here. Lemme tell you somtin. Evelydey you no see dat before Shanklan' dey come he dey shout "hello, hello, hello"? You tink he no know wey tin we dey do? You no know dat evely mo'ring I dey give um envlop? De timber headman dey cheat us all. He no pay up. Shanklan' no get his cut like before, so we reported um. Bu' you, you tell um we dey all bury our own. I for bury you undergroun'! As for now you go suffer.'

Sam tried unsuccessfully to explain that he had thought it was unfair, and that he obviously had not known about this arrangement. But from then on his life was hell. The men kept him working non-stop on the shovel. When one task was finished he was made to start another without rest. He was forced to do unpaid overtime with different teams. They tried to break him physically and emotionally. It was worse when Shankland was around; he took pleasure in ordering Sam about and the others excelled in their abuse with an audience. Fortunately, three months later Shankland left and things eased up for Sam.

He soon obtained his blastman certificate and learned to drive the small locomotives used to move the ore out. Victor was impressed with him for not leaving. Despite the criminal supplementary earnings, he was himself a tough miner, disciplined and punctual; his men worked for him and he got his tonnage out. Sam admired him for his leadership skills.

One day after the communal meal, one of the Dagartis asked Sam, 'Did you enjoy my food today?' Sam nodded. 'Do you know what it was?' Sam shook his head. The Dagarti started barking wildly. Sam coolly shrugged his shoulders.

'Did you enjoy my food?' Sam asked. 'Do you know what it was?' His colleague waited. 'Snake!' Sam pretended. To everyone's amusement the man retched.

Sam got a buzz from these moments of camaraderie. The miners were rough, pure brawn with a latent violence in their manner. A tremendous level of fearlessness was required to work in the dangerous and dark conditions. And Sam had demonstrated his guts for the job. His O and A levels meant nothing to the other men, who were mostly illiterate, but his physical ability and his mental toughness won their respect.

Outside work

At the end of a shift Sam showered, changed his clothes and reached home at about 4.00 p.m. One of the best things about living at home was Beatrice's cooking. It was not only excellent, but also plentiful. It was a shame that someone so passionate about eating was plagued with constant stomach trouble. Out of work Sam hung out with his neighbourhood friends. Kwame Owusu was a year younger, studying at the University of Science and Technology in Kumasi. Kwesi Adu-Gyamfi was a year younger still and about to enter Upper Six at a school in Kumasi. They read everything they could get their hands on and their favourite magazines were *Time* and *Newsweek*. They walked around clocking and chatting up girls. In the evenings they listened to the Beatles, James Brown and Marvin Gaye. The mine provided some electricity to light Obuasi's main street, but apart from this there was very little lighting in the town. Thomas's house was the only one with a generator, so at night the light as much as the music attracted people from the neighbourhood.

Late in September the A level results came out. Sam's grades were respectable but not brilliant. When term restarted for Kwame Owusu and Kwesi Adu-Gyamfi, they left for Kumasi. With four sisters and their friends, the Jonah house seemed to swim with girls. One of Vida's friends was Eno Fosu, a beautiful seventeen-year-old. Eno and Sam, who had just turned twenty, hardly knew each other when the opportunity arose to snatch a kiss. The kiss intensified quickly to intercourse. They had not been friends before and, if anything, this union distanced them from one another.

Early in January 1970 a distressed Eno revealed that she was pregnant. Sam was as shocked as she was. Guilt overcame him. Eno was still in secondary school and this could jeopardise her future and his. It felt as if his whole world, which he had just started to map, was disappearing before him. When Eno came home earlier than usual from school Beatrice soon figured out the truth. Her pragmatic view was that what had happened had happened; they simply had to face the consequences. Thomas had always threatened to send any son of his who made a girl pregnant down the mine to earn a living. Since Sam was already working underground, his father insisted that he hand over his menial monthly wage of 67 cedis for Eno's benefit. The parents agreed that the teenager should finish school after the birth, with Sam responsible for the remaining school fees. Eno's parents could have insisted on a marriage, but customarily such discussions were to occur after the birth so that due attention could be paid to the pregnant woman's care. Sam wanted to get married, but not to Eno. He hardly knew her. In addition, he hated to be forced into anything; a lack of choice made him feel trapped. A son, Ben, a spitting image of Sam, was born on 30 July 1970.

Sam was soon to leave for England. Eno's parents did not push for marriage. Their daughter was bright and completing her education was paramount. Perhaps they also appreciated the enormity of Sam's opportunity to study abroad. Going overseas was a big thing. Sam saw the timing of his departure to the United Kingdom as a timely escape.

Before he left early in August 1970, Beatrice organised a big send-off party. The mark of a good Ghanaian party is lots of food and music, and this was a great party. Friends and relatives came. Everybody had advice for Sam, the most repeated being, 'Whatever you do, don't come back with an English wife!'They were worried that if Sam married an English woman then the chances of his not returning to Ghana would increase. Even if he brought someone back they doubted that a young marriage could withstand the strains created by cultural differences. On a practical level, his family would be unable to complete the customary due diligence on a foreign girl's background, the moral standing of the girl, the community's view of her family and, in particular, a search for any mentally ill relatives that could reveal a hereditary risk. The community's biggest fear was that Sam would adopt the English nuclear family ideal, which Ghanaians condemned as selfish. With an English wife Sam might lose his sense of his social obligations.

On the morning of Sam's departure his father imparted a last few words. Despite his authoritarianism Thomas was never preachy. To Sam's surprise he told him to ignore all the nonsense about white women; it made no difference to him so long as he continued to remember his family responsibilities. 'Be careful,' he added. Before Sam left he went to say goodbye to Eno and Ben. He promised to send money whenever he could and begged Eno to go back to school as planned – partly to appease his own conscience. (She did complete her studies and went on to qualify as a teacher.)

An AGC car with a driver arrived to take Sam to Accra's Kotoka International Airport. His mother delegated her sister, Aunty Jane, to accompany him. It seemed as though everybody in the neighbourhood had gathered to wave him off despite the early hour. There was no sadness on Sam's part, only excitement and a tinge of relief.

To his delight Perbi and Brew had come to the airport to say goodbye. They were equally excited for him and stayed with him until airport procedures forced them to part. As they waved him off they promised to keep in touch by letter. Once on board the British Overseas Airways Corporation flight Sam closed his eyes. Recklessness had nearly cost him his dreams. It was okay to make a mistake but unforgivable to make the same mistake twice. There and then he resolved to get married while in the United Kingdom. The selection of eligible girls in Obuasi was limited and the prettiest had often been with the men from the mine. Besides, Sam reasoned, dating would take time and energy; it would involve excursions to Kumasi, the nearest city, for entertainment and that would not be conducive to the mine regiment and shift work. Sam decided that it was important to come back to Obuasi with a wife; that way he could throw himself into his career when he returned. His single-mindedness left little room for romance and from a corner of his mind a voice asked, 'What about Eno?' He slept.

CHAPTER 4

'When a poor man is decked out in gold, people say it is brass'

1970–73

The plane landed at Heathrow in the evening. As he came through the customs' formalities Sam noticed Nat standing with a woman before the two saw him. The brothers hugged, took a good look at each other and embraced again. It was five years since they had been together. They stood with outstretched arms for a moment. Sam broke the silence by announcing in the manner of a command, 'I'm not leaving without a wife-o!' Ghanaians elongate words in this way for emphasis – he pronounced the 'o' for several seconds for greater impact to show just how serious he was. The brothers burst out laughing and hugged again. The woman, now standing awkwardly behind Nat unavoidably witnessing these private moments, stepped forward and introduced herself as Lily Blitz. She worked in the personnel department of AGC's London headquarters. The three took a taxi into London.

It was late in the evening and Nat planned to give his kid brother a taste of the best of London before they headed off in the morning to his home in Brighton. The two were so engrossed in catching up on home life that Sam had little opportunity to take in the surroundings. They regularly turned to Lily to explain who they were talking about and what they were like, to bring her into the conversation. Even without knowing the characters it was easy to relate to the familial anecdotes. The taxi stopped at the Savoy on the Strand where the three got a table for dinner. At Nat's suggestion Sam ordered a mixed grill. His first English meal was a memorable occasion. The mixed grill had a bit of everything and he thoroughly enjoyed it, so much so that for years afterwards he would only ever order this in a restaurant. Lily Blitz was motherly and welcoming; her boss was Anthony Orchard, the head of personnel at AGC. She informed them that Anthony, by chance, also lived in Brighton. She could be contacted if Sam had any queries or problems regarding his studies or his stay in England. After dinner Lily left and the brothers checked into a twin room to continue catching up.

The next morning they took a train to Brighton from Charing Cross station, a short walk from the Savoy, then a minicab to Nat's flat from Brighton station. Nat's Ghanaian wife, Elizabeth, met them at the door holding their baby son, Fidel. For the next three years their home would become Sam's when he was not in school. Nat took him shopping for winter clothes and showed him around the lively seaside town.

Early in September the day arrived to head off to Camborne. Nat accompanied his brother to London. They crossed the city westwards on the tube from Charing Cross to Paddington. Sam had been sent the address and names of the landlords with whom he would lodge, David and Daphne Hawkins. Since the Camborne School of Mines (CSM) had no halls of residence, students were accommodated with local families. They were encouraged to correspond with their landlords, which Sam had done, telling them about himself and his family, and including some photographs. They did likewise and made arrangements to collect him from the train station when he arrived.

The train journey lasted about eight hours. Camborne is a small town near the south-western tip of the British Isles. It grew from an insignificant hamlet thanks to the tin and copper mining boom of the nineteenth century. The town's fortunes declined with these industries early in the twentieth century, but the presence of many disused mines provided excellent teaching grounds for mining students. When the train pulled into the station, David Hawkins was waiting for Sam. David was in his early thirties with dark hair and a moustache. He worked at a local branch of Boots the Chemist as a sales assistant. His wife, Daphne, was a housewife and they had two young sons. They regularly offered lodgings to the mine school students for extra income. In addition to Sam, in that year they took in two other Ghanaians, James Assan and Kwabena Boakye, who were both on Ghana Mines Inspectorate scholarships. The Hawkins's home at 61 Hughville Street was a three-bedroomed terraced Victorian house. Through the narrow hallway David and Sam turned into the small sitting room where Daphne stood waiting with her sons around her knees. She was a pretty young woman, much taller than David, and very eager to please. Boakye came down the stairs to introduce himself; Assan would arrive the following day.

The three Ghanaians shared an upstairs room facing the street. There was no central heating. The only room that was constantly heated was the sitting room, which had a paraffin heater. Its pungent smell spoilt the pleasantness of the warmth, but it was difficult to pull away from that heater. Throughout their stay at Hughville Street the Ghanaians suffered with endlessly streaming noses as a result of the climate change and the unfamiliar odour of paraffin.

Difficult acculturation

Living with English people triggered a chain of cultural shocks for the Ghanaians. One of the first meals that Daphne cooked for them was roast chicken. Delicious smells emanated from the kitchen. Each of the Ghanaians looked forward to getting his hands and teeth around a large, tasty piece of meat on the bone. The sight of the chicken did not disappoint them as Daphne placed it carefully at the centre of the table; it was golden brown and sizzling in its juices on the tray. Daphne flashed a big carving knife and fork before their eyes. She proceeded to cut slithers of chicken breast onto each plate. Then tin foil appeared and she deftly wrapped up the chicken and returned it to the kitchen. Sam looked down at his plate. The slices of meat were so thin that he could see the plate through them. The torture of seeing and smelling a whole chicken only to be served a scraping was nearly unbearable. 'Would you like some gravy?' Daphne smilingly offered. Back home the chief ingredients of gravy were sweet, ripe tomatoes and chopped onions, seasoned with pepper according to taste. The thin, brown liquid that drowned the translucent slithers of chicken nearly pushed Sam to tears. Had he been ten years younger he would have bawled. The rest of the chicken was consumed over several days in sandwiches and soup.

Three days after Sam's arrival, the new lodgers were summoned to the sitting room. The young men wondered what grave news necessitated the meeting. David Hawkins, standing next to his wife, began to explain. They had noticed that the boys were each taking a shower every day. This was not acceptable and henceforth, David instructed, they were only to shower once a week. Daphne was nervous, fearing that the lodgers would leave when she desperately needed the rent, so she quickly added in her smiling way that they only had a bath once a week too. 'A quick wash with a flannel of a morning does us!' The boys were in total shock as they had been brought up in the tropical heat to shower twice a day. Out of respect they smiled and agreed, but in the privacy of their room they declared their bewilderment. The thought of sitting unshowered in a classroom each morning made them feel physically sick. Could they find alternative accommodation? But maybe all English landlords had this rule. Daphne's speed in the bathroom each morning – she was in and out in five minutes – now made sense.

One Saturday, before lunch, David invited the boys to his local pub, the Tyacks. They eagerly accepted. The pub contained miners just off their shift, the atmosphere was lively and apart from one or two women, it was an all-male zone. David sat them down in a cosy corner. 'Beers all round, then?' he cheerfully asked. The boys nodded. He proceeded to the bar and returned with four pints. No sooner had David finished his than he patted Sam on the back and said, 'Your round, son.' Sam cocked his head with a furrowed brow, not understanding the expression. 'It's your round, Sam,' David repeated.

'My round?'

'Yes. It's your turn to get the pints in. I bought the first round; now it's your turn.'

'Oh!' Sam said as jovially as he could muster. He headed for the bar glancing quickly at the horrified faces of his compatriots. What a strange practice to invite people for drinks and then ask your guests to buy their own. Each hoped that he had enough money on him to satisfy the unfamiliar custom. David introduced some of his friends and the occasion grew more pleasant with successive pints. It was a short walk home.

They were, however, not so tipsy as to have forgotten the evening's cultural revelation. In their bedroom Assan started in Twi, 'Maybe I misheard him but didn't he *invite* us there?' Boakye continued, also in Twi, 'Can you imagine telling your friends back home to come to a bar with you and then making them pay for drinks?' Jonah concluded in English, 'That was probably our first and last visit to a pub.' But soon enough their zeal for pub rites would grow.

So inured had they become to the food situation that their first roast beef Sunday lunch raised a laugh rather than pain. The transparent slices of beef were expected. Accompanying this was Yorkshire pudding – a mirage of a food. It looked on the outside like a beautifully baked bun. The young men expected the solidity of bread but at the touch of a fork it collapsed, and then went soggy in the thin, brown gravy. Sam roared with laughter and the table joined in. Little did the Ghanaians know how proud Daphne was to have achieved this light and fluffy, collapsing effect. She had baked the Yorkshire pudding just right.

Although he was always hungry for current affairs, Sam was rarely able to watch the news. Daphne switched the small black and white television from one soap opera to the next. By default the lodgers became addicts of *Crossroads* and *Coronation Street*, magnetised by the paraffin heater. Every Saturday night David and Daphne went to bingo and they always invited the young men along. The Hawkinses were a very nice working class family and their lodgers were pleasant and considerate but between them they never quite bridged the cultural gap.

Disappointment and regret

Daphne put the young men in touch with a former lodger of hers, a brilliant Ghanaian named Ernest Baafi who had recently completed his Associateship of the Camborne School of Mines (ACSM) with a first class pass. Baafi was now living in private rented accommodation in town. He was pondering what to do next as he did not fancy returning to Ghana (he later became a professor of mine engineering in Australia). Baafi clicked with Jonah. In conversation they discovered shared acquaintances. He was a friendly man but a bitterly frustrated one.

His first words to the new trio were disconcerting, to say the least, 'This is not a university and you will not be leaving with a degree.' The newcomers were stunned. They had assumed that because the course lasted for three years that meant that it was automatically a degree. The more they were told about the ACSM qualification, the more disappointed and deceived they felt. How could they return to Ghana without a degree certificate in their hands? Their old classmates would laugh contemptuously at non-academic qualifications – just as they themselves would. They would not have contemplated such a course at home, how much less to travel all the way to England for a vocational education. When Sam had received news of his scholarship he had assumed that he was going to a university. When the papers arrived outlining the Associateship syllabus he had made enquiries and was reassured that it was the equivalent of a degree from a very famous mining school. In fact, the Associateship was a diploma. Tarkwa School of Mines in Ghana offered diplomas. At that time you did not even need A levels for the Tarkwa diploma; people entered after O levels. Sam was furious. He could have walked into any university and now he was going to study for a *diploma*. Such was the Ghanaian obsessive reverence of university education that for the first time Sam felt he had made a mistake. He contemplated going home but to do so would leave him two years behind his sixth form friends who were already starting their second years at university. And then there would be the shame of coming from England with nothing to show for the experience. How it would please Beatrice to know that he had given up on his mining dream. That would be a shame too great to stomach. It was too late to change his mind.

Baafi felt seriously short-changed. He told them of his A level classmate from their elite Cape Coast school, Mfantsipim, one Isaiah Blankson. The story of their rivalry matched that of Jonah and Perbi. Blankson had gone to the Massachusetts Institute of Technology (MIT) and achieved a double degree; he was now doing his Ph.D. while Baafi was writing home to say that he had got an 'Associateship'. He said the word with great disgust and rancour. His classmates who had been way below him at school and had gone to Ghanaian universities were now on paper better qualified than he was. Sam was angry and upset on behalf of his new friend and for himself.

In fact, Camborne School of Mines, opened in 1888, is arguably the most famous mining school in the world. This meant nothing to the Ghanaians. The value of the ACSM qualification, its comprehensive syllabus, the excellent teaching and practical work and its reputation in the mining industry would only be fully appreciated by Jonah much later when he started work.

The School of Mines was just off the main road, Trelowarren Street, in the heart of the town, a ten-minute walk from their lodgings. It was aptly called a school as it consisted of a single, long, grey, stone building. Inside were laboratories, a lecture theatre, classrooms and teachers' offices. There was a school club with a snooker table and bar area. What the three new students saw on their first day deepened the truth of Baafi's words. The young men had envisaged spacious, landscaped grounds with beautiful architecture, like the universities back home. But here there was no campus to speak of. Even when Jonah compared it to Adisadel, Camborne was structurally a sorry institution. The only positive discovery was that the sports centre had showers. 'Hallelujah!' Jonah exclaimed. Henceforth they would arrive at school early to shower and after lectures they could shower again.

The first day at the mine school was an orientation day. Sam met other new Ghanaian students. These included Kwame Kissi and Tony Wood. Wood arrived at school dressed in a brand new black dinner suit. He had spent the bulk of the funds allocated for clothing in his Ghana government scholarship on this one tuxedo. Sam and the others could not help laughing, but they offered him items of their own to wear instead. Some sort of pre-departure cultural orientation would have benefited them all.

There were about one hundred and twenty first year students of whom about half came from overseas. Of the foreign nationalities, the best represented were, in about equal proportion, Ghanaian, Zambian, Rhodesian, South African and Malaysian. Jonah was confident and stood out because he mixed well, socialising with everyone irrespective of their colour.

The school subjects included geology, surveying, mechanical engineering, electrical engineering, metallurgy, mine economics, computing and statistics. The first year work, particularly the maths, felt far too easy, which added to Sam's frustrations. He struck up a friendship with Kum Tung Pan, a Malaysian who was good at maths; racing Pan to complete exercises brought some much needed excitement to the day. With time, the course did get progressively more challenging, but CSM did not have the competitive academic atmosphere of Adisadel.

When Sam later learned that the Royal School of Mines at Imperial College as well as Newcastle and Nottingham universities were awarding mine engineering degrees his disillusionment with the Camborne course was complete. He felt that AGC had not been open and honest with him. The company had had a whole year to present the full facts and there had been time to apply to alternative mine engineering courses. Now he had no intention of applying himself; his aim was to do just enough to pass.

Ron Gaskell taught a range of mechanical engineering subjects. He showed a special interest in the African students and mentored many of them. Baafi introduced Sam to Gaskell who warmed to him. Sometimes Sam taught the Gaskells' son, Howard, maths and physics, or they played football together. The two of them joined the CSM soccer team with Sam playing centre back and Howard as a striker, even though he was not a CSM student but still at grammar school. Irene Gaskell was like a mother to many of the overseas students. She was sensitive to their homesickness and invited them over for meals. With his decided disdain for the course, Sam spent many afternoons and evenings watching television at the Gaskells' until the transmission closed with *God Save the Queen*. Then he walked the 35-minute journey home or sometimes got a lift back.

Meeting his future wife

About two years before Sam started at Camborne, the Ghanaian government sent a Colonel Bernasko to investigate the use of government scholarships in the United Kingdom. He visited Camborne since the school received a significant number of students on these scholarships. The students he met gave him a list of complaints, which included the absence of Ghanaian women in the area. To the colonel's credit he promised to do something about it. The Ghanaian government's investments were at risk if these young men met and married English women and so failed to return home. The very next year a programme started for Ghanaian women at the Treliske nurse training school about fifteen miles away from Camborne. Unsurprisingly, their Camborne compatriots snapped up the first batch of these 'home girls'. One of these women was Mercy Adu-Darko, Baafi's girlfriend. Mercy and Sam were the same age and got on extremely well.

In January 1971, Mercy excitedly reported to Sam that a very pretty Ghanaian woman had arrived at Treliske and there was no time to waste; she was going to 'make the connection'! If only it had been that simple. It took a few months of chasing on Sam's part following Mercy's initial contrived meeting at Baafi's flat in Dolcoath Road. Theodora Arthur was pretty, light-skinned and petite. Her disposition was quiet and solitary, in contrast to Sam's gregariousness. Therein lay the attraction.

As soon as Baafi announced that he was moving on, Sam jumped at the chance to rent his flat and asked Kissi to be his flatmate. Not everybody could have afforded it as those on government scholarships had a much tighter budget than those on company scholarships. The two enjoyed their independence, but most of all relished their own cooking at Dolcoath Road. Theo would stay over when she was off duty. During the weekends she cooked several dishes and left them in the freezer for Sam and Kissi to enjoy during the week. Sam also liked to cook. In return Kissi was assigned to clean the kitchen, which he rarely did. He had an imagined phobia of kitchens.

So it was a big surprise when Theo and Sam returned from a visit to Brighton to find that Kissi had been in the kitchen. He had gone shopping for ingredients to make a stew. The table was laid and the stew was about ready. Only the rice remained to be cooked, which Theo helped him to do. The stew was scarlet with red bits floating on top. Maybe they were tomatoes, Sam thought. After the first mouthful there was a pause as each person considered whether to swallow or spit. Theo did not want to hurt Kissi's feelings but it was like eating jam with rice. Sam coughed his mouthful out into his hand, 'Kissi, what the hell is this?' Even the cook couldn't pretend that it was palatable. He recounted how he had made the stew, but that did not explain the sickly sweetness. It wasn't until Theo got up to rummage through the cupboards to prepare something edible that she came across bags of cherries. 'I didn't know you could bake, Kissi,' she said, holding up the evidence. Kissi had made them cherry stew – he was positive that he had picked up bags of tomatoes.

Secondment to Australia

In the summer of 1972 the CSM arranged practical work experience for those students on track to graduate the following year. Jonah opted to go to the Warrego gold and copper mine in the Northern Territory of Australia. Other students went to Canada, South Africa and Zambia. Jonah flew from London to Sydney via Singapore with Qantas. Thereafter he boarded a postal plane that landed him and the post in what seemed like open desert. The small plane quickly took off again. A few minutes later the postman drove up in a pick-up truck, collected the sack of mail and sped off, raising dust behind him. Jonah waited and waited. He had not felt the sun so hot since leaving Ghana and the sensation on his skin was good. In his mind he began to double-check his travel instructions; was he sure he was in the right place? A burst of noise startled him and a group of Aborigines emerged from behind a small airport building. Wrapped in blankets and totally drunk they shouted and stumbled their way towards Sam. In between peals of laughter they appeared to be questioning him. Sam's blank responses gave them another idea. They started prodding him, which amused them enormously. They soon got bored and left as loudly as they had arrived, swaying and swooning in a huddle as they propped each other up. To Sam's great relief the next vehicle to pass was from the Warrego mine company.

The Warrego mine was a cosmopolitan oasis in the desert with employees from every continent. Tennant Creek, about 20 miles distant, was the nearest town to the mine. You could have confused Tennant Creek with a Hollywood Wild West set, complete with swinging saloon bar doors and arguments settled with broken bottles.

At the mine, the work experience programme was structured so that students would spend a short time on different aspects of mining; they could get involved in a limited capacity but mostly observed operations. A basic student allowance was paid and their work hours were restricted. When Jonah arrived he went to see Brian Speechley, the mine's manager, without delay. He explained that he had his blastman's certificate and had already worked in a mine for a year and so he didn't want to waste time or money on the round-robin training. He asked to be a contract miner and to be put on contract miner wages. Speechley agreed and Sam joined a crew excavating a crusher station underground. He started on a Friday night and worked twelve-hour shifts, volunteering to work weekends. Saturdays paid time and a half and Sundays double time. With a year to go before returning home, and with marriage, Ben and Eno to think of, Sam had all the motivation he needed to work hard. One evening when he went underground to do overtime, the roof of the chamber they had been creating had been daubed in spray paint, 'Sambo, the money-hungry bastard'. Sam shrugged his shoulders with a smirk – after all, it was true; he was working like mad to make money, and he felt no shame about that whatsoever. The racially derogatory literary allusion was lost on him.

On Sam's first pay day he noticed that three caravans had appeared at the mine camp. They stood side by side, and in front of each was a long queue of men. He asked a Polish colleague what was going on and discovered that the new arrivals were prostitutes from Alice Springs who made the 400-mile journey north once a month. They were kept busy around the clock for two days following pay day.

The Warrego experience confirmed to Jonah that he could enjoy working long hours in uncomfortable and sometimes dangerous surroundings. Getting on with people came naturally to him and he realised at Warrego what a vital asset that was, enabling him to work effectively in teams with varied skills and backgrounds. His sense of humour served him well. On his flight back to the United Kingdom he felt satisfied with and enriched by the time that he had spent in Australia.

Wedding preparations

Sam spent the few remaining days of his summer vacation with Theo in Brighton. They visited AGC's head of personnel, Anthony Orchard, in his spacious waterfront flat. Orchard showed a real interest in Jonah's welfare. Jonah suspected that Orchard had assisted him over and above the call of duty because his scholarship funds far exceeded those of anyone else at Camborne. In addition, other work experience students had to pay back their travel expenses from their wages earned abroad, but Orchard did not insist on this in Jonah's case.

Sam talked frequently about his career plans to Theo. He often brought up Kwesi Mensah, the AGC mine captain who had become a mentor to him during his year underground. The fact that Mensah was one of the few senior Africans at AGC showed the desperate need for better qualified Ghanaians. Sam was excited about the opportunities before him and infected Theo with his enthusiasm. His work experience at Obuasi and at Warrego had removed all romantic notions about the job and Sam tried to convey this honestly to gauge Theo's reaction and to prepare her. Mines operated 24 hours a day so he would work shift hours, sometimes overnight, and, if needed, overtime; there would be no time for gallivanting to Kumasi or Accra. Neither of them recalls a marriage proposal as such, but the pair discussed and agreed to get married. Theo's parents wanted them to return to Ghana to satisfy the customary rituals, but they managed to dissuade them because of the cost and instead planned a small wedding at the Church of Christ the King in Hollingbury shortly after Sam's graduation.

So relieved was he to leave Camborne that Sam did not bother to attend the graduation ceremony. He threw himself into the wedding organisation, which included, to his shock, paying for the church and choir. What had been planned as a small affair grew in size and about eighty family and friends attended the service and reception on 4 August 1973. Theo's mother and aunt travelled from Ghana for the occasion. Victor conveniently was in the United Kingdom at the time, completing a course at the Tyne and Wear Nautical College, so it was agreed that he and Nat would represent the entire Jonah family to save those in Ghana the expense of travelling. Camborne friends came, as did Mercy and her nursing friends. Typically of Ghanaians, friends of friends brought their own friends along. Anthony Orchard enjoyed the day. In a decorated Opel Kadett the couple drove the short distance to the beachside hotel they had chosen for their honeymoon.

A sad event tinged the celebrations. A wedding guest complained of severe headaches at the reception and collapsed. He was taken to hospital where he later died. When Theo and Sam heard the news they cut their honeymoon short to visit his widow and children.

The time to start real work was fast approaching. Sam had familiarised himself with the regulations and requirements for mining promotion. There was a minimum number of years and qualifications needed for each step of the hierarchy before miners were permitted to sit exams for promotion. Sam planned his career moves accordingly to minimise the period between categories. The first milestone was the shift boss level that required at least one year's work experience after graduation before you could enter for the exams, provided you had the blasting certificate and a mine rescue certificate. As he did not have the latter, Sam pressed Orchard about completing this before leaving the United Kingdom. Orchard found him a place on a course being run in Aylesham in rural Kent. There Sam met another Ghanaian, Ben Adoo, who was working for the State Gold Mining Corporation. The course was not very intense. Their afternoons were free so Ben suggested that they make better use of their time by finding a job. They knocked on a few farmhouses to offer their labour. At one property the farmer asked, 'Can you drive?'

Just as Sam was about to reply in the negative Ben enthusiastically nodded and said, 'Yes!'

'Come with me, then.' The farmer showed them to two tractors with contraptions attached at the rear to bale hay. The farmer explained how to cut and release the bales when full. 'No problem!' Ben assured him climbing onto one tractor and waving the farmer off. Jonah had never driven a car before, let alone a tractor. He reluctantly sat on his.

Ben instructed him in Fante, 'Don't worry, it's easy. There are only two pedals. The one on your right is the accelerator; that will make you go forwards. The larger one on the left is the brake. Put your foot on the brake and turn the key.' Sam's tractor chortled to life. 'Good! Now you see that lever to the left of the steering wheel, that's the handbrake. Pull it towards you.'

With only one hand on the steering wheel the tractor surged forward without control. 'Ewuradi!' (My God!) Sam exclaimed. Ben shouted to press the left pedal, 'Press the brake!' After a second attempt Sam was on his way at Ben's side. Ben turned to smile broadly with a confident wave as they passed the farmer standing nearby. Sam kept his eyes firmly ahead and tightened his grip on the steering wheel.

'All you have to do now is concentrate on steering straight,' Ben shouted. Somehow they managed it. The farmer was so pleased with the speed of their work that he asked whether they would return the next day. 'Sure!' they beamed. The young men laughed and laughed at their brazenness and returned for seven days to complete the farmer's fields. They earned £21 each, which when compared to Adoo's annual stipend of £52 was a great deal of money. The pounds would go a long way in Ghana.

At the end of the mine rescue course they cadged a lift back to London with some English youngsters who had been working on a nearby apple farm. Seven of them, five boys and two girls, squeezed into an old Renault. Joking and bantering, the journey passed in no time at all.

Anthony Orchard knew that Sam was leaving his young wife in the United Kingdom alone for a year to complete her nursing course, and that their honeymoon had been cut short. As a wedding and farewell present wrapped into one he kindly arranged to put the couple up in the Dorchester for a week before Sam left for Obuasi. All expenses were paid by AGC. Orchard may not have intended the experience to serve as a carrot, but it did. This taste of pure luxury whet the newly-weds' appetite for success.

CHAPTER 5

'Short though the elephant's tail may be, he can flick away flies with it'

1972–82

The euphoria of 1969's civilian elections quickly dissipated. Ghanaians expected the intellectuals who made up Busia's Progress Party (PP) to resolve the country's economic problems swiftly. But debts accrued by Nkrumah's administration continued to limit the government's choices. The PP, like its military predecessors, attempted to adjust the economy structurally away from its overdependence on cocoa by implementing austere IMF recommendations. Civil service salaries were frozen, taxes increased, the currency devalued, and state-owned ventures sold off. Urban workers were the worst hit by the soaring cost of living. When the trade unions rose to protest, the PP denounced them for being un-patriotic and Busia sent the army in to quell the strike action. Soldiers occupied the headquarters of the Trade Union Congress. Busia himself, and many in his party, had suffered the denial of freedom of expression in exile and in prison under Nkrumah. Consequently, the PP's extreme response to protestors cost democracy its credibility. Discontent grew in the army as perks were slashed, and in January 1972 Colonel Ignatius Kutu Acheampong overthrew Busia's democratically elected PP in a bloodless coup.

There were significant continuities with Nkrumah's regime in the policies of Acheampong and his National Redemption Council (NRC) in terms of the relationship between the state and the economy as well as in the NRC's anti-imperialist stance. The reach of the state widened in the distribution of consumer goods, and in controlling prices and import licences. The Industrial Relations Act of 1971 was repealed thereby increasing trade union rights. Redundancies were outlawed and social security improved. The currency devaluation of 1971 was partly reversed and, in a very popular move, Acheampong repudiated foreign debt.[1] Full of catchphrases Acheampong pronounced, 'We Will Pay and We Won't Pay, Which is Stronger?' It sounded punchier in Twi and Ghanaians enjoyed this spirit of self-determination. For the first two years of the return to military rule the economy did, in fact, improve thanks to the absence of debt and the reduction of imports encouraged by Acheampong's 'Operation Feed Yourself' and 'Operation Feed Our Industries' initiatives.

The partial nationalisation of AGC

Acheampong largely blamed 'evil' neo-colonialism and the 'sharks' of international finance for shackling the domestic economy.[2] His policies of self-reliance extended to increasing the government's participation in the timber and precious metals industries that were dominated by foreign firms. Ghanaians were to 'take over the commanding heights of the economy',[3] (another of his favourite slogans). Consequently, on 6 December 1972, the NRC issued Decree No.132 cancelling AGC's mining lease. The British firm's assets were transferred to a new, Ghanaian company, Ashanti Goldfields Corporation (Ghana) Limited. Lonrho was permitted a 45 per cent ownership stake in the new firm. The matter of compensation and the reinstatement of the mining lease would remain unresolved for years to come.[4] The move gave the government tremendous negotiating power and a substantial share in profits from the free gold price, which had soared since the collapse of the Bretton Woods system in August 1971.

The head of state inaugurated the new company on 26 January 1973. Shortly thereafter the government and Lonrho signed a Technical Management Services Agreement, whereby Lonrho managed the mines in exchange for fees, initially set at $200 000 per annum. Rowland allegedly remarked, 'I am totally in sympathy with this type of revolutionary capitalism (the partial takeover of national resources). If you have that, you won't get nationalization.'[5] Lonrho's consulting engineer, George Cappendell, referred to the change as a 'new joint venture'.[6] Lonrho's calm acceptance reveals that the mine was potentially rich enough to provide decent minority shareholder income in spite of the expropriation, the cancellation of the mining lease, the increased expenditure on African workers' welfare such as the 98 per cent increase in the minimum wage in 1974, and even in spite of the reduction to a five-day working week from 6 October 1975.[7]

An indigenous majority on the board of directors was demanded by Decree 132, with six of the eleven board positions given to Ghanaians. The government would henceforth nominate for appointment to the board a non-executive chairman and an executive deputy managing director (MD). Lloyd A.K. Quashie, a geology lecturer, served as the first deputy MD. The government and Lonrho agreed that the MD role should be filled by a Lonrho employee seconded to AGC. The new company was headquartered in Accra in the airport residential area.

Despite these drastic ownership changes and the increase in the number of Ghanaians on the new board of directors, even in executive capacities, Ashanti continued to be managed remotely from London through Lonrho's Technical Department. There was a real dearth of indigenous technical management skills caused by the absence of any serious African development policy. In addition, the Technical Management Services Agreement with Lonrho prevented any real change in power and control of the firm. Lonrho's Technical Department was the same as the pre-expropriation management team. A parallel or duplicate management structure existed in Obuasi, but only London could authorise technical or operational decisions so power remained firmly in London.

The Accra head office was devoid of authority and mainly occupied itself with government relations as well as obtaining import licences and foreign exchange through the official procedures. The rest of the time was spent receiving telexes from Obuasi, forwarding these on to London and awaiting responses on action to be taken at the mine. The government-nominated deputy MD, Quashie, supported by the Ghanaian majority on the board, did manage to implement AGC's first target-led Africanisation policy and a slow start was made to improvements in African welfare provisions such as basic pensions and housing. When Jonah returned to the mine in 1973 there were not yet any glaring changes, but the workers were perceivably more conscious of their rights.

The first rung of the career ladder

Beatrice was happy to have her son home but the three years that he had spent abroad preparing for his career had in no way reduced her anguish about it. Jonah reported to the mine along with a new recruit named Boakye Ansah, a mechanical engineer graduate from London. Thanks to recent changes at the mine both were entitled, as graduates, to company accommodation. The mine secretary showed them to one-bedroomed apartments in a place called Hell's Kitchen near the Pampora Treatment Plant, where black senior staff were living. Jonah immediately refused to live so close to the arsenic-emitting processing site. Accommodation should not have been built there at all. Although there was surprise at his temerity and ingratitude the matter was reviewed and Jonah was eventually offered a bungalow on the Lady Spears Estate. Jonah and Ansah were the second and third Africans to have lived there. The first was a Colonel Yarboi who had held a senior administrative position at the mine after the Lonrho takeover. With Theo in England, Jonah spent most of his time at his parents, particularly around meals.

Jonah's first assignment was to monitor an underground fire that had been burning for more than a year in the north section of the mine. The fire had seriously affected production. Jonah's team was tasked to erect concrete barricades to deprive the fire of oxygen. His crew worked one Sunday from 8.30 a.m. to 5.30 p.m. It was unusual to do such non-extraction work on a Sunday, especially after 1.30 p.m. When the team surfaced, the shaft gate man was glad to see Jonah. His mother had been at the shaft crying and looking for her son. They had sent her to the security office where someone had taken her home.

Jonah was extremely embarrassed by her behaviour. When he arrived home he ignored his mother's relieved pleas for an explanation. 'Don't do that again,' he commanded. 'It caused me a lot of embarrassment.' Beatrice had panicked when her son had not arrived as per normal for Sunday lunch. 'Just stop worrying about me,' he snapped. 'After all, if you lose me you have seven others!' The words hurt his mother deeply. She did not venture to the mine again, but that did not stop her from worrying.

Theo's return

Theo arrived as a qualified nurse in 1974, a few months before Jonah was promoted to the position of shift boss. She quickly found employment at the mine hospital. Unfortunately, in attempting to elevate the hygiene standards to what she had experienced during her training, she got on the wrong side of the matron who took any suggestions for improvement as a slight on her character and management. Two weeks into the job Theo resigned.

With time on her hands and encouraged by the Operation Feed Yourself campaign Jonah suggested that they set up a pig farm for Theo to manage. His wife enrolled on a short livestock management course in Kumasi and Thomas helped to find a site fifteen miles outside Obuasi town on which to construct pens. Eight sows and two boars started their breeding stock. After Jonah's shift work he would pick up Theo and a worker to do the rounds of the local restaurants picking up swill. They had supplied the mine restaurants, local chop bars, fruit and vegetable sellers, and the butchers and fishmongers in the town with plastic containers to put their food waste into for collection. On Saturdays they would to go the secondary schools in the area, and even travelled as far as Kumasi to collect throwaways there. Spent malt brewed by the Northerner wives of Jonah's colleagues, sweepings from corn mills and cake from palm oil processing plants were all obtained free of charge for the pigs' diet. The first pig that they sold before they had acquired their own scales had to be weighed at Obuasi train station. It came in at 320 pounds! At the going rate of 3 cedis 75 pesewa a pound, the income from that one pig was four times a mine engineer's monthly salary. They were onto a winner. Under Theo's management the piggery grew to be the second largest in the Ashanti region.

Challenging the status quo

One day Jonah decided to request a company car and driver to take Theo on a trip to Accra to see her parents. Jonah had seen expatriate wives enjoying such privileges so he went to the transport department to complete a 'Senior staff off-camp transport requisition form'. Under the normal procedure the form would be endorsed first by the chief engineer and then the general mines manager (the General) who returned it to the transport department. When Jonah handed his form to Julius Opara, who was still working there, he told him, 'Kwesi, you know this is not for blacks.'

'But the form states clearly that it is for senior staff. I am senior staff. I've seen the wives of other senior staff taking a car plus chauffeur, so I'd like one for my wife.'

Julius tried to dissuade him. 'Just send the form off,' Jonah insisted.

When the chief engineer received it he queried Julius to double-check who had completed it. He felt uncertain about endorsing it and so passed the problem on to the General who sent for Jonah.

'Did you fill in this form?' he enquired.

'Yes.'

'You are not expected to make such requests.' His choice of words pricked Jonah.

'If I am not *allowed*, then tell me so. But as far as I know I am entitled.'

The General was taken aback by such effrontery; unable to retort he reluctantly signed off the form. There were other 'radicals' among the African workforce, but Jonah was fast becoming the peskiest of them all.

Infiltrating the all-white golf club

As a senior staff member Jonah was entitled to use the Obuasi Sports Club (OSC). The OSC was the official name given to the club after independence, but everyone continued to call it by its pre-independence name, the European Club. To the annoyance of the Europeans and even some Africans, Jonah breezed about the place freely, unlike the other black senior staff who sat in the unmarked, yet nonetheless clearly demarcated black area. Many of the senior Africans in any case preferred the African Club despite its inferior facilities because they felt welcome there. Some of these senior blacks felt that Jonah was a sell-out, embarrassingly trying to be a white man; and most of the whites felt that he was getting above his status.

Precisely because there were no black members, Jonah decided to join the golf club. Unlike the country's other golf clubs in Achimota, Takoradi and Kumasi, which were racially mixed, the Obuasi golf club was exclusively white. This caused the company considerable embarrassment when black players came to compete from elsewhere. The press labelled the firm's golf club an apartheid regime. Not even the offer of a half set of clubs for the first Ghanaian to win a handicap attracted a response. The black workers did not see the whites as their colleagues so even this prize was insufficient incentive to fraternise with them. Jonah met with a cold chill the first time he walked into the clubhouse. Nobody responded to his cheery, 'Hello!' Nobody had to say that blacks were not welcome; he felt it. He got himself a drink and asked the nearest man if he would teach him the game. The man declined, as did everybody else Jonah asked.

Behind the clubhouse Jonah found the caddies, some of whom he recognised as he had seen them around town since his childhood. They were delighted to see one of their own at the club and were eager to help, since the club had no local pro. For ten consecutive days after the end of his shift, Jonah arrived for a golf lesson. After the tenth lesson he felt confident enough to play a game and asked around the clubhouse for partners. People either politely replied, 'Sorry, too busy,' or indicated that they already had their complement of players. If they weren't prepared to come around amicably then, Jonah decided, they would have to come around on his terms.

He planned to arrive at the golf club very quickly after work so that he was at the first tee before the Europeans had changed to come out for their game. Besides being inexperienced he intentionally played the ball slowly knowing that golf etiquette demanded that the players behind wait for him to finish each hole. Their audible insults pleased him. He repeated the stunt for three days and on the fourth day he received three invitations from club members to join their teams.

With time his game improved and he successfully offered himself for election as the club vice-captain, acting as captain on occasion. After a game he would often get a lift back with some of the Europeans to the OSC. The few Africans in there smarted at the sight of him chatting and strolling in with whites. Boakye Ansah reported to him what people were saying – 'He thinks he's a white man.'

81

When Jonah attempted to repay the hospitality shown to him and Theo by the golf club captain who had invited them to his home for tea, he realised that any notions of success in breaking down racial barriers were premature.

'Theo and I would like to reciprocate your kindness and invite you and your wife over to our house for dinner,' he told the golf club captain during a game.

The Englishman replied incredulously, 'You mean you are inviting *me* and *Maureen* to *your* house?' With a look of utter disgust he stormed off the green without giving Jonah a response.

The feeling of isolation from both black and white senior colleagues did not unduly bother Jonah; his conscience was free as he was being true to himself. Moreover, his natural constituency with the majority, the junior workers, remained strong and he had his immediate and extended family close by. Jonah contemplated how unfortunate it was that his commitment to breach the colour bar only raised other issues with his own people. There was still a long way to go for both whites *and* blacks at the mine.

Jonah encouraged Theo to take up golf and organised lessons for her. After a while she gave up, unable to handle the boos and hoots from fellow Ghanaians. Once he had proved his point with golf, Jonah turned his attentions to the company's all-white squash club.

In 1975 Theo gave birth to the couple's first son, Richard. Ben lived only a fifteen-minute walk away, and Theo suggested that he should come and live with them. Jonah objected, explaining that Ben's mother and grandparents were there for him and they could not just remove him. In truth, and to his regret, he didn't want to disrupt his happy family unit and routine.

Progress on the job

Jonah's reputation for zero tolerance of theft as a shift boss grew. As a result of this he was asked to oversee work at the famous stope 2074 at Ayeinm. Stope 2074 was literally a wall of gold. A series of senior staff, both expatriate and Ghanaian, had all been sacked because they could not resist helping themselves to the yellow metal before their eyes. Jonah rushed to tell Thomas about the appointment. Everybody in town knew about 2074; they also knew who worked there – they owned taxis and ran other small businesses. Thomas invited his son for a walk. As they walked he talked. 'You know, when I die, Kwesi, there will be a big funeral for me. People will come from afar and as they file past me lying in state they will talk about what I have left behind, especially my children. You can imagine the conversations, "That one is Nat; he is the engineer," they will say. "And that one is Ernest, the businessman; and Victor, the sea captain; and Sam there … Oh, he's the one who was sacked for stealing gold." Believe me, that's what people will know you for if you yield to temptation at 2074.' The truth of Thomas's words reinforced the ignominy that Sam was conscious to avoid. There was no heavier burden than shame, that feeling of guilt compounded by self-ruin. He redoubled his determination not to let himself or the family down.

As shift boss he would meet with his blastmen and foremen every morning to discuss the problems and plans for the day before descending into the mine. During one of these sessions the night shift reported that as they were driving rocks away in the locos from Level 21 a lot of dust had fallen down the chute (an ore pass) suggesting that the working spaces above had collapsed. Jonah took his men down immediately. Working areas on Level 20 had indeed collapsed and were inaccessible. To reclaim the area they needed first to locate the chute down which they could feed rubble to be removed below by locos. Jonah left the team to search for the chute while he toured adjoining stopes. At about 1.30 p.m. Dogo Dagarti, one of his foremen, excitedly reported that he had found the chute. Jonah rushed back. Now the real clearing work could start. As this progressed Jonah happened to look up and notice a shower of dust beginning to fall from the wall above. 'All of you move!' he shouted. In a matter of seconds large rocks pelted the area where the men had been standing. Dust blanketed the area. From the cloud Dogo Dagarti howled, 'Massa, massa! I'm here!' They all hurried back with hammers and shovels to excavate him. Dogo lost a leg in the accident. The rock collapse was so heavy that it took weeks to clear the rubble.

The accident could have been prevented. Instead of using timber supports in such weak ground conditions rock bolting was needed. But the combination of foreign exchange scarcity, import licence red tape and no new investment from either the government or Lonrho caused the mine to cut corners wherever possible. This jeopardised safety and as a result accidents and fatalities were common.

As a shift boss supervising precision drilling on a sublevel production section, Jonah's team worked about 25 feet ahead of another gang that was using load–haul–dump equipment to extract the ore already drilled and blasted. The drills and the load–haul–dump engine made a tremendous noise. All of a sudden a wall of dust appeared to be travelling from the extraction team towards Jonah's men. They turned to see helmet lamps beaming from the ground. A huge slab of rock about the size of two snooker tables in length and height had fallen on top of the men, trapping three of them and completely burying the load–haul–dump equipment. The drilling crew dashed to their colleagues' aid. It took an hour to free the men. Two of them had lost limbs. One had no noticeable damage but a drop of blood coloured the tip of his penis. He was clearly in shock. They carried them all to the station as fast as possible. At the lift cage, the least-scathed victim grabbed Jonah's hand and thanked him in Fante, 'You've done all that you could do.' Jonah thought nothing of it. Like soldiers on a battlefield they would never let the risk of danger prevent them from helping the wounded; his whole team's response had been automatic. Jonah surfaced at the end of his shift to hear that the man who had thanked him had died in hospital; his words of gratitude to Jonah had been his last. Of the many accidents and fatalities that he was witness to, this one affected Jonah acutely.

One morning as Jonah sorted out timber to be used for support underground at Ayeinm a short, chiselled figure approached.

'Victor? Victor Dagarti! What are you doing here?' Jonah dropped the lumber and embraced his foreman from his 'official learner' days.

'Massa, I wen' home,' Victor started to explain, 'But I decide to come back.'

'Have you been re-engaged?' Jonah asked hurriedly. He had not, so Jonah took him straight to the mine captain to insist that firstly, he hire Victor and, secondly, he appoint him as Jonah's foreman. They had a wonderful time working together. Both were tough, demanding miners, obsessive about achieving their tonnage. Nothing had to be said about Victor's former illicit activities; Victor knew that Jonah would not tolerate anything illegal. Wherever Jonah moved as he rose through the ranks, Victor went with him until the Northerner retired.

After working the requisite two years as a shift boss, Jonah sat the mine captain examinations at the regional Mine Inspectorate offices in Kumasi. Besides the salary increase, which was generous by Ghanaian standards, the promotion came with new perks – a larger, three-bedroomed bungalow and an allocated car and driver. As mine captain Jonah often left home after midnight to surprise his workers with un-scheduled inspections. Theo respected Jonah's commitment to his job and never once complained.

Challenging times

In 1977 a second, healthy baby boy, Andrew, was born to Theo and Sam. It was around this time that Sam's mother, Beatrice, fell ill. A satisfactory diagnosis was never made although she was transferred from the private wing of the mine hospital to see consultants in two other hospitals in Accra. What started off as backache gradually debilitated her until she was unable to walk. For a practical and busy woman the inability to fend for herself destroyed her spirits; her life force ebbed with her independence. Andrew's birth was a break in the clouds but they soon gathered and darkened again. Beatrice died on 4 August 1978, on Jonah and Theo's wedding anniversary. Sam took his mother's death badly. Of all her children she had had a soft spot for him. He regretted all the harsh words that he had thrown at her and the fact that she went to her grave still disapproving of his career.

The second half of the 1970s was a difficult time for Ghanaians. Acheampong consolidated his power in 1975 by creating the immod-estly named Supreme Military Council (SMC) to replace the NRC. Besides its name the only other grandiose feature of the SMC was its corruption. Acheampong took the purchase of political support through the selective allocation of jobs, contracts and import licences to hitherto unknown levels.[8] Everything operated, or rather, was mismanaged, on a who-you-knew basis. The fiscal, inflationary and exchange rate policies disincentivised production. Farmers reverted to subsistence living; those with cash crops smuggled them over neighbouring borders to sell at better rates. The incidents of gold theft at AGC soared as people struggled to make ends meet, while elsewhere massive misappropriations of public funds occurred. A new word emerged to describe a spectrum of fraudulent survival tactics: kalabule.[9] Unsurprisingly, the economy dramatically declined in terms of every measurement.[10]

Jonah and his family were spared the worst thanks to his senior staff salary, but at a corporate level the mine suffered from the gangrenous political economy. Although AGC was the country's single largest foreign exchange earner, the firm was not allowed to hold unrestricted hard currency accounts abroad. Strict foreign exchange controls and the sycophancy that controlled the allocation system resulted in serious shortages for the company. Foreign exchange was needed to buy materials and equipment abroad for importation. Obtaining the foreign exchange from the Ghana Central Bank was one bureaucratic procedure, and securing the licence to import was a separate set of hoops and swings. The ministry responsible for import licences could grant a licence to import goods to the value of $1m, for example, but the Central Bank might only have $200000 available. There was no foreign exchange policy differentiation between AGC and the small-time sole trader; indeed, the latter might have preferential treatment depending on his or her personal connections.[11] The mine got by on a shoestring, often bartering materials with other mines. If the State Gold Mining Corporation at Tarkwa needed explosives and Obuasi needed shovels, there would be an exchange. There were no capital projects undertaken during these years; rehabilitation and development were not considered and nobody dreamed of exploration work. Despite the soaring gold price at this time – a fine ounce of gold had risen from an annual average price of $64 in 1972 to $460 in 1979 – gold production at AGC steadily declined from a peak in 1972 of 533000 ounces to under 238000 by 1979. Mining strategy, that is, the grade of ore to mine and in what quantities, is determined by the gold price and working costs. The surging gold price from the 1970s expectedly led to a reduction in the grade of ore mined. This should have been complemented by a constant if not increasing tonnage of ore mined, but this did not happen at AGC where tonnage declined. Production was far below optimal levels. Thanks to the gold price the company still remained profitable at suboptimal production levels. If Lonrho had had the incentive to do so and the Ghanaian government had had the will and the money, phenomenal profits could have been earned at this time.

In the wake of the partial nationalisation in 1972, the government's share of AGC's income rose to over half of AGC's gross revenues while new capital expenditure at the mine plummeted. This occurred to the extent that in 1978 three times less capital in real terms was employed per worker than in 1905.[12] AGC was literally de-modernising.

Advancing his career prospects

Sam was terribly frustrated but impotent to do anything about the state of operations. Hitches and glitches interrupted the production process. With time on his hands and being averse to idleness he enrolled with Rapid Results College to study law through an overseas correspondence course. Once his shift bosses had reported back at about 3.00 p.m., and after completing a logbook and other administrative requirements, he would spend a couple of hours on his new pastime. Besides curiosity and a desire for knowledge, a law qualification would add to his career options.

Anthony Orchard visited the mine for two weeks every year along with the usual troop of London consultants and controllers. He always made time to meet his 'protégé' and to discuss his progress. Jonah complained that the personnel department at Obuasi had fobbed him off when he requested support to study for a Masters degree. In view of the effects of current government policy on the mine Jonah felt it was timely to study more about mine economics and finance. A higher qualification would differentiate him from the other mine engineers and improve his promotion prospects. He did not reveal to Orchard that he still begrudged his CSM Associateship for not being a proper university degree. He felt that studying for a Masters degree would put that right. In view of the fact that Jonah was doing well anyway, Orchard disagreed that a postgraduate qualification was essential but, with Jonah's persistence, he acquiesced. This time round Jonah self-selected the Royal School of Mines (RSM) at Imperial College, University of London.

In June 1978 Jonah received confirmation of his place. He knew exactly what area of research he wanted to investigate for his dissertation and wrote an abstract on the effect of successive governments' economic and mineral policies on the profitability of Ghanaian mines. Fortuitously, Jonah was able to test his proposal on a postgraduate researcher from the Centre for West African Studies at Birmingham University who happened to be at Obuasi conducting interviews on trade unionism and the firm's industrial relations. The two revised his abstract and Jonah sent it to the dean at the RSM. He wanted early approval for the topic so that he could gather as much data as possible in Ghana before arriving in London. RSM replied to Jonah commending him for his ambitious idea and enthusiasm; it was unusual for a student to be thinking so far in advance about a dissertation. The dean recommended that he limit the project's period and scope. Jonah did so and then commenced with his data collection.[13]

On 5 July 1978 an SMC member, Lieutenant-General Frederick Akuffo responded to rising public anger over Acheampong's 'one-man show' by ousting him in a palace coup. Inflation that year neared 300 per cent; the country's chief export commodity, cocoa, unable to benefit from the strengthening world price, had halved in volume since 1964. Basic commodities were unavailable. Akuffo abandoned Acheampong's attempts to concretise and legitimise military rule through a concept that Acheampong had termed 'union government' or Unigov. Had Acheampong remained, Unigov would have combined elected civilians with appointed military leaders, thereby, it was argued, removing the need for party politics and the divisive politicisation of public life. Opposition to any form of military rule was mounting from professionals, students and churches. So Akuffo's rejigged Supreme Military Council, dubbed SMC II, abandoned Unigov in favour of fully democratic elections. The ban on political parties was lifted and a committee was organised to draft yet another constitution for a Third Republic. Civilian elections were scheduled for July 1979. In the midst of anxious and subdued national expectations for change Jonah and Theo prepared to leave for London.

In London for a Masters degree

Theo decided to accompany her husband to London so that she could work for a year. She reluctantly left the boys with her mother in Accra, as the student accommodation that Jonah had arranged did not cater for families. The couple stayed in a postgraduate hostel, Lillian Penson Hall, about equidistant from Paddington, Kensington Gardens and Hyde Park. Theo missed her boys desperately and she begged Sam to send for them. They contacted a lady who had looked after Fidel, Nat's son, in Brighton and she recommended a family who would take care of Richard and Andrew on a full-time basis. This would allow Theo and Sam to visit their boys on weekends. Unfortunately, these brief weekend visits proved to be horribly distressing for all of them. Parents and sons always parted with the boys screaming and Theo and Sam feeling choked up. After a while, they decided to send them back to their grandparents in Ghana.

Jonah submerged himself in his studies. Experience from his own career and the harsh work environment at Obuasi invigorated his contributions to the course and this in turn propelled his enthusiasm for his own research. Typical dissertation topics at that time focused on the mechanical side of mining, on underground matters such as 'The development of high speed pneumatic drills' and similar subjects. Jonah's area of interest was therefore unusual and his young supervisor, Ralph Spencer, was equally excited by it. The thesis evolved into a comparative analysis of mineral fiscal regimes from an investor's perspective. It necessitated modelling a mine's cash flow and simulating the impact of various fiscal policies on it based on the actual tax rules from ten gold-producing countries. In the absence of sophisticated computer software Jonah and Spencer set about developing their own program to execute the simulations. In fact, Spencer went on to make a fortune from establishing a company specialising in mine finance software.

The research so intrigued Jonah that he was reluctant to return to the mine as a rock man. He considered changing direction towards mineral policy development and contemplated working for the World Bank. He discussed this with Ron Gaskell, his Camborne mentor and teacher. The two had kept in touch over the years and Gaskell was impressed with the feedback that he was getting from RSM on Jonah's thesis. Around this time an advert appeared in a United Kingdom broadsheet for an analyst to work in a new unit of the Commonwealth Secretariat to advise commonwealth countries on mineral policy. Jonah applied and attended a stimulating interview. He was offered the position but baulked at the salary.

Theo had no problem in finding agency nurse work. It paid well and was flexible. In the summer they moved to cheaper accommodation in north London at Wood Green and Jonah started job hunting while he was writing his dissertation. He tried his luck at the Gloucester Hotel, near Imperial College's computer lab. After hearing Jonah's enquiry about vacancies the hotel employee asked first to see his passport. Jonah's student visa allowed him to work part-time but he hoped to work 60 hours a week to take home some hard currency. Unfazed, he started, 'Do you ask for everyone's passport or are you just asking me?'

The manager was unprepared for the challenge to her authority and didn't know what to say. Jonah continued, 'Why do you presume I am not bloody British?' She was now so ashamed at her implied prejudice that she cowered and apologised profusely for any offence caused. 'Would you have asked me for my passport if I were white?' Jonah didn't let up. Not able to apologise enough, the manager immediately offered him a job as a receiving bay manager.

Jonah proudly recounted his bullying tactics and announced his grand job title to Theo that evening. He started work the very next day and was quickly dispossessed of any illusions. The job entailed heaving large pieces of frozen meat out of lorries, into the goods lift and down to the kitchens. It was back-breaking. He couldn't bring himself to confess the grim details to Theo, but towards the end of one shift, as he bent over to balance a half carcass on his back, his eyes came to rest on slim, stockinged calves. With the weight on his back he could only raise his head a little. Theo tilted her body sideways to meet Jonah's lowered face. When their eyes met his grimace broke into a smile and spontaneous laughter. 'So this is a receiving bay manager!' she laughed.

At night Jonah worked in the same hotel as a time clerk, clocking staff in and out in between catnaps. In the morning he continued his receiving bay duties. After that he travelled to north London to Alexandra Palace for a four-hour stint in the bar there; then he headed back to west London to spend time in the computer lab before his night job at the Gloucester Hotel. The large halls in Alexandra Palace were sometimes used to host professional examinations. After one accountancy exam he served an Indian man in the bar area.

'You are letting us down,' the man told him. Jonah checked to see that he was talking to him and not someone else.

'A young guy like you, instead of studying, look at what you are doing. You are letting the side down. You make the whites think badly of us,' the man said.

How judgemental, Jonah thought, quickly spinning a story, 'I come from a very underprivileged background. I couldn't afford to go to secondary school.'

This was no excuse for the ambitious Indian. 'But you speak good English! It doesn't matter that you didn't go to secondary school. It's never too late.' His sincerity and concern mollified Jonah.

'Thank you very much for your advice,' Sam said as he continued serving. The Indian couldn't see it, but Jonah shared his ambition to progress. It amused him to think how quickly people labelled and pigeon-holed others, and he made a mental note to try not to commit the same offence.

Jonah learned from Boakye Ansah, who was being sponsored at the same time by AGC for a postgraduate course, that the banquet hall at Grosvenor House Hotel, where Ansah was working part-time, paid well and was looking for staff. Jonah enquired about a job and was ushered into an interview.

'What qualifications do you have?' the woman asked. Knowing that he was overqualified he thought it best to downplay his achievements.

'Just two O levels,' he said.

'Don't be hard on yourself,' she replied. 'I don't have any O levels at all. You mustn't knock yourself. With two O levels you've done very well. Where did you attend school?'

'Shit!' Jonah thought. He was in a corner. He couldn't now say that he had been to the Camborne School of Mines after the O level line so he said the Cornwall Technical College, a nearby institution that came to mind.

'Where is that?'

She wrote down all his responses.

'Can you give me any teachers' names there?'

He had gone too far to extricate himself, so Jonah mentioned Ron Gaskell.

'Okay, come back to us on Thursday at 2.00 p.m. and you should be able to start work on Friday.'

He related the unexpected interview to Theo who, ever cautious, advised him to notify Ron. Jonah shrugged that off; after all who would bother to get references for such a menial job? Nevertheless, on Thursday morning something told him to call Ron. He wasn't home but his wife, Irene, answered, 'What have you got Ron into, Sam? He wants to talk to you!'

Sam fretfully called back later. Ron greeted him with uncontrollable laughter. He had received a telephone call from a friendly sounding lady who said that Sam had applied for a job and she wanted to confirm that he knew him. Not satisfied with a simple yes, Ron had started to sing Jonah's praises. He remembered that Sam had mentioned working for the World Bank and assumed this was the job in question. 'Oh yes! He was my student at Camborne School of Mines; he did very well there. He was studious and bright. But he's done wonders since he went to Imperial College. He's doing fantastic postgraduate research work there. He's really found his niche and strength in this mine economics field. I hear very positive things from his tutors at Imperial. I can't speak highly enough of him. He's enthusiastic and a very hard worker.'

After speaking without interruption for a minute or so, the caller's curt, 'Oh, I see. Thank you very much,' surprised Ron. He quickly got in before she hung up, 'Who is this?'

'I'm calling from the Grosvenor House Hotel. Mr Jonah applied to us for a catering position.'

Jonah did not bother to show up on the Thursday afternoon.

Bloodshed at home

The year 1979 was a good one to be out of Ghana. On 15 May junior army officers led by the gaunt, half-Scottish, half-Ghanaian Flight-Lieutenant Jerry John ('JJ') Rawlings attempted to remove Akuffo's

SMC II despite the fact that civilian elections were only five weeks away. They were court-martialled and jailed.

On 4 June a group of soldiers sympathetic to Rawlings and angered by the ill-repute that the army had fallen into succeeded in arresting Akuffo, Acheampong and other SMC I and II leaders. They freed Rawlings from jail and announced themselves as the Armed Forces Revolutionary Council (AFRC). On 10 June the former head of state General Ignatius Kutu Acheampong and the Border Guard commander Major-General Edward Kwaku Utuka were executed publicly by firing squad. In an attempt to justify its actions after the event, the AFRC hashed together a military court that declared the executed men guilty of 'using their positions to amass wealth while in office and recklessly dissipating state funds to the detriment of the nation'.[14]

In contrast to the international condemnation of the violent deaths without trial, the Ghanaian public, in a way that human beings en masse are capable of cruelty unimaginable on an individual level, cried for more blood. The Catholic Standard led an editorial supporting the executions with the headline, 'The Great Lesson'.[15] On 25 June word spread across Accra that more executions would take place the following day. An eyewitness recounted that by 5.00 a.m. on Tuesday 26 June spectators started to gather at the Teshie Military Range.[16] A red flag fluttered. Within two hours a great crowd was singing and chanting, 'Let the blood flow! Let the blood flow!' At 9.30 a.m. a convoy of army vehicles including two ambulances arrived. From the ambulances six senior military officers filed out blindfolded. A soldier lined up the men for slaughter to face their executioners. Within a minute they were riddled with bullets. They were the retired Lieutenant-General A.A. Afrifa and Lieutenant-General F.W.K. Akuffo, Rear-Admiral Joy Amedume, former navy commander; Air Vice-Marshal G.Y. Boakye, air force commander; Major-General R.E.A. Kotei, former chief of defence staff; and Colonel Roger Feli, former commissioner of foreign affairs. Afrifa did not die immediately. The crowd shouted, 'He no die oh! Finish um! Finish um!' A bearded officer walked up to the one-time hero who had helped to end Nkrumah's dictatorship in 1966 and cocked his pistol. It jammed. Taking a rifle from a soldier he fired repeatedly at close range into Afrifa's chest. However popular its actions, the AFRC had shown extreme brutality and a total disregard for human and legal rights.[17]

The inclusion of Afrifa in the extirpation weakened the AFRC's defence of its actions on the supposed grounds of 'house-cleaning' and 'anti-corruption'.[18] Not only had Afrifa been retired from the army for seven years, he was also a staunch critic of Acheampong and the SMC. In addition, his income sources and private assets had been probed in an investigation by the Sowah Assets Commission, which had exonerated him of all charges of corruption. Throughout the AFRC's three-month reign of terror, the mayhem provided an opportunity for many to settle personal vendettas. AFRC wrath extended to the market women and traders at Accra's central market, Makola. On 20 September soldiers sacked the area, publicly beating and humiliating market women whom they accused of profiteering.

Nineteen-seventy-nine was a black year of anger, bitterness, bloodshed and fear, at the root of which lay economic hardship and inequality. The AFRC had made its point. It allowed the elections to continue, putting the politicians on notice, and appointing itself as parliament's arbiter. A quiet, career diplomat, Hilla Limann narrowly won the election with his People's National Party, a conglomerate of ideologies. Only 40 per cent of the electorate bothered to vote.

Although fundamental problems with the economy had been diagnosed they remained untreated: the fixed and over-valued exchange rate, the overweight public sector, the state control of prices and distribution, and the ill-disciplined recourse to printing money. The economy continued its downward spiral. Strikes were illegal but they flared nonetheless. Unable to contain the Trade Union Congress, Limann's government announced that government workers (who formed the bulk of union membership) would be sacked for striking.

Jonah returns to the mine

Jonah's two periods of study abroad, first in 1972 and again in 1979, had coincided with tumultuous coups d'états. He returned with Theo to Obuasi in January 1980. With his Masters qualification he was now a senior mining engineer. His first appointment was as deputy head of technical services, an overground job that involved technical planning and scheduling production. The pen pushing soon exasperated him and he quickly went back underground.

Characteristically and according to plan, Jonah wasted no time in passing the underground managers certificate. This involved a two-hour written paper and an oral examination. AGC had three underground managers at the time and Jonah took over the south section of the Obuasi mine. The opportunity arose for two of the three underground managers to attempt the mine managers exam. One of the managers had to remain on site to supervise operations and the General nominated Jonah to stay behind. Jonah walked into his office with a calmness that belied his anger.

'I would like to know on what basis you made the selections for the mine managers exam.'

'Well, you can't all go. Someone has to stay,' said the General flippantly.

'But on what basis did you decide that *I* should stay?' Jonah pressed. When no answer was immediately forthcoming, he continued. 'From where I'm standing it looks to me as if Eckton and Hussey have been given the opportunity because they are white. After all, Hussey worked for me as my shift boss when I was mine captain. I can't think of any reason why I haven't been put forward. I demand the selection to be reviewed on the basis of merit.'

The General had probably not given any forethought to individual merit. He may have picked the two white managers randomly, or it may have been the natural human inclination to warm to your own that dictated his initial selection. He apologised and promised to give Jonah the next available opportunity to sit the test as, at that point, Eckton and Hussey had already left. Jonah remained behind as acting mine manager. Events would overtake his mine managers exam plan.

Rawlings's second coming

On New Year's Eve 1981 the Ghana Broadcasting Corporation interrupted radio and television broadcasts to announce the termination of President Limann's Third Republic. Toppling a government appeared to involve surprisingly minimal logistics. The simultaneous arrest of the incumbent leaders, grabbing a radio microphone and television camera, and a large dose of audacity were the key requirements. In this way a less gaunt JJ Rawlings made his second coming. Dissatisfied with Limann's efforts Rawlings formed the Provisional National Defence Council (PNDC) consisting of military men and civilians, not dissimilar from Acheampong's Unigov concept. Parliamentary democracy was dissolved and replaced with 'participatory democracy',[19] an incongruent description for another one-party state system.

On 5 January the PNDC chairman gave a fuller explanation of his coup, which he called a 'holy war'.[20] Rawlings's speeches revealed a personal and genuine identification with the masses. He was handsome and young. His height, skin colour and his self-deprecatory oratory with constant references to 'Comrades', 'People's Army' and 'People's Power' appealed.[21] The civilian members of the PNDC had Marxist orientations and they heralded a revolution. With organs such as the People's Defence Committees (PDCs) and Workers' Defence Committees (WDCs) in villages, towns and workplaces, the earliest manifestation of this so-called revolution was the harassment of anybody in authority, the rich and the educated.[22] Despite repeated talk of 'a revolutionary transformation' there were no fundamental changes to economic policy.[23] If anything, the PNDC buttressed the state-led economic system with the use of force. Through terror and a measure of luck the fledgling junta survived several counter-coup attempts.

Abductions, disappearances, murder, physical abuse and random confiscation of property cultivated a culture of fear and silence. One high profile case in 1982 was the unexplained murder of three prominent judges. Although four armed officers were hastily tried and executed for these deaths, Amnesty International reported that Rawlings and the PNDC remained incriminated.[24] The regime had denied the accused their legal rights, including the right to appeal. Bizarrely, the senior investigating police officer was imprisoned from 1983 to 1992. Then, when a group of lawyers attempted to commemorate the deceased judges they were thrown into jail for a short period. Those people who could, fled the country, and a growing number of political exiles added to the brain drain.

The 'revolution' and AGC

AGC was not immune from the effects of the 'revolution'. The participatory politics ruse of the WDCs made it easy to target unpopular managers for harassment and removal. Ashanti's deputy MD, Lloyd Quashie, was judged to be insufficiently pro-revolution. Rawlings asked Kwesi Renner, a respected geologist and the newly appointed PNDC secretary for mines, to nominate a replacement for Quashie. Jonah came straight to Kwesi Renner's mind. The two had had a heated exchange in 1980 at a workshop on mineral agreements organised by the United Nations Centre for Transnational Corporations. To Jonah's astonishment Renner had not taken offence at his brash and youthful challenge. Quite the opposite happened; after the session he complimented the young man on his well-expressed counter-arguments. Renner introduced him to respected professionals and encouraged him to read the latest mineral policy research, suggesting authors and titles. Jonah left that conference humbled by Renner's generosity of spirit. They maintained contact and with time Renner became 'Uncle Kwesi', a friend and mentor.

Two weeks after Renner's appointment, he sent the Ashanti regional director of the geological survey, Kwesi Banning, to AGC to invite Jonah to a meeting in Accra. Conscious of propriety and eager for his superiors to be aware of any government overture, Jonah politely requested the invitation to go through AGC's head office in Accra. The very next day the formal invitation came and Jonah headed for Accra.

Renner asked Jonah if he would like to head up a new commission that he planned to create for the minerals sector. Half-knowing that such a bureaucratic job would not satisfy a man of Jonah's energies he laughed off Jonah's courteous rejection and then he got down to his real purpose. The current deputy managing director, Lloyd Quashie, who was the government representative on the AGC board, had been appointed by Acheampong in 1972 and had also served as the chairman of a minerals policy review committee for the Limann government. The PNDC therefore wanted to replace him with Jonah. Without hesitation Jonah declined the opportunity. While he was grateful and flattered to be considered at the age of 32 for such a senior post, his career path was on track and he did not need or want a political appointment in order to succeed.

Renner explained the reasons for his proposition. Jonah was the most senior Ghanaian member of the technical staff at AGC; he could transform the deputy MD role; although it was a government appointment, the nomination had come from Renner himself and it was entirely based on merit; he could use his skill and experience from this position to implement important strategies for the ailing mine. Renner overlooked the initial refusal and urged him to think about it.

On his way back to Obuasi Jonah passed the AGC Accra office to warn Quashie, in as kind a manner as a young man talking to a senior in an age-biased society could, to mend his fences with these newcomers.

To accept the deputy MD position would mean leapfrogging the GM. Jonah was in a dilemma. His father advised him not to accept. Thomas was not just apolitical; he hated politics. This stemmed from his experience with Nkrumah's CPP. His son would make it without any political interference and to accept would mean getting into bed with the devil – not Rawlings himself, but politics in general.

Renner encouraged the chief executive of the State Gold Mining Corporation, a Ghanaian by the name of John Bentum-Williams to talk to Jonah. Bentum-Williams's positive comments as a government employee in the mining sector persuaded Jonah to reconsider. Bentum-Williams saw real promise in this new, youthful PNDC administration that was, in his opinion, sweeping out the old guard and their stuffy ways of thinking. By appointing Renner with his global knowledge and experience in the ministerial role, the PNDC had shown it wanted the best for the sector. Jonah then spoke to Theo who assured him of her support if he felt that he could cope with the added stress that the new responsibilities would bring.

On Easter Sunday morning in 1982, Bentum-Williams drove Jonah to Renner's house in Accra where he accepted the position. The formalities of the appointment would be completed in due course.

Anointed by Rawlings

A few weeks later Jonah met Rawlings for the first time, at Obuasi. The PNDC chairman combined a political rally with a visit to the mine. As deputy MD, Quashie was his tour guide, introducing staff, explaining operations and answering questions. After leaving the mine offices, Rawlings and Quashie made their way to separate cars for the convoy to move on to the mine hospital. The news had just aired on the radio. The headline feature was the sacking of Lloyd Quashie as the deputy MD of AGC. Word spread fast to everyone but the subject of the news. Quashie's driver delivered the blow when he sat in the car to move on to the next stop on the tour. Quashie graciously continued with the planned schedule.

That evening Rawlings entranced crowds at Obuasi's Horsey Park football ground with his easy pro-small man, anti-big man quips. Jonah did not attend the rally. He went instead to the OSC where all the talk centred on Quashie's cruel and dramatic dismissal. Jonah was saddened by the embarrassment that Quashie had faced.

Rawlings was looking for Jonah. The PNDC chairman, still high from the rally's success, sprang from his car as it stopped in front of the OSC.

'Where is Jonah? Where is Jonah?' he demanded boisterously as he marched energetically into the OSC. Jonah stood up. His colleagues sitting next to him hastily drew back – in those days of revolutionary justice you didn't know what was coming. Before Jonah had a chance to speak a strong arm extended to grab his right hand. 'Congratulations on your appointment as deputy MD!' Rawlings bellowed. Everyone gasped – at the announcement and at the Oscar-worthy histrionics.

'Only when you have crossed the river, can you say the crocodile has a lump on his snout'

1982–92

Rawlings had publicly anointed Jonah. Six weeks later the board of directors made the formal appointment. Soon after, Lonrho invited Jonah to London to meet the head office team. As Jonah walked along the Cheapside House corridor towards Tiny Rowland's office he passed an open door. Inside, sat Robert Dunlop, a Lonrho director, speaking to Rowland, who was standing. Rowland noticed the African. Full of charm he called him in. 'Oh hello!' he said warmly. 'Do come in! Do come in!' he gestured insistently. Extending a hand he enthusiastically enquired, 'And how are *you?*' As Jonah responded Dunlop strangely scurried behind him. Jonah looked over his shoulder to see the director waving a sheet of paper on which he had hastily written 'Sam Jonah'. Rowland's enthusiastic welcome had nearly masked his total ignorance of who the arrival was. The contretemps produced three hues of laughter, Jonah's the brightest. Rowland received so many African visitors, particularly politicians, that he often mixed them up or forgot their names and faces. Dunlop redeemed his boss's blushes by reminding him that he actually hadn't met Jonah before, so he could be forgiven for not knowing his name. Lonrho's MD invited Jonah to his home for dinner. It would be the first of many evenings spent together. Rowland's charm and fatherliness captivated Jonah; his ruthlessness in business would rub off too.

Moving from Obuasi to Accra

The promotion to deputy MD required a move from Obuasi to the Accra head office. Theo was heavily pregnant with their third child and so she stayed in Obuasi until she had delivered the baby, a girl named Tamara. Jonah lived temporarily in a guest house until his wife and children joined him in a company-rented, seven-bedroomed house. Beatrice would have liked the property, but Jonah wondered whether all the trappings of success would ever have made his mother proud of his career choice.

With strict curfews in place in the early months of revolution Jonah headed straight home after work. Now that he was in Accra, he was able to renew his friendships with Otoo, Brew and Perbi. Many of his classmates had fled Ghana to better their lot; Kusi, for example, was working in Israel. Jonah also made contact with Richard Peprah whose father's itinerant police inspection work had brought him to elementary school in Obuasi. Jonah remembered him clearly and fondly. Peprah had gone on to Achimota secondary school, where he met Jerry John Rawlings and his wife Nana Konadu Agyeman-Rawlings.

Building friendships with those in powerful places

Peprah's fleshy and bespectacled face fronted a sharp, uncluttered mind. Rawlings appointed him as PNDC deputy secretary of transport and communication and as chairman of AGC early in 1982. It was Jonah's friendship with Peprah, more than the fact that he was the government-nominated deputy MD of AGC, which would draw Jonah into ever closer association with the key 'revolutionaries'.

The 'First Couple' were an interesting match. JJ was half-Ewe, half-Scottish with a physical presence all the more striking when juxtaposed with his thin, raven black, Asante wife. It was Peprah who introduced Jonah to Nana Konadu, and to Rawlings's inner circle: the Tsikata brothers and Paul Victor ('PV') Obeng, although Jonah knew faintly of PV Obeng, who came from the Obuasi area.

Nana Konadu and Jonah clicked immediately. They discovered that they were born only two days apart in the same year and month. Jonah visited her modest state-subsidised apartment. He sensed that Konadu's excitement for the country's prospects were tinged with loneliness and covetousness for a cut of the action. She solicited ideas on how to help her husband to move the country forward.

With each foiled coup attempt against her husband, the First Lady grew in confidence and began to define her own contributions to re-volution. Most notably, in May 1982, she launched the 31st December Women's Movement (31st DWM), whose gender emancipation ob-jective was fused inseparably with highly political and money-generating ventures.

Jonah became a useful sounding-board and mentor to her; he en-joyed her wit and affability. They frequently lunched together, often with Peprah, and they exchanged birthday gifts. The Rawlings children even called him 'Uncle'. Theo enjoyed her home life in Accra and never desired to socialise with the new elite. She extended impeccable cour-tesy and hospitality when needed but willingly stayed in the background. Interestingly, despite Jonah's frequent contact with Nana Konadu he would not meet JJ Rawlings again until 1986.

A true revolution

Two years of virtually no rain followed by a very long dry season in 1982–83 and unprecedented bushfires across West Africa resulted in chronic food shortages. Ghana's situation was further aggravated by the forced deportation of about a million Ghanaians from Nigeria, an in-crease of nearly 10 per cent of the population.[1] The drought and famine were severe. People sported the 'Rawlings necklace', a reference to pro-truding collarbones; there was the 'Rawlings salad' made in desperation from the wild plants called bokoboko that even goats ate with disdain; sugar became gold dust; wives lost their desirable curves. In addition to the food scarcity basic goods were once again unavailable – the distri-bution and transport systems ground to a halt as foreign exchange dried up preventing the importation of petrol and other necessities. The coarsest toilet paper could not be found for love or money. Everyone used newspaper. If you were lucky enough to come across toilet paper for sale you were more likely to display it than use it. You might honour an important guest with a few sheets but you dared not let the entire roll out of your sight. Life was demeaned. This was the experience of even the middle classes, people like Perbi, an accountant, and his wife, a uni-versity lecturer. One morning their small children wailed for bread.

Unable to restrain his own tears, Perbi shut himself in his bedroom and fell on his knees weeping.

In that terrible year of 1983 the government decided that there were too many counterfeit 50 cedi notes in circulation so from a given date they would no longer be legal tender. People queued at banks to change their old notes for new ones – not that any amount of money would find food. In hunger and frustration the queues disintegrated into stampedes.

The government's initial policy to reinforce the statist system by controlling prices and imports and distribution, combined with the natural disaster to cripple the economy. To say that Ghana was on its knees would be an understatement. It had tumbled from that sorry position and fallen, prostrated, with its face in the dirt. The average annual GDP growth rate of 1957–60 of 6 per cent had plummeted to –5 per cent for 1981–83;[2] exports and imports formerly accounting for around 50 per cent of GDP sank by the early 1980s to 8 per cent;[3] and the purchasing power of the cedi in 1981 was 10 per cent of its 1971 value.[4] Inflation climbed;[5] in 1982, government revenue was 5.6 per cent of GDP compared to 20–25 per cent for other West African states.[6] Cocoa production, the bedrock of the economy, had dropped from a peak of 572 000 tonnes in 1965 to 168 110 tonnes in 1983.[7]

The economic crisis split the PNDC into three Marxist factions divided over the appropriate policy response: the June 4 Movement (extreme left), the New Democratic Movement (right leaning), and The Peoples' Revolutionary League of Ghana (somewhere in between).[8] The thought of turning to the IMF for help was anathema to the June 4 Movement, but when the PNDC's Marxist allies such as Libya failed to come to its aid there was little choice.

The government's realisation of the depths of Ghana's economic problems necessitated an ideological u-turn. Its former disdain for foreign capital was set aside to allow the intervention, with political strings attached, of the IMF, World Bank and several Western donor countries. IMF involvement forced policy changes decidedly towards a free market economy.

A Structural Adjustment Programme was formulated to be implemented in phases, starting with the three-year Economic Recovery

Programme (ERP I). Nearly $2bn credit was offered by the IMF, World Bank and other donors for ERP I.[9] The changes were profound. This was really the first fundamental, radical and sudden change in Ghana's political economy since 1957. Here was a true revolution.

In order to reduce the PNDC's risk of political suicide the various policies were implemented without fanfare. The structural adjustment of the economy required the abolition of nearly 6 000 controlled prices,[10] currency devaluations, exchange rate flexibility, institutional changes, and drastically reduced government intervention in economic activity in general. These changes were made against a background of the junta's internal spats, as well as rising public anger as the reforms squeezed citizens for the true cost of previously subsidised goods and services such as petrol and electricity.

It is quite remarkable that the PNDC survived at all, and that Rawlings and Kwesi Botchwey, the PNDC secretary for finance and economic planning, stayed on the liberalisation path. Prior to Rawlings the word 'devaluation' had triggered the coup that toppled Busia's government. Other African countries resisted and rescinded structural adjustment policies. In Ghana, the PNDC's reputation for violence undoubtedly bought the regime passive support arising from fear.[11] But with time, sections of the economy began to profit from the reform policies, particularly entrepreneurs and primary sector exporters.

An improving environment for the mine

Mining was one area that the government highlighted with the IMF for rehabilitation. Kwesi Renner, the PNDC secretary for mines and energy, recognised that any lasting benefits from capital injections would require changes to the institutions governing mining. He invited Jonah to join a team under the newly established Minerals Commission to update the country's mining laws. Coming from the bowels of the earth to these rarefied meetings with intellectual and industrial heavyweights initially unnerved Jonah. But they soon got used to the roughness of his manner and his heavy handshake and he quickly made an impression on them. Jonah's Masters thesis proved invaluable to his contributions on that committee.

Their efforts resulted in the Minerals and Mining Law of 1986, a statute that opened the floundering mineral export sector to new and sustained inward investments. The legislation, inter alia, exempted mine imports from import duty and allowed hefty depreciation of capital expenditure in the first years. It also permitted tax losses to be carried forward, gold producers to retain foreign exchange earnings abroad in order to buy supplies, and the free transfer of currency for dividend and loan payments. Junior exploration firms flocked with the stabilising political environment to seek fortunes. In the first eight years following the introduction of the new law, $1bn of new investment was made in Ghanaian mines and seven additional mine companies were established.[12] Other African countries later copied this mine code. While the prime goal of liberalisation in mining sectors across the continent was to attract foreign investment, the first versions of these laws paid little attention to mine companies' environmental responsibilities.

Jonah makes a name for himself

PNDC Secretary for Mines and Energy Kwesi Renner, often invited Jonah to accompany him on his overseas travels. He mingled with mining experts and UN consultants, absorbing ideas and changes in the global industry. This made the actual day-to-day AGC work in the Accra office more frustrating.

The AGC MD was Mike Bottomley who had come from AGC's London office where he had been deputy consulting engineer. Bottomley knew that all vital decisions would be made in London by the consulting engineer, and so he and his young, sociable wife, Pamela, took things easy. Besides, he was nearing retirement and had seen what had happened when a recently appointed GM at Obuasi (an Englishman by the name of Charles Russell) voiced his vexations about the managers thousands of miles away in London. Russell was promptly sacked. Hours of free time in Accra allowed Jonah to continue with his law studies. He enrolled at Ghana Law School for a conversion course that on completion would allow him to sit the Ghana bar exams. To Bottomley's bewilderment Jonah would spend ten days every month at Obuasi. The MD hardly ever went there.

For Jonah it was important to maintain his contacts with the workers. Although there had been friction between him and some senior black staff, his support was maintained among the junior ranks. When in Obuasi, he continued to socialise with the staff outside work, visiting their homes and drinking in the zongos. So close were his ties to the staff that even when sitting in Accra he would often hear of problems before the General in Obuasi had.

None of the workers could question Jonah's commitment and concern for the mine and their welfare. Queues of people lined up with individual grievances and issues to see him on his monthly trips. He understood the mine's problems inside out. Unlike in Accra, the time spent in Obuasi was fully occupied, but Jonah felt equally defeated there because he lacked the resources and the authority to initiate change. Charles Russell's complaints resonated with him perfectly.

An expatriate was recruited to replace Charles Russell as GM. His predecessor's dismissal likely explained the newcomer's complete lack of initiative. Bad production figures deteriorated even further. Jonah insisted to the chief consulting engineer in London, George Cappendell, and to Bottomley that the GM had to go. But Cappendell hesitated to remove him because finding a replacement would take time. So Jonah volunteered to go to the mine to act as GM for as long as he was needed. Always conscious to strengthen his credentials, the ambitious miner had wisely taken the requisite exam for the GM post following his promotion to Accra, even though he had advanced as deputy MD above that position. When he moved back to Obuasi to temporarily fill the role Jonah became AGC's first African GM.

Jonah relished the opportunity to show what he knew the mine could do production-wise despite resource and other external constraints. It was during his three-month stint as the General that he really made his name. Under his command the mine produced the best quarterly results in five years. His readiness to take a 'demotion' won all the workers over. Morale rose as they saw the GM was not asking anything of them that he was not prepared to do himself. Instead of dictating from behind a desk Jonah descended into the mine; he seemed to be everywhere at all hours of the day and night and refused to allow hiccups to excuse missed targets.

When the mill manager warned that with the unexpected rise in production they were running out of grinding media, everyone rose to the challenge. The chief engineer asked whether old grinding balls would do. Before the mine had fallen on hard times they used to replace these golf-sized balls well before they had worn out. Some of these old balls were found and polished up for re-use. A driver recalled seeing a jackknifed truck some years back on the road to Weija some 150 miles south-east of Obuasi, and he swore that similar looking balls had flooded the accident area. Jonah sent him with a company truck and a couple of labourers to see if they could locate the spot. Unbelievably they did. They dug up the overgrown verges and uncovered a truck full of the steel balls. The workforce brimmed with ingenuity and commitment.

The turn-around astounded the remote controllers in London – Rowland in particular. Once Jonah had set the standard for the incoming GM he returned to Accra.

A relationship develops with the International Finance Corporation

A unit of the International Finance Corporation (IFC) headed by a banker named John Pott was in Accra. Lonrho had initially approached the IFC in 1982 for financial help for the mine. Back then, Ghana's political and economic instability hardly enthused IFC involvement. But conversations were renewed in earnest after the country embarked on the Economic Recovery Programme to dismantle the state-led development apparatus in favour of a free market economy. Lonrho's consulting engineer, George Cappendell, and Jonah led these discussions. It was Jonah who guided the IFC through its due diligence at the mine. His technical knowledge and insightful assessment of Obuasi's problems, solutions and potential impressed the Washington-based team. So much so that Pott made Cappendell and Rowland aware that he would entrust any IFC investment they decided to make in Obuasi to Jonah's management. Besides his operations ability, the fact that Jonah was an African was important to the corporate aims and development ideals of the IFC Africa Desk.

Promotion to MD

The IFC's recommendation together with the excellent results from Obuasi confirmed Rowland's positive view of Jonah; he already liked the man, but now he had a firm basis for his faith in him. Bottomley, Ashanti's serving MD, was called back to London. The MD, under the terms of the 1972 Technical Management Services Agreement between Lonrho and the Ghana government, was to be a Lonrho employee seconded to Ashanti. Jonah as deputy MD was the government's board nominee.

It was around this time that Jonah met Rawlings for the second time. Jonah was paying a visit to PV Obeng, the de facto prime minister, at the Christiansborg Castle, the seat of government in Accra, when Rawlings walked in. 'You look familiar,' he commented to Jonah. When Jonah identified himself, Rawlings congratulated him heartily on the good reports filtering out of Obuasi. 'Keep it up!' he exhorted, to Jonah's elation.

When Lonrho initimated its promotion plans for Jonah, he sought Obeng's and Tsatsu Tsikata's help in gauging Rawlings's reaction should he be offered the MD position. (Tsikata's precise government role was unclear; he could be described as an omnipresent aide.) Tsikata later reported to him that Rawlings would give him all the support he needed; the PNDC leader felt that his judgement in backing Renner's nomination back in 1982 had been vindicated.

Such was the trepidation of upsetting Rawlings or the PNDC that Lonrho decided to seek its own assurances before 'poaching' the deputy MD, who was a government employee. Philip Tarsh, the Lonrho director most closely involved with AGC's affairs and who served on the AGC board, met privately with Obeng. Tarsh left that meeting perturbed. 'Did you say that man was your good friend?' he asked Jonah on his departure. Jonah confirmed this adding that Obeng could often be found at his house in the evenings. Tarsh remained silent until 1994. In a meeting between Lonrho and government ministers over AGC's possible flotation, Tarsh was at pains to stress how Lonrho had always behaved considerately towards Ghanaian sensitivities; he used the matter of Jonah's appointment as MD as an example. Tarsh revealed that in September 1986 Obeng had spoken at length and with considerable passion *against* Jonah's appointment, even stating a preference for a European in that post. It was only after written encouragement from Peprah (who was then the PNDC secretary for mines and energy) that Lonrho offered Jonah the MD position.

Lonrho's caution was partly driven by Rowland's feeling that Rawlings didn't like him. He knew of the Tsikatas' severe socialist views. Kojo Tsikata headed national security for Rawlings. He had fought in the Angolan guerrilla war on the side of the MPLA (Popular Movement for the Liberation of Angola) against Savimbi's UNITA (National Union for the Total Independence of Angola), which was being bankrolled by Rowland. Rowland believed that the Tsikata brothers had concentrated Rawlings's anti-capitalist sentiments against him. His fears were apparently justified: it wasn't until a few years later when Rawlings came across Richard Hall's biography of Rowland and learnt of his anti-establishment reputation that the controversial tycoon began to grow on him. Rawlings commented to Jonah that Rowland might not be so bad after all.

A real change in the locus of management control

In the autumn of 1986 Rowland invited Jonah to London to welcome him formally as a Lonrho employee. On his arrival Jonah was instructed to wait in London as Rowland had been delayed in the Middle East. A week passed before Rowland returned. As a result of the delay Jonah missed the law conversion exam he had registered to take in Accra, and with the workload ahead as MD, his legal aspirations came to an end.

Jonah thanked Rowland for the trust shown in him. 'But,' he added, 'I work on the principle that I am either in charge or I am not. If you want me to be MD I want the authority that goes with it.' All the key positions at the mining level in Obuasi were replicated on the eleventh floor of Cheapside House: procurement manager, surveyor, mine manager, chief geologist, metallurgist, personnel manager, a grand total of seventeen consultants and their support teams were deemed necessary to manage a single mine. Jonah explained that while acting as the mine's GM the acuteness of the problem had dawned on him. All of his divisional managers spent a disproportionate amount of their energies and time corresponding with the London consultants. Every operational decision, every appointment, even at the level of mine captain, had to be approved by London. And the annual two-week trips when the consultants descended on the mine in the imperious tradition of the late Major General Sir Edward Spears annoyed and panicked the workers. In Jonah's opinion the entire eleventh floor was an unnecessary layer – it was expensive, distracting, demoralising and ineffective. 'I don't need them, Tiny,' he said.

Rowland urged the raring 36-year-old to slow down; Ashanti was a huge investment for Lonrho, and the thought of loosening control worried the company hugely. Remote control had been working satisfactorily since 1897. 'Work with it and let's review it after a while,' Rowland suggested.

As a Lonrho employee, a managing director, a Ghanaian raised in Obuasi and an experienced miner, along with his strong personal relationships with Rowland, Renner and key government figures, Jonah was in an extraordinary and unique position to harness goodwill from all sides for the benefit of the mine. This propelled his confidence to pursue his own agenda.

As soon as Jonah got back to Obuasi he assembled his divisional managers. He announced his appointment and told them that with effect from that very day no one would have any communication with London. They were to stop writing and sending letters and telexes. Under no circumstances were they to respond to incoming correspondence, which was to be forwarded to the Accra office. Managers would henceforth take full responsibility for decisions and Jonah would take ultimate responsibility for their actions. 'Anybody who steps out of line with this directive will lose his job. I will ensure that he is fired,' he threatened. It was a complete shock to the system because the whole culture had been one of letter writing and waiting for instructions to follow. As a result, London was completely cut off. Production soared because managers on the spot now felt accountable. The small army of London office consultants sat idle.

To flex their weakened managerial muscles the consulting geologist and the consulting metallurgist sent a telex to Obuasi announcing a visit. This was a defining moment in the locus of management control.

Jonah fired back a response: 'The MD has determined that it will be inappropriate for these visits to occur now.' They didn't come. Costs were down and production was up. Jonah had proved his point.

There were a few of the London consultants identified by Jonah as useful provided that they relocated to the mine. Those who took up the invitation moved to Obuasi, including Leonard Clay as chief engineer (who later died in a car accident). The others retired or were laid off and Jonah made some bitter enemies in the process.

Now that Jonah had vacated the deputy MD position a lot of lobbying was under way in Ghana for the post. Rawlings did not want to appoint anyone who would undermine Jonah, so Tsikata asked Jonah for his own nomination. Jonah put forward Henry Otoo, an experienced mine engineer. The two men had worked together in Obuasi before Otoo took up a post in Nigeria. Jonah knew that Otoo was back in Ghana working for a salt mine. Otoo shared Jonah's work ethic; he knew the Obuasi operations intimately and got on well with others. Government approval came the very next day.

The first IFC-led project

Jonah speeded up and concretised the IFC discussions. A five-year Rehabilitation Programme for Obuasi at a cost of $160m was planned. The IFC led a commercial syndicated loan of $45m, the Standard Chartered Merchant Bank lent $40m and Ashanti contributed $75m of retained earnings over the project's life. IFC involvement was critical because domestic banks did not have this sort of capital to lend and no international bank would have lent money directly to a firm that had been partially nationalised, that operated without a mining lease, and was located in a country plagued by coups. Significant legal assurances were obtained from the government, Lonrho and Ashanti before the IFC was sufficiently satisfied to proceed. A major precondition was the reinstatement of Ashanti's mining lease that had been cancelled in 1972. Although the IFC stopped short of guaranteeing the loans, it acted as a buffer of reassurance for the international lenders.

Thanks to the participation of the IFC and international banks, AGC's single treatment plant, built in 1947, was updated and a new tailings treatment plant was commissioned. The tailings (waste) from extracting gold from the high-grade ore mined over the decades had been stored in tailings dams in anticipation of metallurgical breakthroughs that would allow retreatment. With fresh funding the tailings could now be economically processed to extract more gold using a low-cost technique. New equipment for haulage, ventilation and mechanised mining were procured.[13] Construction commenced for a new shaft system, the Kwesi Mensah Shaft in the central area of the mine, to reach 5 000 feet, then the deepest mining level.

A chance for stability and growth

Obuasi's rehabilitation coincided with the nation's regeneration. The first phase of Structural Adjustment stabilised the economy. Between 1983 and 1987 GDP grew at an average annual rate of 3.7 per cent and inflation fell to 20 per cent. In 1987 donors contributed $430m in aid and the government was able to repay $500m of loan arrears dating from Nkrumah's era. The regime's commendable performance in the eyes of the World Bank and the IMF led to a second phase of the Structural Adjustment Programme with further currency devaluations, strategies to boost savings and investment, and the divestment of state-owned enterprises. However, the austere measures restricting government expenditure aggravated unemployment and poverty.[14] On the political front, the PNDC continued to be criticised by exiles abroad for its undemocratic regime and internal pressure for political freedoms also stirred.

AGC's rehabilitation and expansion programme achieved its target increase in production of 400 000 ounces in 1990, two years ahead of schedule. All debt repayments were made on time. The operational success led to a second IFC-led project, the Sansu Project. The new goals were to develop surface mining, exploit lower-grade ores underground, boost exploration, and improve efficiency.

To treat surface ore and lower-grade ore cost-effectively two new types of treatment plants were built: a heap leach operation and an oxide treatment plant. Heap leach technology involves placing an impervious lining on a suitable site, dumping the surface ore on it and spraying a cyanide solution over the ore; the solution passes through the heap and dissolves gold in the process. The solution containing gold at the bottom of the heap is then drained or pumped to a gold recovery facility. The Sansu Oxide Plant was designed for surface or underground ores with oxidised properties. The technology is relatively simple: the ore is crushed and milled, then put into carbon tanks where the carbon attracts the gold; cathodes are used to strip the gold off the carbon (called electrowinning), and the cathodes are then smelted to produce unrefined gold bars. Diversifying the type and grade of ore extracted, and using different types of treatment facilities allowed a greater degree of production flexibility; it increased production volumes and improved gold recovery levels. Production reached 654 298 ounces in 1992. Funding for the Sansu Project came from a new IFC loan of $60m, and $33m from retained earnings. Standby loans that were arranged in case of cost overruns in the Rehabilitation and Sansu Projects were never drawn on.

Throughout this expansion phase Rawlings and his government gave Jonah and the firm unstinting support. When JJ learned in 1987 that the WDCs were giving management a hard time he visited Obuasi. Without saying a word, but in order to demonstrate his full backing of Jonah, he sat in the MD's car and drove around town with him. The act of unity quelled the WDCs. Jonah's relationship with JJ was one of mutual respect and admiration. The two men saw similar traits in each other, including their vivacity and dynamism, their hunger for change and their fearlessness. But Jonah's closeness with Nana Konadu did not extend to her husband. Unless Nana Konadu informed him, as she did from time to time, that, 'My man would like to see you,' Jonah chose not to initiate contact with Rawlings.

His friends warned him about how dangerously ensconced he had become in Nana Konadu's affections, and indirectly to Rawlings. Anecdotes circulated about the First Lady's vengeful streak for those who fell out of favour with her. Her influence over her husband led many, including Jonah, to believe that she was increasingly the power behind government. To get to the president you first approached Nana Konadu. Her frustrated days in that lonesome flat back in 1982 were long gone; she had now established her own seat of power with grand offices. The 31st DWM grew in reach and prestige. With the wives of leading men and self-made women as members it served as a useful national information network. Her power was such that if you recommended a candidate to Nana Konadu for a certain position he or she was sure to be chosen; if you asked her to save someone from the consequences of a misdemeanor, he or she was reprieved. Theo never joined 31st DWM, but she maintained a cordial relationship with Nana Konadu, occasionally sending her meat and other produce from the Jonahs' 25-acre farm just outside Accra.

Family life and the loss of Thomas

Jonah's family now lived at Villa Rose, a beautiful AGC property in the Cantonments area of the city. A second daughter, Samantha, was born in January 1987. As with the birth of their son Andrew and the death of Jonah's mother Beatrice, the joy of birth and the pain of death followed in quick succession. Jonah's father Thomas died early in 1988. His failing health from old age portended his demise, but nevertheless the moment of his loss was an insuperable shock. Jonah cried openly for his father who had been the single biggest influence in his life. Even as he thought of Thomas's strict discipline and the childhood beatings Sam could not have wished for a finer father.

Theo's children inherited their father's love of animals. A large aviary with a variety of exotic birds was constructed and the grounds were overrun with dogs. The house was overrun with visitors. Strangers came for help with their children's school fees or money for medicine and food. Theo whom Jonah admired greatly for her motherly qualities continued the open house policy of his childhood home. She kept the children grounded and in touch with their extended family. The boys went to the Ghana International School nearby. When Andrew's performance started to suffer from his newfound prowess with the ladies, Jonah sent him to his Alma Mater, Adisadel College in Cape Coast. The unfeathered boarding school experience toughened him up, made him appreciate his home comforts, and got his academic results back on track.

Learning from Tiny Rowland

As Ashanti's operating profits improved and the company became increasingly important to the Lonrho Group's fortunes Jonah spent more time with his mentor, Tiny Rowland, imbibing his negotiation and diplomacy skills. Often he simply observed; at other times Rowland gave his protégé object lessons encapsulated in pithy adages and enlivened with his real-life experiences. 'When I am your friend I am good,' he used to say, 'but when I am your enemy, I am excellent.' The occasion for that nugget of ruthlessness followed Jonah's supplications that he spare Alan Bond, the Australian entrepreneur who made an unwelcome bid for Lonrho in 1989. On one occasion when Jonah suggested that Rowland write down a verbal message that he wanted passed to Rawlings, the shrewd old man said, 'Don't think, but if you must think don't speak; don't speak, but if you must speak don't write; and if you must write don't ever be surprised.'

Rowland's relationship with Rawlings improved with time. Nevertheless, aware of the ideological differences between him and core PNDC members he hoped that Jonah's good relationship with the administration would improve Lonrho's access to Ghana's new free market opportunities. After a meeting with Rawlings at The Castle about a Lonrho investment in a former state-owned sugar factory, the press awaited a statement. Rowland filled them in, reassuringly concluding with an expression of confidence in the Lonrho man on the ground, 'Sam Nujoma'. Jonah could only chuckle at being confused with the Namibian president.

Moves towards democracy

Criticism from exiled groups and Western donors as well as growing internal discontent over the lack of political freedoms in Ghana led to the gradual lifting of censorship and bans on religious groups and political parties. The partially appointed, partially voted regional and district assemblies under the PNDC's self-styled 'participatory democracy' would no longer be good enough. A 258-member Consultative Assembly with a Committee of Experts set about drafting a new constitution using the

1957, 1969 and 1979 versions as well as PNDC recommendations and its own judgement.

On completion, a nationwide publicity campaign was launched to promulgate the draft constitution's major clauses and to advertise the upcoming referendum for the public to vote for or against its adoption. For a time it seemed as though the country had been wallpapered in referendum posters. They were pasted on billboards and cars, in shop windows and in private homes, on street vendors' baskets and on the sides of buses; some even hung from trees. This was the people's first taste of genuine democratic involvement in over a decade. Ghanaians' propensity to break into song led to a profusion of referendum ditties and jingles. 'Re-fe-ren-dum time! Re-fe-ren-dum time!' shrieked constantly from the television and radio. The sights and sounds of the campaign worked. On 28 April 1992 voter turn-out was high with 92 per cent in support of the draft constitution, which allowed for an executive president, a unicameral National Assembly with 200 seats, and a four-year term of office with a maximum of two consecutive terms for any president. Multiparty elections were set for 3 November.

The PNDC rebranded itself as the NDC, the National Democratic Congress. Ex-president Hilla Limann reappeared to lead a new party, the People's National Convention, which would prove to be the largest of the minority opposition parties. The NDC's main opposition, however, came from Albert Adu Boahen's New Patriotic Party (NPP) in the Danquah-Busia tradition. The Nkrumah platform was divided among the other parties, with Rawlings easily the closest match to the first president in terms of populist appeal.

The debates over and the eventual release of each party's emblem, flag and motto carried the same, if not greater, import as the parties' manifestos: 'Party of the People, for the People, by the People', 'Development in Freedom', 'Unity in Strength'. A coconut tree, a red cockerel, an umbrella with a bird's head, and an elephant appeared on posters, caps and T-shirts. The jingles multiplied: 'Exercise your power as a ci-ti-zen'; 'Exer-cise your fran-chi-ise'. The Akan language has a relatively small vocabulary, which lends itself to onomatopoeic expression. An NPP supporter meeting a friend would exclaim: 'Kukurudu!' (The sound of an elephant's thundering steps.) If the friend was a fellow supporter the reply would be: 'Ewosowoso!' ('Shaking-shaking', of the ground.) Then together they'd chime: 'Osono nie!' ('It's the elephant!' – the NPP emblem.)

The Ashanti Mine Expansion Project

Back at Obuasi the Sansu Surface Mining Project proved to be an exceptional success. This method that was cheap to mine and cheap to treat would soon contribute 40 per cent of AGC's gold production. On the back of this the IFC supported Ashanti with a third, more ambitious project in November 1992, the Ashanti Mine Expansion Project (Amep). The total costs were estimated at $305m with $140m provided by banks and the remainder from retained earnings. Amep aimed to build on the previous seven years' growth trend by fully exploiting the mine's untapped lower-grade quartz and sulphides ores; expanding open pit (surface) production; infrastructure improvements over- and underground, particularly mechanisation and improving shaft access to allow the use of large machinery; further treatment plant developments; human resource development; and safety and loss control. Amep also incorporated a cost reduction drive, exploration, and environmental improvements.

In terms of the environmental measures, a visitor to Obuasi in the mid-1980s would have noticed the denuded hills around the mine. Arsenic compounds released from the archaic Pampora Treatment Plant's roasting process poisoned the air. Under Amep an extensive reforestation programmed started. The IFC-led projects also allowed the adoption of the latest technologies to reduce the environmental impact of the mine's activities.

One technological development that illustrated the pioneering spirit and new environmental consciousness under Jonah's leadership was the adoption of the Biox treatment process. Traditional treatment of refractory ore (ore in which the gold is embedded with other minerals in such a way that it is particularly difficult to separate it out) involves roasting the crushed ore, which releases arsenic compounds into the atmosphere. A South African company, Gencor, had patented a low-cost, environmentally friendly process using bacteria, *Thiobacillus Ferro-oxidans*, to break down the refractory ore. The process takes place in tanks under controlled heat and acidity conditions. The bacteria feed on the ore, breaking up the rock matrix into gold, arsenic and sulphides. This allows the gold to be extracted in orthodox ways (and the arsenic, in a separate process, is transformed into a stable and insoluble state for storage or re-sale). Ashanti was the first mine to use this new technology on a large commercial scale. When Jonah and his team opted for Biox out of four-teen alternative and more orthodox treatment methods, one gold ex-ecutive predicted: 'History will either label you a genius or a fool, Sam!' Biox proved to be a resounding success.

Jonah's relationship with Rowland strengthened following Sam's ap-pointment to the Lonrho board in 1992, which necessitated month-ly trips to London. The manner of his non-executive appointment typified Rowland's cavalier treatment of his board. He simply made up his mind and announced the newcomer. Despite Lonrho's African-based businesses not a single African had sat on its board. One director contemptuously remarked, 'Whatever next, Mark Arap too?' refer-ring to a relative of the Kenyan president who was not highly thought of despite his usefulness in heading Lonrho's exploits in Kenya. Had Rowland been more consultative with his fellow board members then Jonah's reception might have been warmer. Of the Lonrho directors, Philip Tarsh, who also served on Ashanti's board, became an invaluable mentor who was exceptionally supportive of Jonah's changes at Obuasi. With time and frequent contact, the other directors' initial wariness of and prejudices towards Jonah were slowly worn away.

A political offer

Jonah travelled to London in May 1992 to make presentations to banks to encourage syndicate support for Amep. One of the Tsikata brothers, Fui, acted as AGC's company lawyer and the head of the Minerals Commission, Kofi Ansah, also an AGC director, accompanied him. They returned after a session in the City to their hotel, the Hilton Metropole. Sam called Theo at about 7.00 p.m., as was his habit, and then the three went for dinner.

A red voicemail light flashed on the telephone when Jonah returned to his room. It was a frantic Theo. Christian Aggrey, the editor of the government mouthpiece, the *Ghanaian Times*, had called Villa Rose urgently requesting a recent photograph of Jonah for a profile to go out that Thursday – in two days' time. 'This is very good news for you and your family and for Ghana!' he had kept repeating. The publicity-shy Theo cautiously promised to get her husband to return the editor's call and Jonah did so immediately. Aggrey, with a child's Christmas Eve excitement, refused to divulge the purpose of the profile; he had been sworn to secrecy. 'But it's very good news for Ghana!' he said again and again. Jonah declined to provide a picture unless he knew what it was for.

A private press industry had burgeoned in Ghana since the removal of media censorship. New tabloids such as the *Ghanaian Chronicle* and the *Free Press* devoted about equal space to reporting sex scandals as they did to lampooning the PNDC, now the NDC. They included Jonah in this, assuming that his close friendship was with Rawlings and not Nana Konadu. Since the announcement of general elections following the April referendum, the tabloids had temporarily shelved their salacious stories to focus on political rumour, for which the public had a similar appetite. The papers were hot with gossip over Rawlings's running mate. In the strange way that journalists sometimes wittingly or otherwise camouflage specks of critical truths with exaggeration or conjecture, the tabloids continued to speculate on the identity of the vice-presidential candidate despite the official announcement in the broadsheets that it would go to a Fante, Kow Arkaah.

Arkaah was a CPP man. Knowing the strength of the Nkrumah ticket, particularly in the rural areas, Kojo Tsikata had brokered a pact with the CPP to allow its man to run as the NDC vice-president to ensure an NDC victory. The pact imposed Arkaah on Rawlings, who failed to endorse him speedily and unequivocally. This hesitation fuelled the rumours that Rawlings was holding out for a candidate of his own choice who could appeal to the Akan electorate to complement Rawlings's strengths with the other ethnic groups.

When Jonah reported back his conversation with the editor of the *Ghanaian Times* to Fui Tsikata and Ansah, they concluded that Rawlings wanted Jonah for vice-president. A political career was the last thing on Jonah's mind. He knew without a second's hesitation that he would have to decline any opportunity to enter politics. He had no desire to be a politician and disingenuously explained to his colleagues that he was not interested in politics. But a man in his position – as the MD of the country's largest private firm in terms of employees and foreign exchange generation, who knew the direct effects politics had on economics and on his firm's fortunes, not to mention his close friendship with the First Lady (she would call him into her bedroom when she was invalided by asthma) – such a man could not be disinterested in politics.

More accurately, Jonah was not interested in holding political office. His appetite for business grew ever stronger with the phenomenal progress that AGC had made thanks to recent capital injections. And there was more to do. The mine, he felt, was nowhere near achieving its full potential and he wanted to take it to the max. His helmsmanship was at a similar stage to a rocket on its launch pad that has just begun its countdown, 10–9–8–7; at best he was at 7 or 6. Take-off was imminent and the limits to which he could take the company were not yet in sight. He did not want to get off this ride for anything, least of all for Ghanaian politics.

Theo called again within thirty minutes. This time Nana Konadu had telephoned insisting that Jonah get back to her straight away. Fui Tsikata advised against an immediate response. Jonah needed time to compose his reply in such a way that would not cause offence. The three men spent a good length of time preparing a soft-coated rejection pill. Jonah had to show elation and honour; he had to sound reasonably interested. 'Don't be too ready to say no. You know this lady,' they counselled.

The next morning before the start of a major presentation to a large audience of banks to pitch for support for Amep, Jonah found a quiet room to make the call. Nana Konadu was not at home; she had just left for the office. He called there.

'Kwesi, where are you?' she asked hastily. 'Why didn't you return my call?' Jonah explained that he had gone for dinner and received her message far too late to ring back.

'You are going to be very happy, very happy indeed. My man wants you to be his running mate and he has asked me to ask you.'

She had barely finished her sentence when Jonah replied, 'I can't do it. I'm not interested in politics.' No sooner had he blurted this than he remembered the script composed the previous evening. He started again, 'Adwoa, my good sister.' In addressing her by her day name, he attempted to redeem the situation.

Nana Konadu interrupted him, 'Kwesi, I'm very disappointed. An invitation to the second highest position in the land and you treat it so casually, you don't even reflect on it?'

Jonah sensed that he was in trouble as Fui had predicted. 'I only put it to you straight because you are my sister, but when you speak to the chief, I know, as my sister, you will put it to him differently.' She expressed her disappointment again and the conversation ended.

As he always did on his travels Jonah bought gifts for the First Lady and her children. On his return to Accra he went to Nana Konadu's office to explain himself as originally rehearsed and to deliver the presents. The two were so close that no matter who was in her office Jonah would be ushered in straight away. On this occasion, however, he was left sitting in the waiting room. In walked Elvis Ayeh, formerly Rawlings's special assistant but at the time editor of the *Graphic*, a government-owned paper with the largest circulation in the country. Ayeh hugged Jonah warmly. 'My brother,' he said, 'when the history of this country comes to be written I hope somebody will record that you walked away from the number two spot.' He explained how his newsroom had buzzed with excitement over the story. Jonah was the perfect vice-presidential candidate; he would attract the dominant Akan tribes as well as the more conservative business and intelligentsia constituencies – Rawlings's most severe critics. Then, all of a sudden, they had had to pull the story. They were informed that Jonah had declined the offer. Despite his disappointment the editor respected Jonah's decision and admired his courage to say no.

Jonah waited for more than an hour before he had the chance to clarify his stance to Nana Konadu. She downplayed her hurt, saying, 'It's okay. Don't worry about it.'

CHAPTER 7

'The canoe must be paddled on both sides'

1992–95

Despite Nana Konadu's reassuring words to Jonah, things were clearly not okay. She pressed him for a personal contribution towards the NDC's campaign, suggesting that he donate T-shirts to be embossed with the NDC logo. The fact that he was not a card-carrying NDC party member was no excuse not to get involved. 'You don't want to help the cause,' Nana Konadu kept saying. The insinuation was that if Jonah wasn't visibly helping the NDC he must be pro-NPP. Eventually he wrote the NDC a personal cheque for 25 million cedis (at the time about $20 000) to appease his friend. Nana Konadu derided the amount and continued to question his loyalties.

Partisanship and clientage permeate Ghanaian society. There is little room for neutrality in politics. People are expected to take political sides; those trying to sit on the fence are pulled down on one side or the other. Students, teachers, churches, firms, institutions, newspapers, everyone by dint of family connections, home town or ethnic group has a 'natural' political leaning. The inability to focus politics on policy rather than allegiances is no doubt attributable to the relative immaturity of democracy in Ghana and it should self-correct with time. Or, less optimistically, it may be due to an intrinsic feature of the country. The ethno-linguistic fractionalisation in Africa, sub-Saharan Africa specifically, presents a unique problem in nation building not experienced elsewhere.[1] If you picked two citizens at random from a sub-Saharan African country the probability that the two would come from different ethno-linguistic groups is two times greater than in less developed countries outside this region.[2] In Ghana's case the ethnic make-up is as follows: Akan (Asante, Fante and various subgroups), 44 per cent; Moshi-Dagomba, 16 per cent; Ewe, 13 per cent; Ga, 8 per cent; and other groups, 19 per cent.[3] There are 25 linguistic groups with more than 50 000 speakers, and 79 spoken living languages in total.[4] This diversity encourages intragroup priorities rather than national concerns and can influence the allocation of resources.

Unsurprisingly, there was very little policy difference between any of the parties in the run-up to the 1992 general election. Structural Adjustment was nearly a decade old and every political leader pledged to stick with it, so there was a certain degree of reform lock-in. That said, democracy, by giving citizens a voice and therefore the freedom to disagree, heightened the challenge of managing economic change. Rather than policy, then, the main differentiating factors among the parties were the ethno-linguistic cleavages, patronage and historic affiliations.

As a result of Jonah's background – an educated Fante coming from a long-established royal household and with an anti-Nkrumah father – it might have seemed logical that he should form part of the Danquah-Busia-Boahen NPP camp. But Jonah tried to express his non-alignment, denouncing partisanship.[5] He told himself that it was possible to separate friendship from political allegiance. The media, however, saw things differently. Jonah's closeness to the Rawlingses, Peprah, Obeng and the Tsikatas fed into the public's perception that he was an NDC man. His donation to the NDC, had it been known, would only have confirmed this.

The eagle-headed umbrella of Rawlings's NDC comfortably won the elections on 4 November 1992, polling just under 60 per cent of the votes – almost double the support of its nearest rival, the NPP. Reports of rigging, coercion and other abuses led the opposition parties to question the generally free and fair verdict of international observers.[6] The NPP and three other parties boycotted the parliamentary elections that followed the presidential poll in protest over the design of the process and the uninvestigated irregularities. Unfortunately, the boycott led to a de facto single-party parliament: the NDC won 189 of the 200 parliamentary seats.[7] An alliance then formed with two minority parties raised this number to 198. Of the 35 ministerial posts, 21 went to former

PNDC secretaries.[8] Richard Peprah, the fulcrum of the government-AGC axis, continued as minister for mines and energy and AGC chairman. In August 1995, following the resignation of Kwesi Botchwey, he was also appointed as minister of finance.[9]

The progress of the Ashanti Mine Expansion Programme

The ambitious Amep set an annual gold production target of one million ounces by 1995. Within two years of the project's inception in 1992, the strategies in place had reduced cash costs to $167 per ounce, placing Ashanti among the lowest in the global industry. The series of IFC-led capital investments had allowed the exploitation of new ore sources, an increase in mechanisation and the addition of new treatment processes.

Impressive output and productivity growth had been achieved since Jonah's appointment as MD: output increased more than 300 per cent between 1986 and 1993. Productivity, measured by gold ounces produced per employee per annum, rose from 25 ounces in 1986 to 80 in 1993. The extent of exploration undertaken shot up from 700 yards of drilling in 1988 to 59 000 yards in 1993. In that year Obuasi produced 770 410 ounces of gold. Could a 30 per cent increase to a million ounces be achieved in two years' time?

The million–ounce target was partly influenced by the fact that gold producers are categorised according to their output: producers of a million ounces or more are 'senior' producers, 500 000 to 999 999 ounces are 'intermediary', and below that are the 'junior' producers. The categorisation affects the producer's cost and availability of capital, with bankers generally preferring to lend to seniors, whose larger revenue streams give greater confidence in their loan repayment ability. The ambitious target was also due to Ashanti's new appetite for challenge and the addictive taste of success; kudos too undoubtedly played a part in Jonah's motivation. 'Every Ounce Counts' was drummed into staff in a relentless drive to reach the magic threshold.

In addition to improving results, Jonah focused his attention on workers' welfare and training. Health and safety received new priority as Obuasi worked to reverse its reputation for frequent accidents. The number of injuries per million working hours exceeded 60 in 1992; by

1994 it had fallen to 13.14 with a stiff target to reduce it to 3 or less.[10] For the first time in Ashanti's history, company houses with private kitchens and bathrooms and with subsidised mortgage schemes were built for *junior* workers.

Jonah revamped the appraisal and reward system by replacing a flat Christmas bonus, the equivalent of a month's wage, with a performance-related scheme that offered up to 90 days' extra pay depending on production results. Ashanti obtained the agreement of the Mine Workers' Union to separate the company's wage negotiations from the Union's annual collective bargaining with the Ghana Chamber of Mines. In this way AGC could award pay based on performance, which potentially benefited the firm and the workers since the national wage deals tended to suit the affordability of the weakest mines in the industry.

Training opportunities abroad were made available to junior and senior staff. The inclusion of juniors mirrored the diversity of skills on mining teams in everyday work situations. Those sent to Japan and Canada returned to demonstrate and pass on their new skills to their colleagues. Gone were the days when African staff were treated as nameless, dispensable muscle in need of coercion and without ambition. As long as you had the aspiration, the culture engendered by the MD allowed you to improve your career prospects. Jonah espoused Ouchi's management Theory Z. As he explained in a speech during the Amep days: 'Involved workers are the key to increased productivity and … better co-ordination of individual efforts performed under a philosophy of trust, subtlety, and intimacy results in higher productivity.' Individual opportunity together with new production techniques boosted labour productivity at Ashanti by 20 per cent in the space of two years.

A critical element of Amep was communication. Jonah instituted informal open forums for discussion that were called 'Free Speak' sessions. Up to fifteen of the most senior managers along with at least twenty employees selected randomly from all ranks and divisions would meet in a relaxed setting such as a beach resort for all-day discussions. No topic was barred from discussion. The sessions thrashed out issues concerning the mine, workers and, importantly, the future, where Ashanti wanted to be. Free Speak improved communications, allowed a high level of bottom-up contributions to management decision-making, and fostered strategy buy-in. At times taskforces arose out of Free Speak sessions and small teams, which included at least one of the session attendees, were charged to investigate the matter at hand and report back to the appropriate manager.

Jonah knew from personal experience that there was a dearth of entertainment in Obuasi. In an effort to rectify matters he introduced a company radio station that was later donated to the town's administration to operate. He also persuaded the board of directors to invest in the town's football team. The Goldfields Sporting Club of Obuasi had been formed in 1978 by miners and languished in Division Two of Ghana's non-professional football league. Ashanti bought the club in 1989. A 25 000-seater stadium, the best-equipped ground in Ghana and one of the few in Africa owned by a club rather than the state, was completed in 1991. The stadium was named after Len Clay, Obuasi's chief engineer who had championed the project and died in a car accident during its construction. Sir Bobby Charlton's Football Foundation assisted the club technically for a period and advised on the establishment of an academy for promising youths. The investment paid off quickly. In 1993, Goldfields Football Club, known affectionately as 'the Miners', won its first major trophy, the Ghana FA Cup. In 1994, when the football league turned professional in Ghana, Goldfields raised the inaugural league championship cup. The orange and black strip of the club covered the town. There tended to be a positive correlation between the football club's fortunes and morale and production on the mine. True to this, production managers reported that output increased considerably in the days following that victory.

Ashanti returns to the London Stock Exchange

As the million-ounce chase stepped up in pace, the government was pressured to demonstrate to the ever watchful Western economic powers that it was committed to the divestment aspects of Structural Adjustment. Until then, it had approached privatisation selectively, holding off the disposal of its most valuable stake in the newly profitable Ashanti Goldfields. The government started discussions to sell part of its 55 per cent share in AGC privately through the IFC. In the course of this Jonah proposed an alternative strategy – flotation on the London Stock Exchange and on Ghana's fledgling stock exchange. He argued that flotation would realise greater value for the government. Lonrho had no objections, although it did not want to reduce its 45 per cent stake.

Jonah felt that flotation would break the constraints of a perpetually cash-strapped owner, the Ghana government, and a conservative one, Lonrho. Without a controlling shareholder, Jonah looked forward to in-dependence of strategy. He thought back to how in 1991 Kwesi Renner had offered Ashanti ownership of the Abosso and Tarkwa mines. Abosso had been abandoned in the 1960s when the expatriate owners called the striking workers' bluff by carrying out a threat to flood the mine unless they returned to work on the same pay terms.[11] Jonah sent a team to assess and assay samples from both mines. The reports revealed un-complicated ores, which would be relatively cheap and straightforward to process. Jonah met Renner and a World Bank International Development Association officer who offered a virtually free, highly concessionary credit of $3m to assist Ashanti to kick-start these mines. His perception of the huge potential of both the mines, even without the additional offer of cash, led Jonah there and then to conclude a memorandum of understanding with the government that he faxed to Lonrho. The same day Lonrho shot back an angry rebuke. Jonah was not authorised to look beyond Obuasi; Lonrho had no desire to increase its mining presence in Ghana and he was to unwind any commitment made forthwith. It was a great commercial opportunity but the MD had to return to the ministry to rescind the offer, to the shock of the minis-ter and the World Bank representative. (Tarkwa was later sold in a bid-ding process to Gold Fields of South Africa, which also went on to acquire Abosso. In 2004 Gold Fields's Ghana mines were producing 800 000 ounces at a competitive cash cost.) The memory of this missed opportunity only increased the allure of autonomy as a public limited company for Jonah. But he failed to consider adequately the force that shareholders and their expectations would have on his strategy choices.

The company's strong growth path over the previous seven years gave confidence in its future potential. AGC's financial relationships had grown with successive rounds of IFC-led syndicated loans. The same bankers convened regularly at mine industry conferences where the fizz

was all about AGC's projects and recent successes. The company's reputation for delivering operational results and repaying debts on time created significant interest in the flotation. A panel of the world's leading
investment bankers paraded themselves to manage the initial public offering (IPO). James Capel – led by Andy Quinn, an experienced banker
with a disarming manner – won the contest. James Capel's initial estimated valuation of $900m was the highest. Quinn assisted AGC to
select lead accountancy and law firms – Deloitte & Touche and Norton
Rose. At the 'all-hands' meeting the timetable and allocation of tasks
and responsibilities were agreed.

A team of about two hundred bankers, advisers, lawyers, accountants
and coordinators worked not only to introduce Ashanti to the investment community, but also to introduce Ghana, and indeed Africa.
Jonah's ability to engage at all levels from president to junior staff came
to the fore and his enthusiasm for the process energised everyone.
Optimism solidified with the rising gold price, in part buoyed by the
uncertainty over the peacefulness of South Africa's forthcoming landmark elections (in 1994) and the impact that these might have on the
world's gold supply.

In order to ensure effective project management organisational
changes had been occurring throughout the IFC period. Now further
changes were made to Ashanti's managerial structure. From 1994 Jonah
was no longer referred to as the MD but the CEO. Mark Keatley, who
had assisted the company for years as an IFC employee, was headhunted
for the new chief financial officer (CFO) position. A new role of chief
operating officer (COO) was created. Besides the usual due diligence
process and having to restate historic accounting data using international accounting standards, unique legal and practical problems arose.

Ghana's unreliable and archaic telephone system seriously hindered
the flow of information between Obuasi, Accra and London. Quinn
acquired a satellite telephone system and ensured its quick arrival in
Ghana by packing the components in suitcases for a young banker, a
member of the IPO team, to travel with. The case that was randomly
picked for inspection at Accra's international airport looked as though
it contained camera parts, an explanation that the customs officer hes-
itantly accepted. The equipment could easily have landed the banker in

prison and the much-needed technology could have been confiscated until orders and licences from the top approving its legitimate purpose slowly percolated layers of time-rich bureaucrats. Things had improved in Ghana, but one general election does not make a democracy. Political prisoners still languished in jail;[12] the police were poorly paid, which encouraged widespread abuses; institutions supporting democracy, such as an independent judiciary, remained very weak. The possible consequences of his time-saving transportation method sent a chill through Quinn when he heard about his colleague's encounter.

Legally, the IPO necessitated a satisfactory conclusion over unpaid compensation by the government for expropriating majority ownership in 1972. Back then a capital suspense account of $6.1m had been created, representing the book value of net assets taken from Lonrho. Rowland agreed to accept this token amount as compensation in order to move the process along. The quickest way to have listed on the London Stock Exchange would have been to create a United Kingdom holding company, Ashanti UK, with Ashanti Ghana as a foreign subsidiary. In this way Ashanti UK could list its shares on the London Stock Exchange and be subject only to United Kingdom law. However, Ashanti's management and the Ghanaian government were conscious of the symbolism of the company to the nation and so were determined to retain its Ghanaian identity. So it was decided to list Ashanti in the form of Global Depository Receipts (GDRs), that is, as an international listing that would allow investors from all over the world to buy, register, sell and transfer shares through a depository such as an international bank without having to worry about cross-border differences in regulation. The London Stock Exchange had never listed GDRs, but the market was beginning to demand these instruments. To allow Ashanti to list GDRs the London Stock Exchange had to change its regulations.[13] Ashanti would not only be the first black African company, excluding South Africans, to list in London, it would also be the London Stock Exchange's first international listing. As such, the lawyers had to ensure that the flotation complied with the United Kingdom's company and securities laws as well as those in Ghana.

To obtain a list of the country's laws, let alone complete copies of the laws, was fraught with difficulty. Although the laws had been written, many had never been printed. It took nearly three months to see a copy of the constitution. The parties discovered that Ghana's Company Code of 1963, drafted by the eminent British Professor L.C.B. Gower, needed modernisation after lying untouched for four decades. Further amendments were made to Ghana's securities laws to accommodate an international listing.

The lawyers were taken aback to read Article 181 of the constitution that required parliamentary approval before the government entered into any loan agreement or any international business or economic transaction. It transpired that the World Bank had imposed these clauses in an understandable attempt to deter corruption. This came as a surprise to the Westerners who considered the impracticalities of such a prohibition on their own governments. Government business would undoubtedly grind to a halt if approval were needed for every government loan, let alone other 'economic transactions', whatever that meant. The Ghanaian politicians seemed oblivious to Article 181 as many mining leases, among other deals, had been signed with foreign counterparties since the constitution had been enacted without parliamentary approval. The government and the citizens had in a very short space of time adopted a host of new legislation supporting free market development, often without any negotiations with interested groups to allow reasonable exceptions to be incorporated. Norton Rose insisted on obtaining parliamentary approval for both the flotation and the recently renewed mining lease.

After Ashanti and its lawyers were satisfied over the issues of tax stability and protection from expropriation, the legal debate moved to the matter of a golden share. In this regard European precedents were considered. For example, in the 1980s golden shares were attached to French and British state enterprises when they were privatised. Industries such as banking and telecommunications were deemed to be of strategic national importance and so these governments maintained a golden share in the post-privatisation companies to enable them to block unwanted corporate changes. All parties agreed that it would be appropriate to issue the Ghana government a golden share in Ashanti, representing ultimate sovereign rights of control and veto. It proved to be a politically expedient mechanism to win over public support for the

IPO. At the time little thought was given as to how this golden share might be exercised.

Despite the firm's Victorian and British roots, Ghanaians regarded Ashanti as the jewel in the country's economy. It is difficult to find another company whose emotional tie to a country is as strong as Ashanti Goldfields is to Ghanaians. The firm's recent resurgence epitomised the nation's progress. Besides the economic importance of Obuasi in terms of jobs and export earnings, gold as a natural resource carries huge historical and social significance. Gold is gaudily displayed on every ceremonial occasion, particularly those of the Asantehene. Media opposition to the flotation equated the government disposal of its majority shares to a sale of the country's birthrights. One major lobby group headed by a Dr Jones Ofori-Atta was particularly vociferous in its condemnation of the flotation. With these sensitivities in mind Quinn's team devised procedures to allow Ghanaians to buy single shares of the company in a fixed price offer. The system enabled bank branches in rural areas to distribute and collate share applications, even accepting thumbprints instead of signatures for the significant number of illiterate people who wanted to invest.

Some NDC cabinet ministers remained opposed to the flotation, partly because of the political cost of the divestment but also because they preferred a confirmed value from a private sale rather than the uncertainty of a flotation. These fears vanished when James Capel refined its valuation to $1.8bn, double the initial estimate.

There was significant concern that Ashanti might evolve into a mini Lonrho because of the firm's interests in a pineapple farm, hotel, bank and limestone production. As the Ghanaian economy recovered, the now cash-rich mine had been presented with, rather than sought, several non-gold business opportunities. As these diverse domestic proposals arose, they were appraised and investments were made in those deemed to have an attractive payback. However, conglomerates were very off-colour with the stock markets and so a strategic decision was made to check the growth of these small, albeit profitable, sidelines. Ashanti would remain first and foremost a gold producer.

The preliminary flotation prospectus made a million ounces by 1995 a central promise. The document presented Ashanti as technically and managerially a Western company that happened to operate in Ghana, a country geologically blessed with a 200 mile-long gold belt. Ghana in turn was presented as an economic miracle in West Africa, highlighting the great strides made to achieve a favourable investment climate and its political and economic stability. Marketing was as much a process of demystifying Ghana and Africa as informing potential investors.

Quinn and Jonah embarked on a six-week global roadshow with over one hundred stops. It was common practice to train CEOs in public speaking and presentation skills before this stage of the IPO process as the institutional investors' initial impressions could make or break the sale. But Jonah was a natural orator and nobody knew his company as well as he did; he didn't need any priming and his humour soon creased up the straitlaced in his audiences. The two men pitched the company's growth plans to potential institutional investors, answering detailed questions not included in the prospectus. One important New York fund manager insisted that he knew Ghana and confidently pointed to an area near Israel on a map to prove it. Jonah was thankful that his blackness spared his blushes; Quinn had no such help. They both appreciated what an uphill task lay ahead.

While in Asia Jonah pondered how a country such as Malaysia had achieved spectacular economic growth, leaving Ghana behind. Half a century earlier Malaysia had been by several measures of wealth on a par with, and by other development yardsticks even behind, Ghana. Topical media and campaign issues of 'Third' World debt and unfair trade had overexternalised Africa's problems. The crux of the matter lay with the will and commitment of African leaders to put economic priorities before immediate political and personal ones, for which Jonah saluted Rawlings for his adherence to Structural Adjustment. He and Quinn waxed philosophical over the complicated causes and solutions to Africa's economic retardation.

The lead underwriters James Capel and Morgan Grenfell succeeded in assembling a syndicate of banks to help with the sale. The timing of the IPO coincided with a bullish market for gold equities and the offers relayed from interested clients indicated high demand. On 26 April 1994 the opening price and number of shares to issue were fine-tuned: 83.9 million shares out of an authorised 150 million would be issued at

$20, making the market capitalisation $1.7bn. The IPO was a great success in that the offer price neither roared away nor collapsed, suggesting that it had neither been under- nor overpriced. It quietly ticked up. The government realised about $400m for selling its share down to 31.5 per cent. Ashanti was in contention for the emerging markets' IPO of the year; at the time it was the biggest ever flotation from Africa and the largest of any gold mining company in the world. AGC stock now formed 70 per cent of the Ghana Stock Exchange. In the flotation process the firm generated $50m in new capital. Lonrho chose not to cash in any of its shares.

Ninety-five per cent of Ashanti shareholders were in fact individual Ghanaians holding between one and one hundred shares, representing 0.5 per cent of the company's total value. Thousands would attend Ashanti's annual general meetings, famed for filling the Len Clay stadium of Goldfields Football Club in Obuasi. Many travelled considerable distances at great cost to keep informed about their single shares and their dividend worth only a few cents.

Good relations continue between Jonah and Rawlings

While Jonah's relationship with Nana Konadu had measurably cooled, President Rawlings continued to support him on the business front. On a few occasions it seemed to Jonah that the president was extending a hand of friendship, which he neither shunned nor embraced. For instance, one morning in his office Jonah got a call to report to the air force base. When he arrived there, the president invited him on a flight in a light aircraft over the greater Accra region. The trip lasted about an hour as Rawlings pointed out landmarks and commentated on them. He showed particular interest in the eroding coastline. Jonah sensed that the president simply wanted to spend time with him. On another day the president's office asked Jonah to accompany Rawlings and a group of foreign visitors to the Akosombo Dam. The president piloted the aircraft with Jonah beside him in the cockpit, letting him control the plane for a brief period. They toured the dam, had some refreshments, and then flew back to the city. These sporadic informal episodes, which were observed by a few but magnified and fed to the masses via the independent press, created the perception that the president and Jonah were the best of friends.

The first production results following the IPO

Ashanti's first annual report as a public limited company (PLC) showed gold production of 932 323 ounces. The company had failed to deliver on the much broadcast million-ounce promise upon which the successful marketing of the flotation had hinged. The drive for quantity resulted in soaring costs, lack of attention to grade control, the mining of excess reclamation material instead of gold ore, and a demoralised staff. Ashanti had lost its reputation as a low-cost producer with cash operating costs per ounce now at $252, higher than the world average. Net earnings fell by 33 per cent, well below the market's worst-case forecasts.[14] Jonah was rudely awakened to the pressures of public owner-ship and analysts' obsession with short-term results. The experience pre-sented a steep learning curve that he had not been prepared for coming from a part-state, part-private company, in a country without a history of stock exchanges and investment analysis. In the euphoria of the flota-tion little attention had been paid to the changes ahead. The irony was that had Ashanti promised 800 000 or 900 000 ounces the market would have been happy with that. But he quickly learned to manage share-holder expectations and the output target for Obuasi was realistically reduced to around 850 000 ounces. This didn't mean that Jonah or the firm were about to ease up; they planned to redirect their 'can-do' atti-tude. The share price dipped but bounced back with the news that the firm was seeking growth from outside the 100-year-old mine.

'To get to the meat of a water snail you must cut off the top and the bottom of the shell'

1996

Late in 1994 it became apparent that the million-ounce target would be difficult to achieve. In November Jonah called his CFO, Mark Keatley, and John Clark, the strategic planning director. Ashanti had doubled its output over the previous five years; he now tasked these two to devise a growth strategy that would again double the company's production in the next five years. Clark took responsibility for what could be done and Keatley for how it could be financed. The pair presented their three-pronged strategy three months later, in half the time that Jonah had allotted to them. The three strands identified in their strategy were Obuasi, exploration and acquisitions.

Obuasi's underground development still required large amounts of investment; the surface resources while very profitable had a short lifespan. Consequently, with time, growth from the mine was expected to taper. Obuasi, with the geological information at hand, would not be a source of growth, and retained earnings and debt would mainly fund its future development.

Exploration up until then had focused on the mine's existing concession. Clark recommended obtaining new licences elsewhere in Ghana and across Africa. Countries formerly under the Soviet sphere of influence such as Mali, Guinea, Ethiopia and Tanzania were known to be seriously underexplored and minerally underexploited. The mineral resources in Africa's non-Marxist dictatorships also repelled investment capital because of the absence of dependable property rights and governing institutions. But the winds of democracy were blowing across the continent and Ashanti could gain first mover advantages by entering for licences now. Where large Western mine companies feared to tread because of both perceived and real political-economic risks, Ashanti ventured. (Small, junior firms with a greater appetite for risk were already swarming the continent.) Ghana had been a good training ground for coping with political and economic uncertainties. While the flotation had tried to underplay the firm's Africanness, Ashanti's new exploration strategy rather promoted this as an advantage. The firm's Africanised management and homegrown skills could be used as a selling point in pitching for concessions and licences in these prospective countries.

The speculative nature of exploration demanded equity funding, for which $60m was raised out of authorised capital to establish Ashanti Exploration Limited in August 1995. Ashanti's research uncovered excellent prospecting maps produced by Soviet geologists in parts of Mali and Ethiopia. In other countries, such as Eritrea, Ashanti was the first senior mining company to prospect for gold. The process started with reconnaissance work by a geologist or Clark himself. If the reports from this were promising then diplomatic efforts commenced.

Jonah led delegations to meet the senior policymakers and sometimes the president or head of state in a country. Whenever he was asked to, Rawlings would supply letters of introduction presenting Ashanti's track record of empowering indigenous staff through training programmes and incentivisation; the social contribution of the company to health, education and sports projects; and the environmental priorities implemented under Jonah's tenure. The high-level contact was crucial since many of these countries were not used to foreign investors and trust was an enormous issue, particularly in view of the sensitivity that extracting natural resources always arouses. Jonah's personal diplomacy succeeded in making these leaders completely comfortable with the firm; they relished the rarity of negotiating with fellow Africans.

In Ethiopia, before an exploratory deal was struck, the Ashanti delegation was honoured with a banquet and traditional ceremonies. President Alpha Konaré of Mali was so impressed with the firm that he made a two-day state visit to Ghana, spending an entire day in Obuasi. He visited the large Muslim community in the town and was pleased to meet his countryfolk and their descendants who had moved from the Sahel region to work at the mine. The president offered Ashanti a major concession in Mali.

In Côte d'Ivoire Jonah could not have been given a better reception. He was met at the airport by a line of Ivorian ministers, including the minister of mines who proceeded to escort him in a motorcade to President Henri Konan Bédié's residence. As the Ivorian president explained to Jonah, he had personally invited him to his country and received him in his home because, 'I wanted you to know what you mean to us as Africans.' His success was their success because in Jonah they saw hope, progress and improvement for the continent. He countered the predominant view that nothing good comes out of Africa. Jonah was overwhelmed by the desire of one African country after another for him to replicate Ashanti's Ghanaianisation and industrial growth in their own lands by using their own people. These leaders yearned for investment in tandem with a more equitable treatment of workers and the environment.

In the Ivorian town of Yamoussoukro Jonah was treated to a display of dancing and a tour of the Basilica of Our Lady of Peace. Then, in the mayor's office, the Ghanaian was declared an honorary citizen of the town. In a guest book signed by heads of state and other dignitaries who had visited Yamoussoukro Jonah was urged not to write a single line as others had done, but to take a whole page.

It normally takes three to six months to apply for and receive an exploration licence, but Ashanti was granted its first concession in the Ivory Coast within 24 hours. The president kept his promise to do all in his power to support AGC in his country and a very rich portfolio of exploration concessions was acquired there.

But exploration never produces quick results. Assuming that a property explored proves to be worth the huge investments needed to develop it into a mine, the turn-around time to production is on average seven years. So while Ashanti Exploration Limited managed this aspect of the growth strategy, the third prong – acquisitions – was put into motion.

Ashanti short-listed junior mine projects at the pre-feasibility or feasibility stages that perhaps lacked the technical, managerial or financial resources to develop fully. The unexpected welcome from African countries to AGC's exploration efforts encouraged the company to also limit the acquisition strategy to Africa (although opportunities did arise elsewhere, including a large surface mine in Uzbekistan). From an initial list of fifty potential targets garnered from word of mouth, industry contacts, journals and conferences, ten were selected for serious investigation. The company hit brick walls with seven of these, leaving three potentially offering value for money and operational compatibilities: Cluff Resources, International Gold Resources, and Golden Shamrock (respectively, British, Canadian, and Australian registered junior firms with African operations).

Before embarking on acquisitions, Keatley sought to put the firm's debt finance on a more permanent basis than the existing IFC project finance arrangements. In July 1995 Ashanti approached the international credit market for the first time without the auspices of the IFC. Keatley obtained a syndicated revolving credit facility (RCF) of $185m, 30 per cent more than the previous IFC loan, which was repaid. The RCF had a greater number of participating banks, nineteen in total. Most of these banks had been AGC lenders through the IFC schemes since 1986. Keatley also intentionally approached new banks to widen his strategic relationships. The new loan stretched over a longer time frame with considerably looser covenants. The RCF as a corporate loan, instead of project finance, was also cheaper. The success of the new debt arrangement showed Ashanti's maturity as a company as well as its creditworthiness and the financial world's confidence in the management team and its operations.

Keatley had long admired how the Canadian gold company Barrick had grown inorganically into a major gold producer under Randall Oliphant. At a mining conference he took the opportunity to pick the CEO's brains. Oliphant discussed among other things how the company's acquisitions had been largely financed with Barrick's New York-listed paper. A New York presence would boost AGC's trading volume and liquidity and increase analyst coverage of the stock. These perks would allow Ashanti to use corporate security as acquisition currency. It was an attractive idea. Keatley proposed listing Ashanti on the New York Stock Exchange (NYSE). Jonah approved, and it was put to the board who backed the proposal. While Keatley set about meeting the onerous listing requirements with a budget of $500 000, an internal team, and only two external advisers (Goldman Sachs as investment adviser and Clearly Gottlieb as legal adviser), Jonah made his first approach to a company on the target list: Cluff Resources.

The acquisition of Cluff Resources

The spirit of adventure and enterprise that took Edwin Cade to the West African jungle in 1895 seems to belong to a bygone era, so someone like Algy Cluff is perhaps of a dying breed. The Englishman made his money from land in Malaysia, oil exploration in the North Sea and gold in Africa. Cluff was the first foreign investor to acquire gold prospects in post-independence Zimbabwe. His company, Cluff Resources, discovered and brought into production several mines including Zimbabwe's largest, the Freda Rebecca mine, to which was added a small mine in Ayanfuri, Ghana, and an exploration concession at Geita, Tanzania. The immediate ounces available from Cluff's mines in production were desired, but it was the Geita concession that really appealed to Jonah. The Geita area, just south of Lake Victoria, had a long history of gold production but had been abandoned over the decades because of political and economic troubles. Cluff's exploratory work had identified 400 000 ounces of gold resources at Geita. This future growth potential put Cluff Resources high on AGC's acquisition list.

Sam admired Algy for his understanding and exploitation of opportunities in Africa. He invited him to dinner at the Berkeley Hotel in London in November 1995. Over dinner Jonah proposed farming Ashanti into the Geita project. Ashanti could contribute funds to bring the project to feasibility in exchange for 50 per cent ownership. Cluff stated unequivocally that no part of his company was on offer. Cluff Resources didn't need Ashanti and it could raise its own funds. Jonah expressed his regret because he sincerely felt that their two characters and the two companies would make a good fit. 'Don't call us, we'll call you,' was Cluff's polite rebuff.

Spurned, Jonah's strategy team regrouped in Accra to consider what to do. Although Jonah had the appetite for a hostile takeover, his board did not. Ashanti had made a policy decision to make takeovers as friendly as possible. But Jonah did not want to accept defeat; the potential value of Geita pushed him to find some way forward. Advisers were engaged to analyse the shareholder structure of Cluff Resources. Hutchison Whampoa was identified as the single largest shareholder with 26.6 per cent of the company. Ashanti's advisers approached the head office in Hong Kong, who directed them to Lord Derwent in London. 'I'm going to make you an offer you can't refuse,' Jonah put to him. He started by highlighting the lack of dividends that Hutchison Whampoa's investment was earning. Geita remained a prospect; not an ounce of gold had been produced. Ashanti could enable Hutchison Whampoa to realise significant value by buying it out for cash. At the time Cluff Resources's share price hovered around 75p; Jonah offered 105p, valuing the company at £80m.[1] Lord Derwent agreed to put the proposal further up the ladder.

Li Ka-Shing, the head of the Hong Kong industrial group, quickly accepted £21.4m for its entire stake. It was Li who had provided finance a decade earlier to enable Cluff to grow his gold portfolio; now he precipitated the loss of Cluff's company.[2] Within days Ashanti had mopped up a further 2.4 per cent of shares from various Cluff directors, which took it to the 30 per cent threshold that in the United Kingdom necessitated a full bid. Jonah offered the remaining shareholders the same cash price per share or one Ashanti share (then trading at $20, about £15) for every twelve Cluff shares.

By 5 January 1996 Ashanti had bought or received acceptances for 76 per cent of Cluff. Before it was announced publicly that Ashanti had control of the company, Sam called Algy to inform him. Algy was gracious in defeat; he wrote Sam a congratulatory letter and opted to accept mostly Ashanti shares for his 2 per cent stake.[3] His remark that, 'Being in love with Africa is like being in love with a woman who does not love you back. You feel like bursting into tears at times,'[4] expressed his personal sadness. But the offer had been too good refuse – time would tell whether Ashanti had overpaid for Cluff.

The takeover of Cluff Resources marked the first time that an African company had taken over a listed British company. Jonah returned the rights of use of the name Cluff to Algy, although these were included in the acquisition. When Cluff made known his personal attachment to certain company assets, Jonah allowed him to purchase these for a fair price.

Cluff accompanied Jonah on a courtesy call to inform President Mugabe of the takeover, since the country's largest mine was now under Ashanti ownership. The conversation that ensued in the president's official residence in Harare shook and shocked both businessmen. Mugabe, wild with rage, launched a tirade towards the Englishman. He had wrongly assumed that Algy owned Cluff Resources outright and not just 2 per cent of the company; in his eyes this was a material fact and the proximate cause of an unwanted takeover. Jonah could not understand the president's anger. He thought that it could stem from Mugabe fearing that the Freda Rebecca mine would fall into mismanagement under African stewardship. Consequently, he stepped in, recounting Ashanti and Ghana's history, and making a big deal of Mugabe's teaching days in Ghana in the 1950s and his Ghanaian wife. This established common ground. He compared Mugabe to Nkrumah, recalling the two countries' independence struggles. If it had not been for their efforts, businessmen like him would not be enjoying the current opportunities. This worked to puff Mugabe up. And, Jonah concluded, in imitation of their pioneering attitude in the sphere of politics, Ashanti was now grasping the baton to spearhead advancement in the business field. The flattery brought a smile to Mugabe's face. His anger cooled, but Cluff and Jonah left feeling hot under the collar. 'Nobody has ever spoken to me like that,' Cluff confessed.

Listing and issuing bonds on the NYSE

Meanwhile Keatley's preparation for a New York listing neared completion. Twenty-four million of Ashanti's 86.9 million issued shares would be offered in New York in the form of GDRs. Keatley desired to extend Ashanti's banking connections further by spreading its fees among a wide number of companies. Consequently, he appointed Merrill Lynch to assist Goldman Sachs to underwrite a bond issue to raise money simultaneously with the New York equity listing. Keatley planned to borrow $220m in seven-year 5.5 per cent convertible notes, exchangeable into shares at a strike price of $27. On Wednesday 21 February 1996, within four months of Keatley's six-month deadline, he and Jonah were standing on the floor of the NYSE with an entourage of Asante dancers and drummers led by Chief Nana Oduro Numapau II, the leader of Ghana's National House of Chiefs. Jonah rang the bell to open trading. The pomp celebrated Ashanti as the first African operating company to list on the NYSE. 'Ashanti is blazing the trail … Here begins an historical trend,' declared Richard Grasso, the chairman of the exchange.[5]

The bonds were more than three times oversubscribed indicating that investors viewed Ashanti favourably and approved of the new growth strategy. The fact that Ashanti was on the NYSE permitted greater financial flexibility, but at a cost. Compliance requirements increased and the firm introduced quarterly reporting in the manner to which American investors were accustomed. A by-product of meeting New York's stringent listing rules was that it allowed Ashanti to join the stock exchange in Toronto, dubbed the mine finance capital of the world, for very little additional cost in time and effort. Jonah quickly put the value of a North American presence to use.

The acquisition of International Gold Resources

The groundwork had already been done before an approach was made to Ashanti's second acquisition target, International Gold Resources (IGR), a Toronto-listed junior. IGR owned 45 per cent of a mine at development stage in Bibiani, just over ten miles away from Obuasi. Through a company called Ghana Libyan Arab Mining Company Limited (Glamco) the Libyan government controlled another 45 per cent and the Ghanaian government 10 per cent of Bibiani. Ghana never adopted sanctions against Libya, a country that had remained a friend of the government since the PNDC's early revolution days. The Libyan connection staved off Western interest, but the mine's planned open pit operations, the geology, its proximity to Obuasi and thus shared resources could provide Ashanti with very low cost ounces.

Throughout the negotiations Ashanti kept using the Libyan card to push down the offer price. It did not reveal until the very last moment that it already had the Libyans in its pocket. Jonah had made a trip to

Tripoli to come to an informal understanding with them. After IGR had agreed to terms in principle, Ashanti announced its plan to acquire Glamco's interest in Bibiani. Had AGC only announced the takeover of IGR's 45 per cent of Bibiani, it would not have had much impact on the share price but the news that it had bought out the Libyans too, nudged the share price up. To cover all bases Ashanti contacted the Sanctions Unit of the Bank of England and received a reply dated 10 July 1996 that no consent under the United Kingdom Libya (United Nations Sanctions) Order 1993 was needed for the transaction. Ashanti valued the Ghanaian government's 10 per cent stake and exchanged this for comparable Ashanti shares. Of the $125m total consideration for Bibiani, $99m was paid in new Ashanti shares.[6]

The acquisition of Golden Shamrock

Ashanti's manoeuvres had so far been able to block off contenders, but this was about to change. When the company made its next offer to Golden Shamrock, an Australian-registered company with a producing open pit mine at Iduapriem in Ghana and a mine development project in Siguiri, Guinea, the junior made the most of the situation to dally for a higher bid. JCI, an Anglo American subsidiary, expressed a strong interest. A two-horse race was only averted because Jonah had a good relationship with Peter Gush, Anglo American's director then responsible for gold. When Jonah heard that JCI was preparing a bid he telephoned Gush to warn him off. Eighty-nine per cent of the $235m cost of Golden Shamrock was settled in new Ashanti shares.[7] Lonrho was beginning to regret that it had not demanded tight measures in the articles of association prior to the IPO to prevent share dilution – its 45 per cent stake had been pared down to 33 per cent. Not once did the Ghana government exercise its golden share rights to veto, let alone question the company's corporate changes. The government was fully supportive. As Rawlings had told Peprah when the latter raised conflict of interest issues following his appointment as minister of mines while also AGC chairman, 'Ashanti's interests are Ghana's interests. What's good for Ashanti is good for Ghana. There is no conflict.'[8]

Ashanti now comprised four operating mines: Obuasi, Ayanfuri and

Iduapriem (all in Ghana) and Freda Rebecca in Zimbabwe. Output from these four sources totalled 1 024 803 ounces in 1996. Outside South Africa, this made Ashanti the largest gold producer on the continent. Two mines were under development: Bibiani in Ghana and Siguiri in Guinea. The exploration portfolio had grown to thirty-five properties in twelve African countries, with the most promising prospect being the 85 square mile licence at Geita in Tanzania.

An honorary doctorate

In recognition of Jonah's and AGC's meteoric rise his Alma Mater, the Camborne School of Mines, awarded him an honorary doctorate. His former teacher, Keith Atkinson, now head of the school, which had been amalgamated with the University of Exeter, was taken aback when Jonah informed him that he would be arriving with 70 guests. The town was overwhelmed by the numbers, the colourful national dress of Jonah's invitees, and the rank of some of the individuals. Jonah's brother, Nat, arrived in full regal attire as he had assumed the stool as Nana Prah Agyensem VI, chief of Assin Kushea (their mother's home town).

Jonah's humble acceptance speech centred on the contribution that the school had made in laying good foundations for his mining career and life in general. When he finished speaking there was a standing ovation that travelled across the gallery of the Wesleyan Chapel like a Mexican wave. After the ceremony Jonah hosted a reception in a hotel in Falmouth as a tribute to the school's teachers. The award had been decided on the basis of Jonah's outstanding contribution to his field. In a decade AGC had evolved from a single, faltering mine into an African multinational, a rare business entity indeed.

A federalist, multinational organisation

Jonah insisted that each of the recently established country subsidiaries should retain its own national identity. He was not about to impose AGC's former long-distance, centralised management on the new Ashanti. And he was conscious not to blunder on racial issues. Emotional intelligence with regard to cultural sensitivities formed a central part of the MBA programme that he designed with the Henley School of Management in the United Kingdom to groom existing employees for greater responsibilities. 'Multinational' to the CEO referred not only to geographic location; it also described the workforce and the mindset of management. Expansion necessitated a recruitment drive and with the global nature of mining expertise Ashanti became a truly cosmopolitan company. Newcomers as well as existing staff found racial neutrality difficult to adopt at times. One Ghanaian manager had to be counselled over his attitude during a presentation in another African country when members of the audience detected an offensive tone of cultural superiority. Others lacking this sort of emotional intelligence ended up leaving. Ashanti endeavoured to develop its properties abroad as Zimbabwean, Guinean and Tanzanian companies. A federalist organisational structure suited the stand-alone operations and allowed local talent to rise.

Opposition to multinationals tends to stem from pressure groups in the developed world. By contrast, most governments in the developing world clamour for these companies to provide jobs and basic, localised infrastructure. This explains why one African president remarked to Jonah, 'I see you are setting up mines all over the continent; why haven't you come to my country?' Providing decent housing, clean water and power as well as education and health facilities in the vicinity of a mine, even on a basic level, provides it with a permanent workforce. These amenities are not goodwill gestures but bottom-line business common sense. Any additional social assistance provided by a mine also serves indirect business goals by improving the authorities' and the public's perception of the company.

Environment and ethics in mining are relatively new subjects, only added, for example, to the Camborne School of Mines syllabus in 1978.[9] These issues have diffused extremely slowly across Africa. Many African countries do not have environmental protection regulations beyond shallow commitments to international recommendations. Where such laws do exist they are often not enforced.[10] The absence of indigenous lobbying groups is partly due to the political and economic strength of offending companies to silence protestors and explain away their responsibilities; and, arguably, environmental consciousness is the preserve of the wealthy since poverty necessarily focuses the mind on the immediate rather than the long term and sustainable.

AGC has endured a long history of criticism on the environmental front. Frequent complaints about the impact of the firm's activities on flooding, subsidence, deforestation, effluent contamination, as well as arsenic trioxide and sulphur dioxide pollution have been lodged against the firm at least since the 1940s.[11] Whereas the company's responses during colonial days ranged from denial to subterfuge, the approach taken since 1986 has been more proactive.[12] Before Ghana introduced its Environmental Protection Agency Act of 1994, Jonah had already raised the environmental agenda at Obuasi. The IFC loans necessitated it, and he was also motivated by the fact that Obuasi was his home town. Land reclamation of abandoned mines commenced, as did extensive reforestation and the adoption where possible of the least environmentally damaging treatment processes. The new subsidiaries adopted this philosophy. That mines can still do more for the environment meets with the rejoinder that governments have a choice: leave the minerals in the ground or manage their exploitation as economically as possible vis-à-vis the environment and profit. A mine would further add that the royalties and array of taxes paid requires host governments to carry the bulk of the burden of socio-economic development. The arrival of Ashanti in Tanzania and Guinea where mines were under development led to a flurry of, on the whole, positive press about the firm's provision of new roads, electricity, water, schools and health facilities.

Pressures to deliver in business and in politics

The whirlwind of takeovers aimed to guarantee that Ashanti met future growth targets.[13] The corporate costs and increased capital expenses arising from the acquisitions coincided with a 40 per cent Mine Workers' Union pay increase and a down-turning gold price to reduce net earnings by 40 per cent in 1996. Nevertheless, the dividend recommended matched that of 1995 revealing the pressure on Ashanti to satisfy investors. Ashanti still had a lot to prove to justify the flotation expectations.

Early in 1996, an election year in Ghana, Jonah arranged a meeting between Andrew Sardanis, a Cypriot Zambian businessman, and President

Rawlings. Sardanis and Jonah were acquainted through membership of the African Development Bank's advisory board and the African Business Round Table, an organisation formed to promote the role of the private sector in the continent's growth. Sardanis was considering expanding his finance and construction businesses to Ghana, so Jonah accompanied him to The Castle. After talking shop, Rawlings pointed at Jonah: 'You are not going to run away this time.'

The president turned to Sardanis, 'I asked him to be my running mate in 1992, but he escaped. Not this time though; tell him to start making preparations.' Jonah writhed in his seat.

Fortunately, Sardanis came to his rescue: 'You know, Mr President, there's something to be said for not putting all your best men in the front line. I have been very close to Kenneth Kaunda and when he came to power he wanted me to take a prominent position in politics. But I told him that I could do more in business. So he agreed to leave me in the background, and I believe I've been of more benefit to my country that way. Jonah is running your biggest company here. What would happen to that?'

The president grunted. 'We'll see about that. You're not out of this,' he muttered to Jonah.

'The tortoise has not any milk, but when it gives birth, it knows how to rear its child'

1996–98

When it came to the 1996 vice-presidential nomination, Rawlings did not ask Jonah again if he was interested in the position. Kow Arkaah had resigned as the vice-president in humiliation after being physically beaten by the president during a cabinet meeting on 28 December 1995.[1] He went on to join the new opposition leader, the NPP's John Kufuor, as his running mate. Rawlings struggled to find anyone willing to serve as his number two. The vice-chancellors of the universities of Cape Coast and Legon demurred. Rawlings's third choice was John Evans Atta Mills, a Fante professor of law and the head of Ghana's Internal Revenue Service.

Friends fall apart

The newspapers were astir with accusations of the misuse of state funds by Rawlings's NDC for its general election campaign. In December 1994 the *Free Press* alleged that in order to secure funds for the 1996 election, members of Rawlings's party were, 'Hiding their faces behind some gold winning interest in the country, and Nana Konadu is believed to have carried gold to Europe on some unannounced trips. Even cocaine deals have been alleged! …'[2] 'Since Rawlings or his NDC has no gold mine in the country, where else did the millions of dollars come from?' queried one analyst.[3]

The 'gold winning interest' was a clear reference to Jonah. In response Nana Konadu sued the editor and publisher of the *Free Press*, Ebenezer

Quarcoo and Tommy Thompson, for libel. In court the *Free Press* failed to substantiate its claims and the court found in favour of Nana Konadu. It was one of many cases where the First Lady succeeded in using the courts to impose injunctions, imprisonment, hard labour and fines on journalists, sometimes justifiably but often for simply printing accounts that put her in a bad light.[4] Amnesty International acknowledged that unrelenting government harassment had been responsible for journalist Tommy Thompson's premature death.[5]

Following the December 1994 article, Nana Konadu latched onto an erroneous rumour that Jonah was financing the *Free Press*'s defence against her lawsuit. The absurdity of such a situation escaped her. Why would Jonah financially support the publication of lies about himself? Jonah made repeated efforts to explain that the article also slandered him and that her vindication in court would also be a vindication of him, but his explanations fell on unreceptive ears.

On a visit to Tiny and Josie Rowland's home in London in October 1996 Nana Konadu vented her disappointment and anger that Jonah was distancing himself from them. It had started with his rejection in 1992 of the vice-presidency, then his paltry financial contribution to the NDC, and now her conviction that he was supporting a journalist against her. Tiny was startled by her vitriol. He feared for his mentee's safety. In addition, Jonah's soured relationship with Nana Konadu threatened to influence the president. There was a very real risk of losing these useful political allies. Rowland telephoned his protégé: 'Sam, I have to come and bail you out.' Without waiting for any explanations Rowland flew to Ghana in an attempt to reconcile the parties.

Jonah sent a note to be delivered to Rowland as soon as his flight landed in Accra; he wanted to speak to him in private before any recon-ciliation meeting. The government accommodated Tiny and his wife in a guest lodge minutes from Sam's house. On previous occasions, Tiny had always walked across the road to Villa Rose. This time he didn't and Jonah was perturbed. His loyalty to Rowland was unquestioned and he had proved it back in December 1994 when, along with just one other director, he had refused to support Rowland's expulsion from the Lonrho board. (Dieter Bock, a former Rowland protégé and Rowland's co-CEO had led the successful mutiny.) Despite their history, however, if it came to Rowland choosing between ditching Jonah and maintaining the Rawlingses onside, could Jonah guarantee where the ball would fall?

Unable to wait any longer, Sam telephoned the lodge and asked to speak to Tiny. He was put on hold for a while. When Tiny answered the phone Sam thanked him for coming, but explained that he had done absolutely nothing wrong to merit either Nana Konadu's bile or his bail out. Tiny seemed eager to get off the phone. He told Jonah not to worry; they would all see each other at the meeting planned for the next day; then he hung up. Before Jonah did too, he clearly heard a second handset drop. It explained Tiny's reticence.

The face-off occurred in Akuse at the former Volta River Authority guest house, which had been taken over by the president as a country retreat. Richard Peprah and Obed Asamoah, the attorney general, had also been summoned. Together with Jonah they were flown in an air force helicopter to Akuse. This close to an election there were obviously other matters on the retreat's agenda besides Nana Konadu's rift with Jonah. Curiously, she stayed in her room. Jonah nevertheless laid bare to the men the nonsense of the rumour that he was paying for Thompson's defence in the libel action. He repeated that he had no political ambitions; he did not want to be vice-president, or president; he was not interested in politics.

Rawlings was very objective. 'It's obvious we have all made a mistake about you,' he conceded after Jonah's impassioned dispatch of the allegations. The president took Jonah for a walk in the gardens alone. Rawlings sympathised, making a joke of women's vicissitudes. 'Nana is like your sister,' he said, advising Jonah to work on her, to give her time. On that note Jonah left the group for a business flight to Eritrea where Ashanti was conducting gold exploration work.

'This has been a very expensive trip for me,' Rowland disclosed to Jonah before he returned to London. He had parted with several hundreds of thousands of pounds, in his words, to 'save' Jonah. The CEO was sickened at the pawn role that others had imposed on him. He didn't need ransoming because he was not guilty of any crime, but Rowland genuinely believed that his intervention for his friend had averted danger. Besides, in the way that Rowland played business, politics was always the

The first formers of Hamlyn House during Homos Week at Adisadel College, 1963. Jonah is standing in the back row holding a palm frond, with his foot on a classmate's shoulder. In the back row, from left to right, Reindorf Perbi is the first boy standing and John Otoo is third along from Sam, leaning forwards. REINDORF PERBI

Adisadel College prefects, September 1968. Seated, third from left is the head prefect, Reindorf Perbi. Jonah, the chapel prefect, is seated fifth from the left. REINDORF PERBI

Young love. Theo and Sam in the United Kingdom, 1973. SAM JONAH

From left to right, Theo, Sam, Rose Arthur (Theo's mother) and Irene Gaskell at Land's End in Cornwall, United Kingdom, August 1973. SAM JONAH

Two of Sam's brothers, Ernest (left) and Nathaniel, Nana Prah Agyensem VI, Accra, 2000. SAM JONAH

Sam's brother, Victor, the sea captain, Canada, 1989. SAM JONAH

Sam and Theo with their children, from left to right, Andrew, Samantha, Tamara and Richard, on the occasion of Jonah's honorary doctorate graduation at the Camborne School of Mines in the United Kingdom, July 1996. SAM JONAH

PNDC Chairman, Flight-Lieutenant JJ Rawlings, gives a May Day address at the commissioning of the Len Clay football stadium in Obuasi, 1 May 1992. Jonah is seated two places to the right of Rawlings. ANGLOGOLD ASHANTI

The pioneering Biox treatment plant at Obuasi, 1993. ANGLOGOLD ASHANTI

Celebrating with Obuasi miners following the commissioning of the Kwesi Mensah Shaft, 1993. ANGLOGOLD ASHANTI

Ashanti's landmark listing on the New York Stock Exchange, February 1996. ANGLOGOLD ASHANTI

A trophy from deep sea fishing, one of Jonah's favourite pastimes. The blue marlin caught from Jonah's boat, *Silver Cloud*, weighed 1 284 lbs and needed the help of a crane at the port to haul it in, Accra, 1999. SAM JONAH

Jonah delivering one of many speeches to promote investment in Africa, Harare, October 1996. SAM JONAH

The commissioning of the Siguiri mine in Guinea. From left to right, Mark Keatley, Sam Jonah, Fred Ohene-Kena, the President of Guinea, Lansana Conté, and Guinea's Minister for Mines, Fassine Fofana, April 1998.
ANGLOGOLD ASHANTI

The CEO and COO, Trevor Schultz, far right, congratulate Sean McGinley (centre), AGC's Group Health & Safety Coordinator for his NOSA Safety Professional of the Year in Africa Award 2001, Gold House. ANGLOGOLD ASHANTI

From left to right: Sam with his good friend Asantehene Otumfuo Osei Tutu II and Theo at Manhyia Palace, Kumasi, March 1999.
ANGLOGOLD ASHANTI

Jonah with the President of Tanzania, Benjamin W. Mkapa, at his official residence in Dar es Salaam, 2000. ANGLOGOLD ASHANTI

Jonah presents a specimen of Asante goldsmithery to his friend Bobby Godsell at the opening of Anglogold's Gold of Africa Museum in Cape Town, 2001. ANGLOGOLD ASHANTI

Lonmin directors greeting Ghana's President John Kufuor at The Castle, Accra. From left to right, Edward Haslam, Jonah and Sir John Craven. ANGLOGOLD ASHANTI

Jonah with Cyril Ramaphosa on a tour of Obuasi's operations, 2002. ANGLOGOLD ASHANTI

Jonah with, from left to right, Alec Erwin, South Africa's Minister of Public Enterprises; Essop Pahad, South Africa's Minister of the Presidency; and Trevor Manuel, South Africa's Minister of Finance, Cape Town, March 2005.
ELMOND JIYANE, GCIS

Jonah with Professor Jurgen E. Schrempp, Chairman of Daimler Chrysler and fellow member of President Mbeki's International Investment Council, Cape Town, March 2005.
ELMOND JIYANE, GCIS

Jonah with Zambia's founding President Kenneth David Kaunda, Johannesburg, 2005.
SAM JONAH

referee. 'And another thing,' Tiny remarked, 'be very careful what you say on telephones.'

On Jonah's return to Accra he attempted to make an appointment to see Nana Konadu, but her secretary seemed to have been instructed to keep him away. Eventually he telephoned the president's office for assistance. He was trying, as Rawlings and Rowland had recommended, to patch things up, but Nana Konadu was refusing to see him. That evening, Victor Smith, the First Lady's special assistant, called with an appointment to meet Nana Konadu the next day. Jonah was kept waiting and when she eventually did see him it was only to hurl further accusations. Besides the Thompson allegation, Nana Konadu was suspicious of Jonah's relationship in general with the Ghanaian private media sector. It was true that under Jonah's direction Ashanti had reached out to journalists in order to improve information flows and their understanding of the business, with the objective of achieving more favourable press coverage. For a period, outside the company's direct public relations needs, Ashanti sponsored and Jonah chaired informal forums, usually held in the private rooms of restaurants where journalists were invited to speak openly with a guest speaker. The guests came from business circles or government, and the only ground rule was that comments made in the forum were to remain unattributable. Jonah hoped that the caustic criticism of newspapers would be replaced by more constructive comments if there were better understanding between journalists and their subject matter. Some interpreted the initiative as a sophisticated manipulation of the press but Jonah continued to support the forum even when it ceased to be operated under his firm's auspices. He assured the First Lady that he had not used these occasions to speak against her, but left her office knowing that his counter-arguments and explanations had achieved nothing.

In a final effort to reverse the disaffection between him and Nana Konadu Jonah penned his defence. Rather than resurrecting the friendship the letter buried its ashes. He received a curt, unplacated reply and there was no direct contact between them following that letter dated 21 April 1997. Friends frequently reported to Jonah that Nana Konadu spoke his name in an accursed manner, but there was nothing that he could do about it.

Success all round

The NDC won the 1996 general election with 57.2 per cent of the vote. Outwardly, at least, democracy was maturing. Ghana was seen to be a political and economic 'success story', although eyebrows deserved to be raised at the rampant inflation statistics and growing fiscal deficit. Earlier in 1996, Minister of Finance Peprah, had sold down the government's Ashanti stake from 31.5 per cent to 25 per cent in order to plug a hole in his annual budget. Such expediency only delayed grappling with difficult measures to increase government revenues and reduce expenditure.

The year of 1997 was a celebratory one for the country and for Ashanti Goldfields. Ghana celebrated 40 years of independence and the firm 100 years since its incorporation in London. Foreign dignitaries, international businesspeople and Africans of the diaspora arrived for a variety of events and celebrations. An invitation to invest was the leitmotif of these gatherings. Now was the time to come to Ghana. Political interference and acute economic instability were fears of the past. And what better example of the potential success awaiting foreigners than the phenomenal achievements of Ashanti Goldfields? President Rawlings wrote a foreword to the corporate publication commemorating AGC's centenary. In it he praised Jonah and the firm for raising Africa's light from under a bushel. In his introduction to the book Jonah expressed profound gratitude to Rawlings personally and to his administration for taking the steps to rehabilitate the mining sector and for engendering an investment-friendly environment.

On 23 March 1998 President Clinton made Accra his first stop on a six-nation tour of Africa. After lunch with President Rawlings he gave a stirring speech at Ghana's Independence Square to the tens of thousands assembled in the heat. It was the first time that an American president had visited the country. He saluted Ghana for grabbing a foothold on democracy and leading the way for the rest of the continent towards economic liberalisation. He referred to Ashanti Goldfields as the only African-owned company on the New York Stock Exchange.[6] Ghanaian critics condemned the visit as a baptism of purification for their bloodstained leader who had not been held accountable for past and current human rights abuses. (Cynics abroad claimed that the visit's sole purpose was to deflect attention from the brewing Monica Lewinsky scandal.) Overall, however, Clinton's commendations generated an enormous sense of pride among Ghanaians. The most powerful leader in the world had acknowledged them as a beacon of change that the rest of Africa could look up to.

Meanwhile, on the football pitch, Goldfields Football Club grew in success. After a short period as a wholly owned AGC subsidiary, the club set itself up as a self-financing charity with its own management board. The trophy room boasted the domestic league championship cup for three years in a row from 1994 to 1996, and the club also reached the quarter-finals of the Africa Cup of Champions in 1995 and 1996. In 1997 that competition changed its name and format to become the Africa Champions League and the Miners made it to the finals to play Raja Casablanca.

Jonah took his usual seat for the first leg at the Len Clay stadium. For most of the game there was nothing to separate the teams, then the Miners scored and the stadium erupted. The game ended 1-0. The Miners had beaten a club with an illustrious and long footballing history. The final leg could not come soon enough for them to complete their victory.

Jonah travelled with the team for the away game at Raja Casablanca in Morocco. It felt like déjà vu as the score remained 0-0 until the second half. And then the home side scored. With the aggregate score at 1-1 the inaugural Africa Champions League final would be decided on penalties. It was almost too nerve-racking to watch and Ghanaian hopes were high until the very last strike. The Miners lost 4-5 on penalties. Jonah congratulated the players on their mighty fight. He reassured them from his own experiences that future successes would soon banish the moment's disappointment. Their performance on that day was something to be proud of.

Over 1997 and 1998 Ashanti succeeded in meeting production targets and containing costs. The mines in development were brought on stream on time and within budgets. This was the results-achieving, pre-flotation Ashanti that everyone was expecting to re-emerge. Analysts labelled Ashanti a buy stock, a market outperformer, 'one of the most undervalued top-tier gold producers'.[7] Whereas production growth from South Africa was slowing due to the maturity of the mines there and the high costs of deep level mining, Ghana was seen as the place for gold investors to put their money. Ashanti produced over 60 per cent of Ghana's total output in 1997.

Jonah became one of Africa's most prominent businessmen. The praises flowed: the man with the Midas touch; Africa's golden boy; Mr Goldfinger. Behind the words were impressive growth achievements that were recognised internationally. In twelve years as chief executive Jonah had increased gold production from 240 000 ounces to over 1.5 million ounces a year. In 1998 AGC's stock price grew 17.2 per cent, ranking it the twelfth best performer out of 123 metal companies on the NYSE, one place ahead of Barrick.[8]

Anglo American of South Africa did not hide its covetousness of Ashanti.[9] Rumours circulated that Barrick also had Ashanti on its radar. While Jonah recognised that in a free market at the right price anything could happen, he hoped that Ashanti's size would deter predators. In response to a question posed by an analyst on this recurring subject Jonah retorted, full of confidence: 'I could take over Barrick. *They* should feel threatened.'[10]

Further acquisition plans

Following Tiny Rowland's removal from Lonrho's board in December 1994, Lonrho underwent dramatic transformations. A change in leadership, ethos and business rationale led to the divestment and reorganisation of the once sprawling conglomerate. To attain greater industry focus, all of Lonrho's mining businesses were grouped together as a separate company, later renamed Lonmin. Naturally, this strategy raised the question of what to do with Lonmin's significant but non-controlling shareholding in Ashanti: the options were either to up the stake or get out. These deliberations coincided with Ashanti's own desire to add Lonmin's South African platinum mine to Ashanti's stable of gold mines to create an African precious-metals giant. There were considerable risk diversification benefits. Unlike gold, platinum's market was predominantly industrial; there was very little forward selling, and the price was on the up pushed by technological innovations for its use. Serious discussions about a possible combination of Lonmin and Ashanti started early in 1998. (Incidentally, platinum, which was trading above $350 when these merger plans commenced, peaked in April 2004 at $937.)

As the discussions progressed Jonah let it be known that he wanted Ashanti to take over Lonmin and to be the surviving entity (although Lonmin was nearly three times the size of Ashanti).[11] The talks stalled. Amongst other things a major sticking-point for Lonmin was the choice of domicile for any newly created firm. But these were hiccups that Jonah hoped to resolve in due time; meanwhile, his aggressive growth strategy turned his attentions elsewhere.

In November 1998 Ashanti acquired an adjoining property to its Geita concession that was owned by a Canadian registered junior, Samax. Geological results from Geita excited the company to get the mine into production as soon as possible. If calculations held up, Geita would supersede Obuasi as the jewel in the group's crown thanks to the extent of its resources and the relatively uncomplicated ores. Negotiations with Samax were protracted. At times the deal was off, then the door re-opened slightly and talks would resume. Jonah surmised that for the controlling shareholder, Jean–Claude Gandur, a man of considerable means and mining expertise, quibbling over price would likely get them nowhere. Instead, he travelled to meet Gandur in Geneva and offered him a board position along with AGC shares. The negotiating teams met after this in Paris. Over dinner the discussions deadlocked, again over price. Jonah asked Gandur to step out for a walk with him. In the cold November air he recapped the economies of scale benefits that uniting Geita would bring, which Gandur did not dispute. If their joint properties would be more profitable than the individual projects then couldn't the two of them compromise on the price? Jonah moved a little from Ashanti's starting price but stayed below Gandur's asking price. The two men shook hands on it, returned to the restaurant and announced the deal.

In 1998, soon after the creation of the world's largest gold company, Anglogold, from the amalgamation of the Anglo American Corporation's gold interests, Bobby Godsell, Anglogold's chief executive, invited Jonah to meet him in London. At the Atheneum Hotel on Piccadilly they discussed the state of the gold industry: the large number of producers, the falling prices, rising costs, the behaviour of central banks, the dearth of strong industry leaders, and the need for rationalisation.[12] Godsell proposed to Jonah that they meet with Barrick's CEO, Randall Oliphant. The industry needed consolidation and Godsell's bold plan was for the three of them to carve it up between them. Jonah was flattered that Godsell deemed him a worthy member of this triumvirate – Ashanti ranked eleventh in terms of global production volumes. But Godsell believed that they shared the necessary leadership strength along with an immense faith in the African continent. This was critical for his vision to materialise because over 50 per cent of the world's known gold resources exist in Africa. The men planned to continue their strategic discussion.

Golden boy, golden firm

Everybody wanted a piece of the Ashanti action. Chase Manhattan renegotiated a second revolving credit facility (RCF) for the company. The attractiveness of the deal surprised even Ashanti. The company had sought $250m but due to oversubscription ended up with $270m. The facility, structured in tranches, averaged a price of Libor +0.83 per cent, 20 per cent cheaper than the previous RCF arranged by Barclays. The security and covenant terms were reduced and new participants came on board including the Bank of Nova Scotia, CIBC Wood Gundy as well as Goldman Sachs; in total there were 23 banks. Besides the RCF many of these banks acted as counterparties to Ashanti's hedging programme, and three of them had bilateral loan agreements with Ashanti for specific project purposes. The RCF money was used to repay the existing $185m facility and the remainder went towards Geita's development and working capital needs. Net debt levels totalled about $400m compared with a cash flow of $200m. Cash inflow was expected to rise with the growth in production from the newly opened Bibiani and Siguiri mines and the eventual addition of Geita.

The impressive RCF arrangement reflected the international financial world's high regard for Jonah and Ashanti. The CEO and his company symbolised Ghana and sub-Saharan Africa's regeneration. Significantly, all of this action occurred in the face of gold prices plummeting to eighteen-year lows.

As a hedged producer, Ashanti, along with other hedgers, faced opposition from non-hedging gold companies for dampening future prices by their growing forward sale portfolios.[13] Inflation in the United States of America, Europe and Japan was low, removing the demand to hold gold for its stable value. In addition, the market had been rocked by the Bre-X scandal: a shadow was cast over all gold equities when it emerged that a Canadian company's claims to have discovered a 200-million ounce deposit in Indonesian Borneo were fraudulent. Perhaps the biggest pressure on the gold price though was the policy of central banks from the mid-1990s to dispense with large gold holdings. Low inflation did not require it, and it made better sense to convert gold into low-risk securities that earned a return.

Ashanti's share price fell, but no more so than other gold stocks and indices. The falling gold price squeezed everyone's profitability margins. The illiquidity of Ashanti's shares due to the situation that two shareholders (Lonmin and the Ghana government) held over 50 per cent of the stock did not help matters. With a world average cost of production of $250 an ounce and the gold price under $280 an ounce from January 1998, mines the world over had to close or tighten operations. Retrenchment of 15 per cent of the Obuasi workforce commenced. Another defensive strategy adopted by Ashanti was to extend the forward sales of gold, and the hedging programme as a whole increased in scope and complexity. The predominant analyst view of the firm at this time was positive: in the face of acute industry pressures Ashanti was seen to be exceeding expectations.[14]

CHAPTER 10

'If the fish in the water grows fat, it is in the interest of the crocodile'

1998–99

Rawlings had been supportive of, indeed instrumental in, Jonah and Ashanti's dramatic rise. He had in Jonah's own words, 'gone beyond the call of duty' to assist the company with industrial relations, flotation and multinational expansion. The relationship between the two leaders was one of mutual respect, and at the opening ceremony of Ashanti's Siguiri mine in Guinea on 15 April 1998 Jonah was fulsome in his praise of Rawlings. But between that date and 25 February 1999 when the Asantehene Otumfuo Opoku Ware II died, the good understanding between them had ruptured.

Although much reduced in power, the Asantehene, the king of Asante, is an important personage continuing a dynasty over three hundred years old. After the British captured the Asante capital, Kumasi, in 1896, they imprisoned and then exiled the then Asantehene, Agyeman Prempe, and the Queen Mother, Asantehemaa Yaa Kyaa, to the Seychelles. Even then, the British realised that their failure to capture the Golden Stool undermined their authority in the region. In 1924 Governor Guggisberg allowed Agyeman Prempe home as a private citizen and soon acquiesced to petitions to reinstate the Asantehene as the king of Kumasi.

In 1935 the colonial administration permitted the creation of an Ashanti Confederacy Council as part of its strategy to rule indirectly through customary authority structures. This move was partly motivated by the immense difficulties and failures experienced by the British in their attempts to control the diverse peoples. Under the 1935 arrangements the British defined the Asantehene simply as the president of the

Confederacy Council. They put their own slant on the codification of Asante laws, for example, promoting the rights of individual states within the confederacy as if they were equal stools, ignoring the Asantehene's overlordship in order to stunt the possible growth of centralised opposition to colonial rule.[1] In the decolonisation period it was mooted and rejected to transform the Asantehene into a national monarch in the British tradition.[2] The rise of Asante was a fear shared by the British and other Gold Coast ethnic groups. Often forgotten in the anti-colonial debate is the point that for some indigenous groups, the Fante, for example, subjugation to the British Empire was preferred, even welcomed, in comparison to Asante domination. Constitutional changes since independence were part of a continued attempt to check the Asantehene's political influence, barring him from direct political involvement.

Nevertheless, the Asantehene remains the most prestigious of Ghana's traditional leaders whose opinion and presence are sought. Modernisation has only heightened global appreciation for heritage. These days non-Asante and locals alike swarm to witness the Asantehene's frequent ceremonial events. People increasingly hang onto his every word.

When the fifteenth Asantehene Otumfuo Opoku Ware II died in February 1999, there were seven contenders whose direct lineage to Maanu, the mother of Osei Tutu I, made them eligible for the Golden Stool.[3] It is said that the Akan practise matrilineality because, unlike paternity, you can be sure of whose womb you came from. A member of the royal household is someone who can show a uterine link to Maanu, the first Queen Mother or Asantehemaa. Generally, the eldest woman alive from Maanu's lineage is appointed as the Asantehemaa.

Of the seven possibilities, the government's preferred candidate was an NDC man, the chief executive of the Kumasi Metropolitan Authority, Nana Akwasi Agyeman. A government delegation led by the regional minister for Ashanti, Daniel Ohene Agyekum, and including Finance Minister Richard Peprah, was sent to the Asantehemaa and royal elders to express the wish of President Rawlings and the First Lady that they elect Agyeman. The audacious request met with indignation. It was not for the government to interfere in a 300-year-old selection process that, after blood eligibility, looked at character, in particular, the ability to listen and consult with others. Agyeman had a reputation for being arrogant and dictatorial.[4] The leading contender was, in fact, the Asantehemaa's own son, Nana Kwaku Duah who had been groomed for the responsibility since birth and who was known to be humble, conciliatory and consultative. It was unlikely that his mother would by-pass the honour of appointing her own son to the Golden Stool. The Queen Mother made the nomination but it was for a council of chiefs, the kingmakers, to accept or object.[5]

Soon after Otumfuo Opoku Ware's death, Nana Kwaku Duah visited Jonah at home. Duah was in mourning cloth. 'Our mother says I should let you know that the time has arrived.' As a child Jonah had come to know Duah from his frequent trips to the Kumasi home of his uncle, Nana Prah Agyesem V. He knew that one day his boyhood friend would become king, and Duah knew that when the time came Jonah's support would be unequivocal. After being nominated for the Golden Stool, the procedure was for the nominee to make gifts to the 33 Asante para-mount chiefs who would become his subjects. Generosity at this stage indicated the Asantehene-elect's humility and gratitude for his elders. Jonah's contributions helped to finance the purchase of lambs, alcohol and cash gifts to the paramount chiefs.

On 26 April 1999 Nana Kwaku Duah completed the 40-day process from nomination to enstoolment, assuming the stool name Otumfuo Osei Tutu II. Hundreds of thousands lined the Kumasi streets from the Manhyia Palace to the city's sports stadium to witness the procession of sub-chiefs, sword bearers, horn blowers, drummers and dancers. It was a once-in-a-lifetime spectacle. Jonah attended as did an NDC govern-ment delegation, but not President Rawlings.

Laden with pure gold accoutrements the Asantehene was carried on a palanquin through the crowds. Once in the stadium he waved to Jonah as he passed the stand for government and special guests. The king then got down to perform rites for the gods and ancestors. At midnight, away from the public gaze and before a select audience of traditional leaders the Asantehene was carried and lowered three times on the Golden Stool. Customary oaths were sworn to the sub-chiefs who in turn pledged their allegiance to him.

Besides the strength of his eligibility, Nana Kwaku Duah had clearly been the people's choice; his succession to the stool did not hinge on

Jonah's support. Jonah felt privileged that he could be of practical assistance to his friend, but it was not in his power to buy anyone the kingship. Whether he had helped financially or not, the Queen Mother would undoubtedly have nominated her well-regarded son. However, President Rawlings took Jonah's support of Otumfuo Osei Tutu II, in opposition to the government's preferred candidate, as an enemy gesture.

The morning after the government delegation's untoward visit to the Asantehemaa and elders (which was weeks after Nana Kwaku Duah's trip to Jonah's home), Duah had telephoned Jonah in total shock at the events related to him by his mother. 'Who the hell do they think they are?' Jonah had said frankly. He made some other angry comments about the government not knowing the bounds of its authority. The delegation needed to be exposed in the press for disrespecting the kingmakers. Days later, Jonah chanced upon Yaw Donkor, the head of Ghana's intelligence service, at the home of Brigadier Wallace Gbedemah. When the conversation came to rest on the vacant Golden Stool, Donkor revealed that Jonah had been the first person that Nana Kwaku Duah had spoken to after the government's delegation to Kumasi. In a flash Tiny Rowland's admonition about tele-phone conversations came to Jonah. He realised that his unguarded opinions had lit a fuse. He sent a driver to Nana Kwaku Duah in Kumasi warning him not to use his home telephone. Jonah would have to check his own too – at least one of them was bugged.

The causes of the Rawlings-Jonah rift

The World Economic Forum is known as the Business Oscars for its A-list gathering of the world's richest and most powerful people in politics and business. In January 1999, as part of the forum in Davos, Gold Fields, the South African mining house and owners of Ghana's Tarkwa mine hosted a dinner. Mzi Khumalo, the Robben Island freedom fighter turned business magnate, sat beside Nana Konadu. Jonah attended another function that evening, but after midnight he received a call from Mzi who was a good friend. 'Be careful my brother,' he warned Sam. 'I don't know what you have done to this lady, but she spoke about you with such venom that I would be very careful if I were you.'

Nana Konadu had questioned Jonah's loyalties ever since his repudiation of the offer of the vice-presidency in 1992. Her doubts had increased further with time and she now seemed to harbour a deep hatred towards him. It is understandable that her intense distrust and dislike of Jonah could have eventually influenced Rawlings's perception of the man.

Following the Davos conference, John Wilson, the CEO of Placer Dome, a Canadian gold mine, telephoned Jonah. He had been in conversation with President Rawlings at Davos and wanted Jonah's assistance to arrange a meeting with Rawlings. Jonah declined to get involved, advising Wilson to make contact himself. Wilson succeeded, and at his meeting with Rawlings they discussed Placer Dome participating in Ashanti. Wilson relayed the conversation to Jonah who reacted frostily: 'John, you're a CEO, like me, and Ashanti's a PLC; you know the procedures. If you want to buy shares or Lonmin's stake or take us over, you know what you have to do.'

Rawlings must have heard about this because Jonah and two AGC directors, Peprah and Ohene-Kena, were summoned to a meeting at The Castle. After the president had related the innumerable ways in which the Canadian government had assisted the country, he said to Jonah. 'I want you to contact Lonmin. Facilitate Placer's takeover of Lonmin's stake. Make it happen.'

It was not Jonah's place to tell Lonmin what to do. Furthermore, he despised being dictated to. 'It would be unusual and inappropriate for me to make such a suggestion,' he explained. 'Wilson is the head of a public company himself; he knows the way to go about these things.'

Rawlings replied, 'Sometimes I don't know who is the president – you or me.' The message was clear: he felt that Jonah was challenging his authority, forgetting his place, and getting above himself. The meeting ended.

One popular explanation of the disintegration of the Rawlings-Jonah relationship is that Sam posed a political threat to the president. He had spurned the vice-presidency, which could have been interpreted by Rawlings as a delaying tactic to contest the presidency itself. Although Rawlings was constitutionally bound to step down at the end of his second term of office in December 2000, whether he would go was by no means certain. If he did vacate The Castle he would no doubt prefer a weak successor to allow him to continue to dominate Ghana's political scene. If Jonah ran for president and won he would not be a puppet.

But Jonah had no desire to be president; political office was anathema to him. Had he held such aspirations then what better strategy could there have been than for him to have courted the vice-presidency in 1996, knowing that he would be in the best position to take over the leadership of the NDC when Rawlings stepped down in 2000?

Jonah's support for Nana Kwaku Duah had also concerned the NDC. What if Jonah used his financial wherewithal to boost the chances of victory for the opposition NPP? Such an outcome would push Rawlings even further into the shadows after nearly two decades in the seat of power. The enmity that spored definitely had a political dimension, but there was also a personal aspect perhaps driven by jealousy.

Jonah was one of the wealthiest individuals in Ghana. He held lucrative international directorships; his family owned profitable investments in Ghana including an insurance company and a farm. Financial power can polarise people. On the one hand, it attracts patronage and, on the other, it repels the cynical and the envious. It is possible that Rawlings envied Jonah for his wealth and, perhaps more importantly, for his rising global profile. Jonah's regular appearances in international newspapers and magazines, an interview on BBC Hardtalk and the accolades bestowed on him expanded the businessman's limelight just as Rawlings's own position of esteem dimmed, and was soon to be extinguished if the constitution and international community were obeyed. After such a long period of continuous power it is likely that Rawlings experienced pangs of insecurity.

Rawlings's treatment of other prominent Ghanaian businessmen seems to indicate that he begrudged their growing success. Perhaps his instinctive Marxist sentiments made a certain level of capitalist success jar with him. In addition, the Ghanaian society is very much like the British in its tendency to slate successful businessmen, labelling them 'fat cats', while paradoxically worshipping sports stars with their stratospheric salaries. Brawn evokes admiration while brains arouse suspicion of manipulation and exploitation. Some cultures, the American and Nigerian, for example, praise business success much more than others. In Ghana's case an indigenous capitalist class has been slow in the making and has suffered from government interference and scapegoating. From colonial days practical constraints on the growth of domestic entrepreneurs, not least of all in terms of access to funding, bred a preference for foreign capitalists. Amongst many Ghanaians there is a palpable mistrust of a *Ghanaian* businessman: when Thomas warned his son that AGC would come to ruin under an African he was expressing a widespread sentiment. In a similar vein, a Ghanaian would prefer to buy products manufactured abroad than those 'made in Ghana'. Such attitudes are only now beginning to change.

The few Ghanaians who have been highly successful in big business are very visible. The list of those sabotaged by Rawlings makes interesting reading. They include the expropriation without compensation of J.K. Siaw's Tata Brewery and B.A. Mensah's International Tobacco Ltd as well as forced closure of Safo Adu's Industrial Chemical Ltd. Rawlings even went on television to exhort Ghanaians not to buy Apino soap manufactured by his compatriot, Appiah Menka. It seemed that business success would only be tolerated if a person was conspicuously pro-Rawlings.

Another important element to understanding the two men's rancorous split is that between those pivotal dates, April 1998 when Jonah praised Rawlings at the opening of the Siguiri mine in Guinea and February 1999 when the Asantehene died, Tiny Rowland also died – on 25 July 1998 to be precise. Whatever financial assistance Rowland had maintained for the Rawlingses and the NDC came to an abrupt stop. As the *Guardian* in London rightly reported from a political analyst in Ghana, 'To have your biggest company refusing to give money to the party is never popular in Africa. Ashanti has refused to let itself be bled by the government.'[6] In Rawlings's eyes Jonah was personally indebted to him. 'I made him! I made him!' he repeatedly told others in disgust and anger that the chief executive whom he had anointed back in 1982 for Ashanti's deputy MD position, and who, in his opinion, had only risen to the top thanks to him, should now treat him so ungratefully.[7]

When Ashanti became a PLC it allowed Jonah to channel all requests for corporate donations through the AGC board's new charity committee and to remove himself from such decisions. What he did with his own money was a private matter, but he had neither the depth of pocket nor the inclinations of Rowland for political largesse. Rawlings took this personally.

There were growing reports of the Rawlingses' vengeful conduct that made the beating of Vice-president Arkaah in a cabinet meeting in 1995 (already mentioned in Chapter 9) appear very much in keeping with a pattern of behaviour. Some would say that simmering violence from the revolution days had never dissipated. Others alleged that the end-game scenario created by the constitutional limit of two terms in office only encouraged Rawlings to take advantage of presidential immunity enshrined in the same constitution to deal with his enemies once and for all.

Danger looms

On Saturday 10 April, Sam called up a few friends to travel to Obuasi, as they did from time to time, to watch Goldfields Football Club play the following day. He found one of his friends, Alhaji Yusif Ibrahim, a businessman from the Northern Region, in a panic. Alhaji would not be going to the match. He had just been tipped off by a Castle source that his new hotel was about to be knocked down on Rawlings's orders. The 67-room hotel, strategically located near the international airport, had cost $6m to build and fit. Accra was hosting an African–American summit the following week and representatives from the Ghana Investment Centre had pushed Alhaji to have his rooms ready on time for this. The vice-president's wife, the minister of tourism, and the chairman of the Accra city council had all visited and inspected approvingly in the weeks before. A South African hotel manager was due to arrive on the Monday morning. It seemed inconceivable that Rawlings would demolish the hotel. To comfort his friend Sam suggested that he talk to people who were close to the president, such as Brigadier Wallace Gbedemah and Warrant Officer Tetteh. Alhaji did the rounds seeking confirmation of the rumour, but nobody seemed to know anything, which he found reassuring.

Jonah returned to Accra on Sunday evening. He went for his usual 5.00 a.m. walk on Monday morning. Not long after he had returned Nana Prah (Jonah's brother Nat) arrived at the house, pale-faced despite his black skin. 'Alhaji's hotel,' he stuttered in shock, struggling to speak. 'The whole area has been sealed off. Soldiers with machine guns have surrounded the place. Bulldozers are razing it to the ground. There's dust everywhere.' The commanding officer of the operation had been instructed that nothing was to be salvaged: brand new television sets, beds, refrigerators, kitchen equipment and furniture were all destroyed. He did not even allow the air conditioners delivered on the Saturday and still in their boxes to be removed. President Rawlings had ordered the demolition and he allegedly hovered overhead in a helicopter as the destruction started. In no time a thick throng gathered, gazing in disbelief. The president then drove to the site and congratulated the soldiers on a job well done. The South African hotel manager arrived with his family as scheduled, only to witness their new life, work and home crumble into dust.

Different reasons for the drastic action, which had been taken without legal notice, were bandied around. Some said that the hotel lay in the airport's flight path and others that the land belonged to the military. The official reason supplied by Accra's Metropolitan Authority was that the hotel was too near a waterway. The irony of this was that several houses, just yards from the hotel, stood on either side of the small stream, which flowed through the grounds of another neighbouring hotel, the Shangri-La. If proximity to a waterway was such a danger then all of these buildings should have been destroyed. Furthermore, the same Accra Metropolitan Authority had not only granted planning permission but also advised Alhaji with the project and cooperated throughout its construction. Objections to the project could have been raised at any time during the lengthy building process.

Alhaji was convinced that the cruel contempt for his private property rights stemmed from Rawlings's envy and his erroneous belief that Jonah was the real owner of, or at least a stakeholder in, the hotel, neither of which was true. At the time of writing a suit for compensation remains in the Ghanaian courts.

Then there was the later case of Selasse O'Sullivan-Djentuh taken up by Amnesty International. According to his application for asylum to the British Home Office in March 2000,[8] Selasse had dated and been engaged to Rawlings's eldest daughter, Zanetor. (It was during this time that Selasse told Jonah's sons, Andrew and Richard, that Mrs Rawlings had ordered him not to associate with them.) When Selasse broke off the two-year relationship a string of frightening events ensued. Selasse claimed that a truck driver had signalled him to pass while on his motorbike; as he did so the truck swerved into him, but fortunately his injuries were not too serious. The police investigator revealed that the incident docket had been sent to the Office of the President at The Castle. Without tracing the truck driver, a court convicted Selasse and fined him for reckless driving. A few weeks later he was abducted by AK47-wielding soldiers and beaten up. They drove him to The Castle where his head was shaved with a broken bottle and rusty razor blades. The soldiers threatened to kill him. He believed that it was only thanks to his mother drawing media attention to the abduction and her pointing a finger at the conspicuous suspects that his life was spared. His hitherto law-abiding parents then found themselves facing trial on a number of criminal charges, and buildings belonging to his mother's real estate business were bulldozed.[9]

In the context of such examples the events during and following the Obuasi miners' strike in May 1999 take on a sinister perspective. From 13–25 May 1999 Ashanti experienced a miners' strike like no other in the company's history. For a decade relations with the Mine Workers' Union had been generally constructive, but with the appointment of a new union secretary, Adelaide Borden, a demand was made for a 500 per cent average wage increase. A 6 per cent settlement was eventually agreed to on Wednesday 11 May. The wildcat strike that then occurred on the Friday took management by complete surprise. Union officers reported the presence of unidentifiable individuals wearing Ashanti overalls among the strikers. Company property was destroyed. An effigy of Jonah was carried around Obuasi and then burnt in public. The ashes were put in a wooden coffin and literally buried. Jonah had been aware of the difficult wage negotiations but, in his opinion, this strike appeared to be about him, not wages. Placards read, 'No More Sam Jonah!' The strikers successfully blocked the shipment of gold bullion. A 10 per cent wage increase was renegotiated and the strike ended after twelve days. The company estimated that the disruption had cost it $50m.

A wave of strikes over pay that year – from civil servants as well as hospital and university workers – reflected the Ghanaian economy's difficulties. Adherence to the strict discipline of Structural Adjustment had been backsliding for some time. There was a notable mismatch between the money supply growth figures provided by the government and soaring inflation, which confounded IMF economists, as did Ghana's non-compliance with fund disbursement rules.[10] Real wages fell, growth stagnated, and the government resorted to greater and greater amounts of debt. Ghana was quickly losing its reputation as the shining example of Structural Adjustment.[11]

In view of the economic hardship in 1999 a strike at Obuasi in itself was not unusual, especially when coupled with the added fact that the mine was pursuing a strict cost-cutting drive necessitated by the fall in world gold prices. Furthermore, the personal tone that the protests took could be explained by the fact that the miners related to Jonah as an Obuasi boy. They wanted to show their disappointment in him, as if he had turned his back on them. Notwithstanding these considerations, the rent-a-mob evidence, the subsequent sighting of Adelaide Borden at Nana Konadu's office, and the nature of the government inquiry that followed, suggest the possibility of political interference.

Allegations of criminality

The government launched a three-man official inquiry into the strike. The team was led by Brigadier Anyidaho under the auspices of the ministry of employment and social welfare. The remit to investigate the causes of the strike did not justify the 'Top Secret' classification red-inked on the proceedings. The committee's questions focused inordinately on Jonah, specifically on the involvement of his family in the mine and related businesses, and on the manner in which he had purchased his company residence, Villa Rose.[12]

In June 1999, Rawlings ordered Anyidaho's unpublished interim report up to the Serious Fraud Office (SFO) to add to a separate investigation that he had instigated into Jonah's role in a company called Sterling Financial Services. Newspapers suggested that the president was hoping that if he cast his net wide enough something would legally entangle Jonah.[13] Furthermore, he wanted the SFO to conclude its investigation as quickly as possible so that he could see Jonah condemned and punished before the end of his term of office.[14]

On 28 July 1999 in a meeting with the Council of State at The Castle Rawlings veered off the agenda to fire a verbal assault at Jonah.[15] This was on the back of insults hurled at the Asantehene when the Council had met on 19 June.[16] Those present at the meeting were shocked to hear the president label the country's leading businessman a 'corrupt and criminal person'. The episode was reported in the media and brought Jonah's reputation into disrepute both locally and internationally.[17] When pressed about this serious accusation it transpired that the president was drawing his conclusions from the unpublished Anyidaho interim report.

The committee's integrity and credibility was thrown into question in view of the fact that it had evidently changed from an industrial relations remit into a probe on Jonah and that premature judgement had been passed while evidence was still being gathered. When Jonah next appeared before the Anyidaho committee on Thursday 12 August, he refused to cooperate until it cleared the air by denying it had already published conclusions while still sitting, and requesting the president to retract his allegations or substantiate them. Neither the committee nor the Office of the President came forward with clarifications.

The silence unnerved investors. These were serious allegations being faced by the CEO of an international company. Shareholders, international stock exchanges and commentators flooded AGC with requests for information. In the depressed gold market, the smear only weakened confidence and further dampened Ashanti's share price.

With regard to the allegations as the company understood them, since it had not been allowed to see the Anyidaho report, AGC could confidently explain its robust, documented procurement procedures that detailed objective assessment criteria and did not permit decision-taking by any one individual.

Sterling Financial Services was a company 51 per cent owned by Metropolitan Insurance. Jonah had been a major shareholder and a director of Metropolitan, but in May 1998 he resigned the directorship and transferred his shares to a trust for his children. Metropolitan's participation in AGC's insurances pre-dated Jonah's involvement with the insurance company and its selection followed Ashanti's set procurement rules. In a typical year AGC placed 85 per cent of its insurances in London. Of the 15 per cent placed locally in Ghana, the State Insurance Company had 7 per cent, Metropolitan had 6 per cent and two other local companies shared the remainder. Metropolitan's 6 per cent of premiums was further reduced from its cessions to local reinsurance companies, Ghana Re and Mainstream Re.[18]

Sterling had been established along with a flurry of other local financial companies to try to win government mandates in connection with the wave of privatisations of state-owned enterprises. In the event, the company was only ever involved with two such mandates. Sterling advised the ministry of finance on the sale of the government's stake in Barclays Bank Ghana Ltd. There was also indirect participation with a mandate awarded to Rothschild to advise in the divestment of Ghana Oil (Goil). Sterling's role here was to act as Rothschild's local agent. The Goil plans were later aborted. Sterling's management believed that the company was disadvantaged in the bidding for government business because of Jonah's links with Metropolitan, Sterling's majority shareholder.

In the matter of Jonah's purchase of his house, Villa Rose, AGC board minutes show that following the success of the 1994 flotation, the directors discussed offering Jonah a gift as a bonus to show appreciation for his contributions.[19] Jonah in response asked, and approval was given, to buy his company-owned residence at the higher of the market valuations made by a government surveyor and a private firm.[20] Jonah requested that the furniture be valued separately and added to the purchase price. AGC directors Richard Peprah and Philip Tarsh thought his behaviour odd as post-merger bonuses were common practice. But Jonah's sensitivity, hypersensitivity even, to the appearance and practice of financial rectitude in the hazardous political climate necessitated that he left no room for external censure. He duly paid the higher market price for Villa Rose.

As for the involvement of the chief executive's brothers in mine business, Jonah's brother Ernest owns a chain of Mobil petrol stations across the country. One of these is in Obuasi, his home town. This Mobil is not on mine property and has never had anything to do with the mine.

A spurious link between Ernest and AGC might have been made because Mobil, in an unrelated corporate contract, supplied the mine with its on-site fuel.

Following the 1986 liberalisation of the mine sector in Ghana, Nana Prah established a company called Interoc, importing and supplying hydraulic pipes to mines throughout Ghana. Far from profiting from Jonah's position Interoc struggled and later went into receivership.

When Sam's other brother, Victor, was summoned to the Anyidaho Committee he submitted evidence to them showing that while he had accepted an unsolicited offer from a French mine equipment company to act as its Ghana agent, his agency had been terminated after years of inaction.

On 19 August Ashanti issued a press statement to defend the chief executive's integrity. Four days later the government responded in a press office statement that denied that the president had called Jonah a criminal, despite the fact that there were several witnesses to this. The government's reputation to investors was more important than the 'interest of the Chief Executive of the AGC', the statement barbed, personalising the issue. It ended with a managerial reproof: AGC was criticised for handling its relationship with government immaturely. Rawlings had called Jonah a criminal, and now he decried his management ability. Either Jonah was corrupt or Rawlings was a liar. The reputations of both men were at stake, and the stakes had just been upped.

Tests of loyalty

As this exchange of insults and insinuations, denials and defences played out in the media many of Jonah's friends ducked out of sight. One of Jonah's security guards at home, a former soldier, recognised an army colleague among those indiscreetly watching Jonah's house from the property across the road. Surveillance men dotted his usual 5.00 a.m. walking route. Jonah's contacts in the security services, Tony Gbeho and Johnny Kwadjo, confirmed these operations.

Jonah noticed when friends arrived lying across the back seat of cars, hidden under blankets, afraid to be seen entering and leaving his house. It was painful to watch. The frequent stream of visitors at Villa Rose, particularly in the evenings, dried up, and his 5.00 a.m. walking group companions thinned.

Jonah had maintained his close friendship with John Otoo since school days. He had happily assisted Otoo over the years in many practical ways, as he did for many others, whether they asked, or, as was often the case, as soon as Jonah learnt of their unfortunate circumstances. Jonah had not heard from or seen Otoo for a long time and he did not want to believe that even he had disassociated himself, so he sent word to him to come and visit. After some time Otoo arrived. He confessed that he was in line for a promotion in the military's chaplaincy service, so, quite frankly, at that point in time, he could not risk being seen as Jonah's friend. Sam's heart sank. He was gutted by Otoo's rejection of him, but it was a sign of the times.

Kofi Ansah, Kwame Peprah and Fred Ohene-Kena, all government ministers who knew first hand just how much Rawlings now hated Jonah, remained loyal, as did Fui Tsikata, Perbi, and Alhaji Yusif. Alhaji had always been wary of Jonah's closeness to the regime, but now was not the time for I-told-you-sos. They trusted in their friend's probity; it would take more than hearsay to shake that. 'I hope these stupid articles aren't getting to you,' Jonah's twelve-year-old daughter Samantha chided in reference to a derogatory headline about her father. 'They don't know you. We do. So don't let it get you down.' His gutsy and cheeky namesake never failed to amaze him. She was right. Besides, two important developments for Ashanti's strategic future demanded his full attention: finding funds to bring the lucrative Geita mine in Tanzania into production, and completing an acquisition of Lonmin.

The on-again negotiations with Lonmin at last neared closure. Jonah's plan was to combine Ashanti's gold mines with Lonmin's platinum mine and to dispense with the latter's non-precious metal properties. As the gold price bobbed under $255 an ounce, the strategic sense of creating an Africa-wide, precious metals company and thereby diversifying price risk made greater and greater sense. The sticking-points over domicile and the cash element of the purchase had been resolved. Names for the new board had been suggested, the valuation method decided, and mid-October set as an appropriate date to issue a press statement – to coincide with Ashanti's third quarter results.[21]

Then, on Monday 27 September, the newswires flashed that most unexpected announcement: fifteen European central banks had pledged to restrict and control their future disposals of bullion. The salvo of cheers over the price-strengthening news was soon drowned by the realisation of the negative impact of a rising gold price on the extensive short positions in the bullion market, and by the sound of detonating hedge books.

CHAPTER II

'When a bird remains too long on a tree, it has a stone thrown at it'

September–October 1999

The first margin call came from AIG's derivatives desk.[1] If Ashanti had had a normal year of operations without a major strike it could have met this initial demand. It was the failure to do so that sparked the rumours followed by a rush of other hedge counterparties whose rights to margin may have been negotiated away had Ashanti been able to satisfy AIG and avoid panic. Cash at hand came to $70m; margin calls totalled $270m. Failure to honour the seventeen hedge banks' collateral entitlements triggered a breach of Ashanti's twenty-three-bank revolving credit facility as well as two project finance agreements involving three separate banks.

The hedge banks feared that bilateral deals would result in unfair priority payments being made to some and not others. Goldman Sachs's lead advisory role in the Lonmin merger, its position as the largest hedge counterparty as well as its recent appointment as AGC's corporate broker created enormous distrust among the other bankers. No bank knew the other parties' exact hedging position with Ashanti (let alone competitors' aggregate potential losses from other gold mines caught in the fix – Chase Manhattan's total gold derivatives exposure was reportedly as much as $20bn).[2] Rival banks were rightly convinced that Ashanti had revealed its entire hedge portfolio to Goldman Sachs, exposing all of the banks' positions and creating an unfair information advantage.[3]

How would derivatives traders or bullion dealers explain to their internal credit committees that they were exposed to a potential loss of tens of millions from a single client? And that it was an African-based client at that. Counterparties spent sleepless nights assessing the loss dynamics in their individual positions. Jobs were on the line and tension mounted to tearing point.

Some of the banks in the hedge group had provided security guarantees to other hedge banks trading with Ashanti. These security arrangements stated that within a certain time frame, the guarantor bank would pay whatever Ashanti owed should Ashanti default. It was not in the beneficiary banks' interests to hold off margin calls. If Ashanti couldn't pay – and it couldn't – then it was to these beneficiary banks' advantage to see Ashanti liquidated in order to fall on the guarantors to pick up their losses. The longer the banks waited, the greater the chance that the guarantee period would expire and they would be lumbered with the loss.

Project finance lenders took a long-term view of the situation. They wanted Ashanti to survive to repay their huge capital investments. Traditional lenders and derivatives traders from the *same* bank did not necessarily share the same opinion – there was no guarantee of mutual aid because personal survival was at stake. In game theory terms the situation, from the hedge counterparties' point of view, appeared to be a non-repeat game – the company was finished – and therefore the benefits of self-interest exceeded cooperation.

Cultural differences in the banks also came to the fore. The British investment houses tended to lay their claims in a placatory tone (perhaps conscious of the City's unwritten code to support troubled British institutions, although this did not strictly apply to Ashanti because it was a Ghanaian firm). American banks negotiated more aggressively.

Bankers pressured Lonmin, as Ashanti's single largest investor, to come to the rescue, forcefully reminding it that refusal to help would evaporate its $200m investment in Ashanti to zero. Ashanti's first thought was that Lonmin could in principle guarantee the margin calls. Lonmin's response was a cautious offer to provide a secured loan of $30m, an insufficient gesture. However, it promised to move the merger plans along as quickly as possible although it would no longer be an Ashanti takeover of Lonmin. Negotiating power had flipped and the previously leisurely pace of talks geared up to a sprint.

Ashanti's merger advisers at Goldman Sachs attempted to persuade Lonmin that the margin calls were a collateral cost – not a sunk cash cost; that the rally was a short-term bubble driven by existing gold buyers and not new investors, and therefore was unsustainable. The intrinsic value of a combination with Ashanti therefore remained unaltered. True, Lonmin could now cut a more favourable deal, but in Ashanti's immediate favour, the strength of Lonmin's balance sheet and United Kingdom–domiciled status could remove, or relax, the banks' demands for security.

Jonah was in need of a trustworthy adviser with Ashanti's interests at heart. He called on his long-time friend, Andy Quinn, formerly of James Capel but then with CIBC. Quinn had led Ashanti's 1994 IPO and provided training for the firm for its new responsibilities as a public company. He had been irked somewhat by Keatley's sidelining of his services since then, but remained loyal to Jonah. Quinn, a respected banker with a rare knack of straight talking without causing offence, assumed a friendly broker role.

Mark Bankes, a bespectacled, precision-thinking corporate finance lawyer, and a partner at Norton Rose, the external United Kingdom law firm retained by AGC, worked frantically to produce a standstill agreement acceptable to all the bankers. By midnight on Monday 4 October all signatures had been received. But before AIG would sign the agreement it held Keatley to ransom. Unless the embattled CFO neutralised AIG's position of 430 000 ounces it would pull the plug. Keatley, under terrific pressure, obeyed, deferring the premium payable to AIG for the transaction. It was only then, just before midnight, that AIG agreed to the standstill.

Once in place, the standstill agreement prevented any party, including Ashanti, from making any bilateral payments and from taking any action that could lead to the company's liquidation. It would hold until 5.30 p.m. on Monday 11 October. Meanwhile the hedge parties appointed the City lawyers Linklaters, led by Richard Bussell and Robert Elliott, to represent their divergent interests. The RCF bankers instructed Clifford Chance, headed by Dominic Ross with Alan Inglis. If one thing was certain, this crisis was going to generate a lot of fees for lawyers.

Ashanti issued a press release to the market conveying the 'continued support' of its hedge banks by way of a standstill.[4] The announcement would likely have calmed listeners had it not added that Ashanti's non-executive director, Jean-Claude Gandur, had resigned. As far as journalists were concerned, the firm wishing 'him every success in his endeavours', translated into 'the ship is as good as sunk when insiders start jumping overboard'! In fact, in June 1999 Jonah had travelled to Geneva to ask the Swiss businessman to resign. Ashanti's other directors accused Gandur of trading AGC stock during a closed period and were also critical of his insistence that a company in which he held an interest should be awarded the fuel supply contract at Geita. He allegedly threatened to cause problems for Ashanti in Tanzania if this firm wasn't appointed as supplier. Jonah put it to him that his actions were not in keeping with a director's duties, so he should voluntarily and quietly resign. Gandur refused and the matter was tabled for discussion at the next board meeting. But then the crisis hit and Gandur chose to disassociate himself from AGC's situation.

Some bankers manoeuvred to make money whether the ship sank or floated. The leaders of the pack let it be known that they had taken positions in the market that would be in the money if Ashanti went under. The firm's demise would restrict the supply of physical gold in the short term and prices would rocket to the benefit of these traders' new positions. It is difficult enough to negotiate with a party that has nothing to lose, how much more so when that party has huge amounts to gain from your downfall.

Ashanti suffered all the more when Cambior, a Canadian intermediate producer in a similar situation, published comprehensive details of its hedge book. Until January 2000 no stock market jurisdiction demanded the disclosure of hedge portfolios. There were arguments against treating hedge contracts as either assets or liabilities and Ashanti chose, quite legally, to keep them off-balance sheet. Nevertheless, Cambior's transparency tipped a dumper truck of criticism on Ashanti.

Irate shareholders

An acerbic letter to Ashanti's company secretary from a livid shareholder is reproduced here in full:

As a shareholder of Ashanti may I begin with these words: I cannot find enough scorn to heap upon you. You and those others who for the past few years have been masquerading as beings fit to run a company – any company!

Ever since you were allowed to get your paws on the company it has headed south. If there was ever a case of allowing children to run a sweet shop this is it. But, not content with the destruction of the company, your utter disdain for the shareholder by your deceitful silence is no more than can be expected from you.

I demand up-to-date information on what you think you are going to get up to next before your inevitable return to the bush, where you rightfully belong.[5]

The letter reminded Jonah of a newspaper headline that he had read when Magic Johnson outed his HIV status. Jonah recalled that the article had spoken of the inability of blacks to handle success – as if Magic's colour had anything to do with his sickness.[6] But Jonah noticed that no connection to race was made when the white American heavyweight hopeful Tommy Morrison announced that he was also HIV-positive. Since his appointment as MD of Ashanti in September 1986 Jonah had spoken of feeling the weight of his race on his shoulders, the expectations of failure because he was a black African. It added to his resolve to conduct corporate affairs with the utmost rectitude. Those willing his downfall through misdemeanour would have an interminable wait. What had landed Ashanti in a crisis boiled down to a management decision taken in good faith, but which events had proven to be mistaken. It is reasonable and proper to expect uprightness from a CEO, but it is too much to ask a CEO never to make a wrong decision. Even the two Nobel prize-winning experts who founded Long-Term Capital Management (Myron Scholes, famous for the Black-Scholes option pricing model, and Robert Merton) were not immune from financial catastrophe when in 1998 their company was nearly bankrupted. Now, in Ashanti's case racial daggers were being drawn because of a misjudgement about the direction of gold prices. Criticisms about Jonah's judgement, or dissatisfaction with the level of communication from the firm were warranted, but what did returning 'to the bush' mean?

Confronting an arena of creditors

The initial meeting of all hedge counterparties and lending banks took place in London, in the first floor conference rooms at Linklaters, 1 Silk Street. Ashanti's corner was fielded by Jonah, Keatley, Richard Peprah (Ashanti's long-serving non-executive chairman and Ghana's minister of finance), Frederic Ohene-Kena (Ghana's minister of mines and energy and an Ashanti non-executive director) and Kofi Ansah (the chief executive of Ghana's Minerals Commission, the state regulator, also a non-executive Ashanti board member). Each banker attended with a member of senior personnel, perhaps a credit partner, and often a lawyer in tow. Upwards of seventy people filled the theatre-like set-up.

At first, there was no clear agenda to speak of. The 'meetings' consisted of sustained and bitter criticisms and condemnation hurled from the bankers at the Ashanti representatives. To the middle-aged minister of finance, the vituperations from these 30-year-old bankers, however justified their anger, was unbearably humiliating. Ghanaian culture is largely one of unquestioned respect for seniority; consequently, the bankers' tone pained the greying man almost as much as the company's predicament. The unveiled accusations of incompetence and the cheap opportunity to correlate the firm's demise spuriously to the colour of the men's skin and the continent of their birth were low blows. The stakes are so high in any bankruptcy situation that in all likelihood it was fear and edginess, not racism, fuelling the anger. Choice expletives ricocheted between the bankers themselves. It is easy to imagine how the concoction of unaligned incentives, disparate negotiating styles and 2.00 a.m. arguments boiled over into near-physical blows.

The hedge counterparties and the revolving credit facility bankers organised themselves into two subcommittees to represent the respective groups. The subcommittees would each meet the Ashanti group in a separate, smaller room across the corridor from the main arena. When it looked as if a way out, an accommodation, had been found with one of the subcommittees and hands had been shaken in agreement, the subcommittee would return to the waiting bankers and their lawyers to relay the progress made. It would take just one banker in the room to disagree for the illusory step forward to disappear. The subcommittee members would be swapped around and negotiations restarted. The lowest common denominator (not in terms of morality – this was an amoral situation – but in terms of pernicketyness) had the *legal* right to be satisfied. During one of many such impasses a mobile phone rang. The ring tone was inauspiciously the *Mission Impossible* theme tune. A rare, light moment of laughter spread across the room; Jonah's roar of a laugh contradicted the heaviness that he felt inside.

As the chief executive, Jonah felt acutely and expressed firmly that any failings within the Ashanti organisation lay squarely on his shoulders. His insistence on diverting blame away from Keatley to himself confounded and infuriated many bankers. They felt that Keatley had kept them in the dark about the firm's unusually broad banking relationships and the complexity of Ashanti's entire hedge portfolio. Keatley, as far as they were concerned, deserved to be hung, drawn and quartered, and it appeared as if many would have gladly volunteered to mete out such punishment. Jonah would not make a symbolic sacrifice to satisfy anyone. His priority was to work out a solution. If heads needed to roll then he volunteered his own to go first, but the banks rejected his offer to resign.[7]

The thought of unravelling the situation – perhaps through liquidation in Ghana and in the other African countries where AGC operated – without Jonah was too opaque to contemplate. Despite everything, the bankers still trusted Jonah. The CEO argued that Keatley knew the company's financial situation better than anyone else and was therefore indispensable at this critical time. This thinking failed to wash with the majority of bankers and they continued to criticise Jonah for what was, to them, grossly misplaced loyalty.

Ashanti's board gathered at Goldman Sachs's Fleet Street offices on Saturday 9 October for emergency deliberations. The board endeavoured to resolve not one, but two liquidity issues: the need for cash, firstly, to appease the hedge banks and, secondly, to bring Geita on stream. Work at Geita was about half-complete, requiring an immediate addition of $85m if production was to start on schedule in June 2000. Based on a mine plan that only included five million ounces out of the eleven million of gold resources identified, the mine would increase Ashanti's output by 400 000 ounces (30 per cent) per annum at a competitive cash cost of $180 an ounce. But with the group's gross gearing standing at 154 per cent, which was unsustainable and excessive in view of Ashanti's business and its peer group debt levels, and with the existing $270m revolving credit facility expiring on 2 December, securing new capital for Geita appeared to be as steep a challenge as dealing with the margin calls.[8]

An expedited merger with Lonmin was the obvious answer. The solution-storm continued on Sunday. Overnight, J. Aron, Goldman Sachs's derivatives arm, had devised another way out, which it was convinced it could persuade the other hedge banks to buy. J. Aron's proposal was to shelve the margin calls *and* provide a $100m loan for Geita in exchange for warrants over 15 per cent of Ashanti. Jonah and his board sat up. This would not preclude a merger and it would bring about a speedier conclusion to the immediate crisis. The 15 per cent, Jonah mentally plotted, could perhaps be negotiated to 10 per cent. The request for equity was a welcome vote of confidence in the underlying assets of the company, in its operations, and in Ashanti's future.

The flicker of hope didn't last long. Before the idea could be put to other hedge banks, higher powers at Goldman Sachs rejected it, and the derivatives traders were spoken to strongly. They had no right to commit corporate finance to loans or equity acquisitions.

A merger solution

The merger option remained. On Monday 11 October Lonmin and Ashanti jointly announced Lonmin's offer to take over Ashanti in a share-for-share deal at an exchange ratio of 32 new Lonmin shares for every 43 Ashanti shares not in its possession. This valued each Ashanti share at about $7 (an 86 per cent premium on the last traded New York Stock Exchange price of $3.75), valuing the firm at around $835m. The merger would be subject to, amongst other things, approval from the Ghanaian government and an extension to the standstill agreement by all banks. The standstill agreement was duly extended for one more week, until 5.30 p.m. on Monday 18 October. In the meantime, Ashanti suspended trading its shares on the six stock exchanges where its securities were listed (London, New York and Toronto as well as the Australian, Ghanaian and Zimbabwean bourses) pending further developments.

At The Castle, Richard Peprah presented the benefits of the Lonmin merger to ministers and the president. His exhortations fell on stony ears. The government, unaware of the history of the merger plans, could not ignore the public vibe that Lonmin was moving in when the company was on its knees to get it on the cheap. It was duty bound to explore the Lonmin proposal as well as other options in greater detail. It would normally fall on a minister of finance to lead such an investigation, but Peprah's chairmanship of Ashanti and, more significantly, his friendship with Jonah, caused the president to delegate the task to Vice-president Mills.

The pro-government *Daily Graphic* in Ghana had reported on Friday 8 October that Fred Ohene-Kena, the minister for mines and energy and an Ashanti director, was supportive of the merger. Ohene-Kena stated that the government's 17 per cent stake might even be reduced to 10 per cent. Whatever hopes Jonah and his bankers drew from this positive stance were short-lived. The minister returned to London expecting his presence and message to bolster the bankers' confidence. But the day after the merger offer, President Rawlings abruptly sacked Ohene-Kena for having the audacity to prejudge the government's decision. Ohene-Kena heard the news third-hand; after a radio announcement in Ghana, a colleague telephoned Peprah with the information. Peprah received the call while in a taxi with Jonah returning to the hotel where he was staying with Ohene-Kena. It was on Peprah's arrival that he relayed the dismissal. The absence of government support for the merger – the only solution Ashanti had on the table – seriously destabilised negotiations. Jonah was furious, but that was just the beginning.

On Friday 15 October Rawlings dismissed Kofi Ansah as chief executive of the Minerals Commission. Much to the government's annoyance, sacking Ansah and Ohene-Kena from their government jobs did not automatically remove them as Ashanti board members – that could only be done if they voluntarily resigned from the board or were voted out at the next AGM. But they were no longer the government's representatives on the board. Any prospect of gaining government approval for the merger and a prompt resolution to the crisis thinned.

The government had three tools to block Lonmin. Firstly, as a 17 per cent AGC shareholder, it held more than 25 per cent of the non-Lonmin votes and so could prevent any merger using a scheme of arrangement (the simplest route for a merger requiring over 75 per cent of the non-Lonmin shares to be in favour). Secondly, as a regulator, any changes in majority control of a Ghanaian mine needed written ministerial approval according to Section 60 of the Mineral and Mining (Amendment) Act of 1994; this could be withheld, especially now that the AGC-friendly Minister of Mines Ohene-Kena had been removed. And, thirdly, there was the government's golden share.

The exact use and powers of this instrument had never been tested. Of all the mines in Ghana, foreign and/or indigenously owned, only Ashanti was encumbered with a golden share. As guardian over the nation's minerals the government, quite correctly, was provided with legal teeth in the Minerals and Mining Law to protect its interests and to intervene in prescribed circumstances to protect those interests. This law governed every single mine. By contrast, the golden share was shrouded in mystery and only applied to Ashanti. If its purpose was to protect sovereign mineral rights, then it should have been a prerequisite in the share profile of every Ghanaian mine. For instance, when the South African company Gold Fields acquired 100 per cent of the former state mines at Tarkwa, no golden share was imposed. It was at the time of Ashanti's flotation in 1994 that a golden share was given to the government. It had proved a useful political device to carry public support for the loosening of the government's grip on the country's richest mine. Nevertheless, its grip remained substantial – at the IPO the government continued to hold 35 per cent equity in the firm, unlike its 100 per cent abandonment of Tarkwa. In the minds of Ghanaians, however, Ashanti Goldfields was unlike other mines. Its unique ores, profitable history and geographic association with the great warrior-tribe endowed it with a legendary status. The golden share frankly served emotive purposes rather than any equitable or legal ones. For Ashanti as well as international investors and financiers, it added an unhelpful layer of uncertainty. It would have been better for all if the government transparently ruled out a Lonmin merger on the basis of its shareholding or by invoking Section 60 of the Mineral and Mining (Amendment) Act, instead of wielding the golden share as a weapon of unknown force.

As Ashanti's share price plummeted Lonmin revised its offer

downwards to 16 shares for every 27, about $5.95 a share or $665m in total.[9] Lonmin's chairman, Sir John Craven, and chief executive, Nick Morrell, travelled to Accra to put their case across to Vice-president Mills. Lonmin's view of the merger as the best all-round solution for Ashanti was received terribly. The government felt that Lonmin's assessment was not just inaccurate but arrogant. It was suspicious of Lonmin's motives because Jonah was a Lonmin employee and director. It seemed to the government that Lonmin was only looking out for its own interests by insisting on this merger. 'We should throw them in jail,' a government minister growled.[10] The hostile reception and predatory motivations foisted on Craven and Morrell removed their desire to fight for the deal. Picking a political battle made no commercial sense. Whether the hedge banks would rescind all claims for margin, another prerequisite for the merger to proceed, remained uncertain. In these circumstances Lonmin backed off. The two men were sufficiently shaken by the government's reaction to insist that Jonah's wife, Theo, left the country with them on their private plane.

As the *Financial Times* perceptively noted, the bankers and Lonmin had failed to take three important factors into consideration: the animosity between Jonah and Rawlings, the status of Ashanti in the national psyche, and tribal politics,[11] the last point referring to the newly enstooled Asantehene.

The Jonah-Rawlings enmity prevented Minister of Finance Peprah from executing an easy option out of the crisis. The Ghanaian government could have provided a letter of guarantee to the hedge counterparties. Even though the IMF would frown on any government intervention in the misfortunes of a publicly listed company, such an action was not without precedent elsewhere in the world. All it required was presidential support. It would be an unusual request, a favour, as the government was under no obligation to assist in this way. But Peprah did not even ask – he was as perplexed as the rest of the nation by the incredible rupture between the president and Jonah. The chief executive regretted that a personal feud could jeopardise his life's work and AGC's very existence.

A resolution to the crisis looked increasingly unlikely. Monday 18 October, the expiry date of the extended standstill agreement came. The deadline of 5.30 p.m. passed.

CHAPTER 12

'The lizard does not eat pepper and sweat break out on the frog'

October–November 1999

The cash collateral demanded from Ashanti peaked at $270m on 5 October. Although in the following weeks the gold price slipped, it didn't fall sufficiently to remove Ashanti's burden. There was no way that Jonah could fight for his reputation and his company from Ghana, so the chief executive rented a flat between Grosvenor Square and Hyde Park, his work-out flat, as he termed it. During the day the non-stop discussions and negotiations at least provided comfort that something was being done, action was being taken, even though it felt mostly like treading water. Jonah darted from appointments with his advisers – Andy Quinn at CIBC's Tooley Street offices; Richard Campbell-Breeden at Goldman Sachs in Fleet Street; and Mark Bankes, Ashanti's lawyer at Norton Rose based in Liverpool Street – to meetings with his creditors. There were the group meetings of hedge banks and RCF banks and one-on-one encounters with individual bankers at their various offices. Ashanti board meetings were now being held almost daily via teleconference with United Kingdom and Ghana-based directors.

Jonah assured his would-be executioners that Ashanti's business was fundamentally sound and that the company's assets remained valuable. The chief executive was on first-name terms with many of the bankers and his evocation of the strength of past relationships jarred with some as he implored them to try to look behind and ahead of the present situation. He offered to fly to the United States if needed to put his case for continued support in person to the CEOs of the banks headquartered in America. Few people could speak as skilfully extemporaneously or with such fluency and confidence about the operations of a gold business as Sam could.

While Jonah wrestled for corporate survival in London, operations continued on target at the mines. The attractiveness of AGC's core business led the press to gleefully declare a fire sale of Ashanti assets as the only remaining remedy now that merger hopes were dead. A large group of well-known and more obscure mining houses along with a so-called 'white knight' from the Middle East hovered, waiting to dive in.

Considering the options

Nana Prah had been staying with his brother in the work-out flat and providing invisible but immeasurable support. When Theo arrived he returned to Ghana. The evenings were in many ways more difficult for Jonah to cope with because it was on his return to the flat that he learnt of news from Ghana. Radio phone-in programmes had hooked onto the crisis; the calls expressed the people's anger and bewilderment at events. The efforts of Ashanti's small public relations department needed reinforcement to reduce the emotion, confusion and inaccuracies. Consequently, in addition to the usual press statements, insiders anonymously penned articles in defence of Ashanti and Jonah in an attempt to balance the negative coverage and the column space devoted to examining the stains from the latest mud slung by Rawlings. Sam was protective of his reputation and the bad press gnawed at his very being. It was in his nature to counter the personal insults immediately, but he was conscious of the danger of diverting his energies from the crisis.

He walked outside the perimeter of Hyde Park late at night, sometimes alone, sometimes with Quinn or Morrell, mulling over the options and the ramifications of each one. To ignore or challenge the margin calls was an idea abandoned as quickly as it had been raised. The Lonmin merger solution had been blown out of the water by the Ghana government, although no written rejection of the proposal had yet been received. Richard Peprah reported that there was no chance of a Ghana government guarantee. Attempts to obtain backing from the World Bank and the IFC also failed to come to anything. The possibility of providing the hedge banks with political risks insurance to cover the

margin liability proved prohibitively expensive. They investigated introducing the equivalent of the American Chapter 11 bankruptcy law in
Ghana, which would buy time for the company to reorganise. But such
an initiative had to come from the government and that was highly
unlikely; besides it would be a lengthy process. Overtures were made to
Warren Buffet and George Soros, but without success. Preliminary discussions took place with an investment vehicle of the Libyan government for a loan of up to $150m. Legal investigations suggested that
while there would be no breach of United Kingdom laws,[1] Ashanti's
American advisers, Goldman Sachs, would have to resign as American
laws prohibited involvement in any Libyan transaction.[2] Furthermore,
the appeal of AGC stock to North American investors would be dam-
aged with significant Libyan participation.

The sale of individual mines was another option. Barrick, Anglogold
and Normandy approached Ashanti with unsolicited offers – Barrick
and Anglogold for 50 per cent of Geita, and Normandy for 100 per cent
of the Siguiri mine in Guinea and Bibiani in Ghana. The jewels in
Ashanti's empire were Geita, Obuasi and Bibiani. If asset sales were un-
avoidable Jonah's preference for disposals would be Siguiri and, if pushed,
Bibiani. Of all his achievements at Ashanti, the acquisition of Geita and
the expansion of its resources following its purchase gave him the most
satisfaction, and he would safeguard its ownership if at all possible.

After the Lonmin merger a strong alternative that emerged was to
restructure the ownership of Ashanti. The company considered separating the non-Ghanaian assets from the golden-share-attached Ghanaian
ones. It would be easier to raise equity for the former, but it would not
be a quick or straightforward way out. Geita in Tanzania had related
negative hedge contracts and the company's existing tax structures had
not been designed with divestment in mind. Furthermore, the Ghana
government could erect obstacles to breaking up the group, and even if
these proved surmountable it would take several months to execute
such a major corporate reconfiguration. Jonah, his advisers and lawyers
explored and re-explored the various alternatives while keeping an eye
on the company's daily cash balances.

On 17 October Ashanti's cash at hand stood at $28.5m. The directors'
legal duty to ensure that the company remained solvent necessitated the

production of daily cash status reports, which were also circulated to the creditors. A $19m loan from Barclays due on 12 October had by mutual agreement been deferred and was being rolled over daily. However, another project finance loan of $10.5m owed to UBS and Dresdner would fall due on 30 October.

On Monday 18 October the extended standstill agreement expired. If the hedge counterparties could help it there would be no more weekly standstill extensions. They closed in on Ashanti for their margin, now giving the company 24-hour deadlines to pay up or face foreclosure.

The arrival of government advisers

Ghana's leading investment bank, Cal Merchant Bank, and a dominant domestic stockbroker, Databank, offered their advisory services to the government, along with a pride of lawyers. Jude Bucknor headed the Cal contingency. Bucknor had previously served on Ashanti's board while also a director of Lehman Brothers investment bank. He had left Ashanti following conflict of interest issues with his role at Lehmans. Ken Ofori-Atta, whose father had been a staunch anti-AGC flotation campaigner, led the Databank team. Databank, feeling out of its depth, then recruited T. Hoare Canaccord, a British, boutique brokerage firm specialising in the mining sector, to assist. Canaccord was thus initially an adviser to a government adviser.[3] Vice-president Mills was so impressed with Mark Horn, Canaccord's workaholic representative, that he soon awarded Canaccord a direct mandate.[4] A lawyer by training, Mark Horn quickly emerged as the group leader of the government team. Its remit was reportedly to help the government to understand the hedging crisis,[5] and to make recommendations on a course of action that would foreground the interests of the government and the people of Ghana.[6]

If Ashanti failed it would not only cost the government in terms of its 17 per cent shareholding. In addition, the downfall of the country's largest firm would dent Ghana's GDP; the small economy would lose about $30m a year in royalties and taxes; and 11 200 jobs were directly at stake, not to mention the ancillary services and businesses linked to Ashanti's operations. Ashanti's bankruptcy would immeasurably damage the image of Ghana as an attractive foreign investment destination. If the

government played any role in that demise it would be scrutinised un-
forgivingly by potential investors.

These small-firm government advisers felt that they were *personae non
gratae* in the presence of the large, premier banking houses such as
Goldman Sachs and Barclays. On the team's arrival in London on
15 October, Jonah invited the group to Fleet Street to brief them on the
situation. The chief executive hoped that as professionals they would be
able to see and treat the crisis as a corporate one without conflating the
issues along personal or political lines. Bucknor and Ofori-Atta assured
him of this, but relations quickly deteriorated.

Horn lodged formal complaints with the American financial markets
regulator, the Securities and Exchange Commission (SEC) and the
Bank of England against Goldman Sachs. Goldmans had acted as
Ashanti's corporate adviser for several years but its advisory role during
the crisis created potential conflicts of interest since the same bank suffered the greatest credit exposures as Ashanti's largest hedge counterparty and a participant of the RCF.[7] Conceding to this, Goldmans
ceased to advise Ashanti, and CIBC, through Quinn, shouldered this
role on its own. The United Kingdom Financial Services Authority later
launched an investigation into the American investment bank's behaviour during Ashanti's crisis.[8]

Horn and his men further accused Ashanti and the banks of withhold-
ing information and fobbing off their enquiries. The government advisers
were adamant that the ching-ching of fees was biasing the bankers' judgement. They refused to accept that in this bankruptcy situation the creditors would drive the solutions and so they voiced suspicions over any
proposals promoted by the banks. In their view, the banks were intimidat-
ing Ashanti. The team cited as an example the banks' support of the
Lonmin merger, which they scorned as a give-away. So strongly did they
feel about this that they were prepared to bring the 'strong-arm' tactics of
the banks to the attention of the Non-aligned Movement as an example
of North-South exploitation: wealthy, white banks bullying the blighted,
black firm. To Horn, Ashanti's predicament became almost a personal,
geopolitical crusade, not a mere search for a financial solution.[9]

Like a fly that intermittently buzzes straight into your ear, the government advisers began to irritate the various bankers. Jonah respected the

legitimacy of their remit but he wondered how conscious the individuals were of being used as pawns in a battle that would surely conclude the war between himself and Rawlings.

At least one of the group of government advisers, Frank Adu, a director of Cal Merchant Bank, recognised the hidden personal agenda. During a meeting in a conference room at The Castle with President Rawlings, Vice-president Mills and other government ministers, Adu stood up to protest at the personalisation of the crisis by Rawlings.[10] He was not prepared to get involved in a fight between 'an elephant and a lion', as he put it.[11] He saw his role clearly as the provision of professional evaluation services, and to make recommendations based on his best judgement in exchange for a fee – nothing more, nothing less. If only that could have been true, but clear-cut was not an adjective appropriate for any aspect of this crisis.

Ashanti gold represented 'national sovereignty' to President Rawlings and he used this point to raise objections to the Lonmin merger plans.[12] However, it was Rawlings who invited the founder and chairman of Barrick, Peter Munk, and his chief executive, Randall Oliphant, to meet him personally to discuss how Barrick could come to Ashanti's rescue, an invitation that necessarily involved foreign ownership.[13] It was Rawlings who entertained the investment proposals of Saudi Arabia's Prince Al-Waleed Bin Talal Bin Abdulaziz.[14] And less than a year earlier it had been Rawlings who had asked Jonah to initiate a potential takeover of Lonmin's stake by Placer Dome, another Canadian firm. During the crisis Placer Dome renewed its interest to buy into Obuasi.[15] Objections over the price of the Lonmin merger offer held more water than the cheap, untrue and populist anti-foreigner spin fed to the Ghanaian press by the Office of the President. The hypocrisy was symptomatic of the president's irrational behaviour, itself induced by his hatred of Jonah – a hatred that seemed to surpass any desire to ensure Ashanti's survival.

After Barrick's meeting with Rawlings the press reported the president's words that, 'Sam Jonah would have been shot' in the past for Ashanti's current situation.[16] When Oliphant, Barrick's CEO, had lunch with Jonah in London soon afterwards he warned him to watch his back. Barrick had been so disturbed by Rawlings's anger directed personally at Jonah that it vowed not to get involved in Ghana. Even if the roads of Ghana were paved with gold, Oliphant confessed to his bedevilled industry rival, Barrick would not do business in that country. In the present circumstances it was only prepared to consider involvement in Ashanti's mines outside Ghana.

Jonah also received sympathetic words from another personal friend and industry rival, Bobby Godsell at Anglogold. The South African sent him a handwritten note as the crisis escalated wishing him well and reassuring him that history would not forget his achievements for the African continent.[17]

The British Foreign Office gets involved

Two weeks before Queen Elizabeth II's planned three-day state visit to Ghana, scheduled for 7 to 9 November, the Ghanaian ambassador to the United Kingdom, James Aggrey-Orleans, was awoken by a telephone call to his London residence. It was well after midnight. The anger in President Rawlings's voice shook off the ambassador's drowsiness. 'Get Tony Blair on the phone,' he insisted, unconcerned about the time of night or the strictly emergency circumstances that would merit disturbing the British prime minister. The diplomat conveyed the unlikelihood of this happening, but promised to try. As expected, the duty officer at Downing Street refused to oblige. Aggrey-Orleans called President Rawlings back. Rawlings, still incensed, instructed the ambassador to tell Tony Blair that if the British government did not look into the criminality of Sam Jonah then the Queen's visit would be cancelled. Aggrey-Orleans was dumbstruck by the threat as well as by Rawlings's venom. To communicate such ill-considered bluster would denigrate the office he held, not to mention his own reputation as a seasoned diplomat, so the ambassador decided not to act.

Unbeknown to Aggrey-Orleans, the First Lady, Nana Konadu, attempted another approach through Cherie Blair to soil Jonah's reputation.[18] Whatever Nana Konadu had told Cherie Blair was believed because a letter was sent from Downing Street to the Foreign Office and forwarded to Britain's man in Accra. The letter did not enquire into the truth of Jonah's criminal allegations, but rather appeared to be putting the Foreign Office on notice. Craig Murray, acting British High Commissioner in Ghana, drafted the response himself. He advised No.10 to ignore the misinformation: Jonah was highly respectable. Murray rather expressed concern about Nana Konadu whose character he could not similarly vouch for.

Murray received several telephone calls from London for information. One came from Leon Britten, a former cabinet minister under Margaret Thatcher and vice-president of the European Commission, who called on behalf of an Ashanti-embroiled bank. The bankers all delivered the same refrain: there was a strong impression in the City that the Ghana government wanted AGC to fold. They wanted to know what the hell was going on and sounded the man on the spot for his opinion.[19]

Meanwhile, the government advisers continued doggedly with their investigation of Ashanti's options. Either they were deluding themselves that they were fighting in the cause of Ashanti's survival or they were ignorant of the president's cloaked operations. Parallel to the public and official view of events, Rawlings made use of a clique of trusted men, such as Tsatsu Tsikata, to orchestrate his private schemes.

Bank of England and United States Treasury involvement

Behind the scenes, Michael Beckett (a non-executive Ashanti director), Sir John Craven (Lonmin's chairman), and Richard Peprah contacted Bank of England superiors to request unofficial assistance to rein in the most belligerent hedge counterparties that were foaming to foreclose.[20] Help was specifically requested with regard to the behaviour of the American banks. There is anecdotal evidence that Ashanti's predicament and the negative impact its failure would have on African foreign direct investment was put to the United States banking authorities. Whether any action was taken by them to assist Ashanti directly is unknown. However, further evidence from industry insiders suggests that to prevent the worst fears of a gold market crisis from materialising, the United States government instructed J.P. Morgan to intervene massively in the bullion markets.[21] It is very likely that pressure from above was exerted on Ashanti's hedge counterparties.

This, coupled with the hedge banks' late realisation that under paragraphs 67 and 68 of the Ghana Minerals and Mining Law, Ashanti's insolvency or bankruptcy would allow the government to cancel Ashanti's mineral rights and on termination practically all the Ghanaian assets, including the prized Obuasi mine, would 'vest in the Republic', concentrated minds. If the banks forced Ashanti to the wall they would come out with very little and the shareholders (apart from the government) with nothing.

An old offer re-emerges

A group of four hedge banks led by J. Aron rehashed the proposal originally suggested on Sunday 10 October. The banks would be prepared to drop their margin requirements if Ashanti converted the hedge book into a more straightforward portfolio, and if the banks were granted up to 20 per cent equity in Ashanti. Jonah didn't get too excited because too many straws had already broken from his clutch; he requested the offer to be put in writing to the board. He added his dismay that this time around there was no Geita funding attached and that the equity demand had significantly increased. Linklaters, on behalf of the hedge banks, delivered a formal written offer on Wednesday 20 October. Ashanti was given just two days, until 5.30 p.m. on the Friday, to agree to the proposal.

The detailed term sheet specified that the hedge banks would suspend margin requirements until 31 December 2002 if they were issued five-year warrants over 15 per cent of Ashanti's post-exercise issued ordinary share capital. In other words, they were prepared to waive the $270m collateral demanded for the hedge book losses, and for the next three years Ashanti would be allowed to trade derivatives without having to put up any security. For this leniency the banks wanted the right to buy 15 per cent of the firm at a certain price per share. The warrants would be exercisable any time after twelve months, but within five years, at the mid-market share price on 19 October 1999 of $4.50. After the three-year grace period, margin (or security) requirements would be re-introduced, but at more generous levels than AGC's existing $300m limit. The major precondition for the deal was that within a month

Ashanti had to secure the much needed short–term liquidity (for Geita and for working capital) on terms agreeable to the hedge banks *and* with Ghana government consent. Ashanti was to deliver a business plan by 2 December showing how it would restructure to reduce gearing in the medium and long term. Within three months of that date the firm would have to demonstrate to the satisfaction of the banks that the business plan had been successfully implemented. The margin-free period would be effective from that point. Until then Ashanti would continue to operate on a standstill.

To evaluate the offer Ashanti compared the cost of issuing the warrants with the value of no longer having to post margin. This calculation would depend on the cost of borrowing to post margin, movements in the gold and share price between then and December 2002 and the cost of surrendering equity at various points in the future vis-à-vis market price and strike price. With regard to the hedge book going forwards, Ashanti was of the opinion that it would need to continue to hedge 50 per cent of total reserves against downside risk for the next four years for several reasons. These included its high debt commitments until the completion of Geita; the fall in physical demand for gold due to the Asian crisis; and the increase in gold production expected from new mine start-ups on the back of higher prices. Thereafter it would be possible to reduce hedging to about 25 per cent. Whether the hedge banks' independent auditors would agree to this strategy remained to be seen. Other concerns aired by AGC directors included what would happen after the three-year margin-free period. Would the hedge banks cease to trade with Ashanti? How would the company's deteriorated creditworthiness affect its chances of raising funds within a month as specified as a precondition? Of ongoing concern was the erratic and volatile behaviour of the hedge bankers, some of whom were themselves under mounting pressure from their senior management and credit executives to close out their positions with Ashanti without loss to themselves at the soonest opportunity.

At 5.00 p.m. on Friday, Ashanti made a counter-offer to Linklaters. It was serious about this proposal but was only prepared to offer 10 per cent of shares at a strike price of $4.75. The standstill was extended to Monday 25 October for this to be considered, by which time the RCF banks, upset by their exclusion from the offer, had added their demand for an equitable share of warrants. After all, they had a $270m facility with Ashanti due for repayment on 2 December. This put them in as strong a negotiating position as the hedge banks.

The cash egg timer

With the prospect of suspended margin calls, the emphasis now shifted to addressing the immediate liquidity issue. Suppliers at Geita were now demanding cash on delivery, seriously jeopardising the timetable for completion. Two unattractive bilateral offers lay on the table. Following an approach by Jonah, the Libyan Arab Foreign Investment Company offered to provide $100m over six years, unsecured at 7.5 per cent with an upfront fee of 8.5 per cent. The loan could be completed for disbursement within three weeks, but the negative press from Libyan involvement tarnished the deal. The African Infrastructure Fund, an American investment vehicle, offered $25m at an exorbitant 15 per cent. The ideal solution would be for the $270m RCF facility to be rolled over for another year with an added tranche of $100m for Geita.

Gerard Holden at Barclays pitched for the role as financial adviser to restructure Ashanti's commercial debt and to secure an additional $100m to $125m. Barclays was still peeved that Chase Manhattan had dislodged it as the leaders and arrangers of Ashanti's last RCF. The bank had a high profile in Africa and in mine finance, along with a thirteen-year relationship with Ashanti in various capacities, first as a lender, then a bondholder and hedge counterparty. In addition, Barclays was owed a favour – a $19m bridging finance loan due since 12 October was being rolled over on a daily basis. To Barclays's credit it produced in record speed an impressive model of Ashanti's operations and cash flow requirement for the next four years based on various gold price levels. The bank gave assurances to structure a term sheet incorporating the refinancing of the existing RCF, repayment of outstanding bilateral loans and the assumption of new debt of up to $125m by 30 November. On the basis of its advanced initiative Barclays was appointed restructuring lead, but so as not to offend Chase Manhattan a role would be found for the latter bank as the incumbent RCF leader.

In order to allow a bank delegation to brief the Ghana government on the recent and rapid developments, Ashanti requested another stand-still extension. The company argued that with the gold price on Monday 25 October at $298.50 only three of the hedge parties were legally entitled to make margin calls so it would be morally reprehensible for any of them to call margin particularly since Ashanti had started serious negotiations with them.

Ashanti called the bankers' bluff and simply ignored the next deadline set for 12 noon on 27 October. The banks didn't foreclose. Rather, they came back the following day conceding to one of AGC's counter-offers. The banks would accept an exercise price of $4.75 for the warrants, but they would not budge on 15 per cent of Ashanti's share capital. Jonah signed the warrant agreement on 29 October. A mix of emotions swirled in him. The size of the ownership stake demanded by the banks stung, particularly in view of the fact that Ashanti had not lost the banks any money – the margin requirements were not realised losses but only requests for collateral. Had Ashanti delivered the money at the peak of the gold rally most of it would have been returned before the day the warrant agreement was signed. But the 15 per cent stake in Ashanti could also be viewed as consideration to the banks for having not exercised their legal rights to foreclose.

The timetable to provide liquidity, restructure the balance sheet and to deliver a business plan was tight. While Barclays spearheaded the liquidity resolution, Jonah's attention turned to reducing gearing levels. Splitting the Ashanti group in order to raise equity for the non-Ghanaian subsidiaries, which would be more attractive to investors because they were unencumbered by any golden shares, stood out as a preferred option. In the hope of obtaining Ghanaian government approval to divide the company up, Ashanti planned to offer the government a larger ownership stake in its Ghana assets.

Another gearing reduction option was a partial sale of Geita to generate funds to clear debt. Barrick tabled an unsolicited formal offer of $200m for 50 per cent of Geita along with an $85m bilateral loan at 10 per cent that could either be repaid in cash, or converted into Ashanti shares of an equivalent value. In money terms Anglogold made a similar offer, but, unlike Barrick, Anglogold would not demand managerial control of Geita.

Quinn calculated that the net present value of Geita as a whole, assuming a discount rate of 6 per cent and based on gold prices at $300, was $450m, making both offers in the ballpark. However, tax advice received from Deloitte & Touche discouraged any sale of Geita at the risk of double capital gains tax bills from Tanzania and the United Kingdom (since Geita was linked to Ashanti subsidiaries in the Isle of Man).

Looking ahead, in March 2003 Ashanti's $250m bond issue would be due for redemption or, more realistically, refinancing. In that light the company might have to raise equity *in addition* to the sale of a significant asset. But at least the margin call guillotine had temporarily been removed.

A false sense of relief

Just when Jonah, exhausted from treading water, felt as if a hand had reached out to lift him from the sea, a surging breaker engulfed him. Mona Caesar-Addo, the head of Ashanti's treasury department responsible for formulating and executing the group's hedging programme and at the epicentre of the crisis, announced the resignation of the entire treasury team of six. The team simultaneously offered its services on a consultancy basis – and at consultancy fees. In the past Caesar-Addo had complained about the discrepancy between expatriate and Ghanaian wages at Ashanti. Perhaps she now saw a means to rectify her grievance, but she had seriously miscalculated her boss. Jonah's instinctive reaction to being cornered was to pounce, not recoil, and he accepted the resignations without hesitation.

In response to Keatley's questions about how the company would manage, Jonah said, 'Consider them dead.' Keatley waited for an explanation. 'What if all six had been on a plane that crashed? Would the company come to a stop? Certainly not! This firm is bigger than any of us. Neither Ashanti nor I will stand for blackmail,' Jonah barked. But he was hurt – not so much by the timing of the treasury team's self-interest, but by a sense of betrayal and disappointment by those whom he had for many years obviously misjudged.

Jonah's dismissiveness of Mark Horn, the Canaccord representative, also constituted a misjudgement. Horn's pursuit for information led him to disgruntled shareholders. One of these was Jean-Claude Gandur, the Ashanti director who had resigned within a week of the crisis erupting. He joined forces with Horn to create a formidable threat. Gandur had formerly owned a significant part of the Geita prospect, which Ashanti had acquired in November 1998 through the purchase of Samax. Geita had now turned out to be one of the most exciting gold deposits in the world. If Horn succeeded in shaping events Gandur would potentially have the opportunity to regain control of the mine. It seemed to Jonah that Gandur and Rawlings shared one goal: to get him out; the only difference between the two men was that Rawlings was prepared to do so even at the risk of destroying Ashanti.[22]

The meeting of a bank delegation with Vice-president Mills and his advisers at The Castle in order to explain the new state of affairs ended disastrously. Not only did Horn oppose the plans for Ashanti to assume any new debt, the government also made it clear that it had no desire whatsoever to acquire a larger stake in the company's Ghanaian assets following any proposed restructuring. The state's divestment strategy aimed to reduce its ownership in business. This particular work-out solution ran counter to that principle and would not be entertained.[23] Moreover, the government was unhappy about the dilution of its stake from the warrants agreement and would legally challenge the issue of more warrants to the RCF banks.[24]

Rawlings simultaneously stepped up his public vilification campaign of Jonah. He used the prestige and profile of Queen Elizabeth II's visit to Ghana to hurl insults about Jonah. At an official banquet in honour of the British monarch on Monday 8 November, Rawlings, seated next to Her Royal Highness, stood to deliver his speech. It was unclear to the British Foreign Office staff in attendance whether the president had gone off-script or had always intended to deliver such an acrimonious tirade. It was apparent to all that his subject, without naming him, was Sam Jonah. Rawlings was apoplectic. His veins bulged; his fists clenched tightly and reddened on the podium. The crescendo of insinuations then cut off abruptly and an uncomfortable silence froze his anger. Nobody knew where to put their eyes. For a good half-minute the audience wondered what he was going to do next. From all accounts it was extraordinary. Rawlings then visibly forced himself to gather his composure. In a normal voice he resumed and finished his speech.[25]

It is hard to imagine that the president's diatribe accusing a certain individual of gold theft in collusion with Britain could have been any worse or any more inappropriate, particularly considering the Queen's speech earlier that day in which she had commended Ghana for pioneering the 'renaissance in Africa of democratic values' and praised the good relationship between the two countries.[26] But the distinguished guests would have been even more horrified than they were had it not been for the intervention of certain ministers who at the eleventh hour switched the president's original script (which, incidentally, was preserved) for a more 'diplomatic' version.[27]

Jonah seethed when he heard of the banquet events. The work-out negotiations had taken a physical and mental toll on him; he had not slept well for weeks despite his exhaustion. And now Rawlings's incessant taunts dealt another blow to his spirits.

Nana Prah had left his younger brother with some sleeping tablets. 'I know you'd prefer a woman for stress relief, but take these instead,' he'd jested before he left for Ghana. The tablets remained unused, but on this night Jonah took one and went to lie down. Theo watched television for a while before heading to bed. She opened the bedroom door to see Sam slumped, unconscious, between the bed and the bedside cabinet. He was breathing and she discerned a pulse, but when she tried to rouse him he failed to come round. In two minds as to whether or not to call an ambulance she gave him an almighty, last-ditch slap.

Jonah shot up. 'Fuck Rawlings!' he bellowed. Events and the sleeping pill had combined literally to knock him out. Theo managed to get him into bed and he immediately fell again into a deep sleep. She lay beside him, watching him, her diminutive size belying her strength of character. It wasn't until 3.00 a.m. that Jonah awoke fully to see his wife's face above him, and the lights on. 'I thought I had lost you,' she said, before recounting the night's events.

Like a heavyweight boxer who is knocked down but staggers to his feet to rapturous applause before the count is out and who, inflamed by the blow, fights with greater determination, Jonah now rose to his feet for the biggest fight of his personal and business life.

CHAPTER 13

'When a scorpion stings without mercy, you kill it without mercy'

November 1999–January 2000

It was time for Jonah to retaliate. His absence from Ghana had given wind to detractors' accusations and now he flew home to speak his mind. He took out a full-page advert in the country's most widely read newspaper, the *Daily Graphic*, to challenge the president's accusations and to expose Rawlings's hidden agenda. Jonah wrote:

> *The president appears to think that some mining companies keep govern-ment revenue in their own accounts and make profit from it before sur-rendering it to the government. AGC certainly does not do that ... It is important that if the president knows of such or any other criminal con-duct, it is in everybody's interest that he provides details of it as soon as possible so that those involved are dealt with in accordance with due processes of the law ... I wish to assure his Excellency, my friends, well-wishers and indeed, all shareholders of AGC, that there is no basis what-soever for anybody to suspect me of criminal conduct ... AGC is still in delicate negotiations with its counterparties. Any unsubstantiated allegations of the nature which may have led the president to express the sentiments attributed to him recently, could heighten our counterparties' perception of risk associated in dealing with our company. This will cer-tainly undermine the company's position in those negotiations and the country will ultimately suffer as a result.*[1]

So conscious was the chief executive of the perception and actuality of his financial probity that the foot of the announcement read, 'Issued and paid for by Sam Jonah.'

Rawlings had been goading for a fight knowing that his previous opponents had all been soundly defeated or had retreated into exile. But with this announcement Jonah stepped up to him, disregarding the knowledge that nobody publicly challenged Rawlings and survived intact.

In Jonah's eyes, Rawlings had nothing on him but jealousy and hatred, and so he asserted his innocence in total confidence. His sentence correcting any illusions that the government might hold over ownership or rights to Ashanti revenue delivered a sweet right jab to NDC fundraising efforts for the general election a year away. Significantly, Jonah's statement revealed that Rawlings's behaviour – contrary to his frequent press releases about assisting Ashanti out of the crisis – was undermining Ashanti's chances of survival.

The gloves were up.

An immediate need for liquidity

True to his word, Gerard Holden at Barclays delivered a term sheet within the month reorganising Ashanti's existing debt and incorporating additional cash needs. The new facility would be in four tranches: tranche A would repay the bilateral loans totalling $29.5m owed to Barclays, Dresdner and UBS; tranches B and C would renew the existing $270m RCF; and tranche D represented a new debt facility of up to $125m. The total cost of the package, including the loan rate, a commitment fee of 1 per cent and the arranger's legal and out of pocket expenses totalled Libor +5 per cent, more than six times the price of Ashanti's existing RCF at Libor +0.83 per cent. If the lending banks were awarded warrants, as the hedge banks had been, then they would consider reducing the total price to 2–3 per cent above Libor. An onerous list of conditions and covenants followed.

No dividends would be permitted until Ashanti had refinanced or redeemed its bonds as well as outstanding balances of tranches A, B and C, and in any event not before total borrowings were below $300m. Apart from agreed local currency lines, the company would be prohibited from assuming any other debt. It also could not acquire or dispose of assets without majority bank consent. Outstanding balances from tranches A to D would be mandatorily repaid in the event of Ashanti raising equity or disposing of an asset. The banks reserved the right at any time to sweep the company's bank accounts for cash in excess of $10m deemed sufficient for working capital.

Then there were reporting impositions. Management information reports were to be received within 21 days of the month end, and had to include an independently audited cash flow statement and forecast. Independent experts would assess and define the hedge book parameters to the satisfaction of the banks.

A negative pledge clause prevented Ashanti from pledging its assets elsewhere if that would diminish the banks' security. In addition, a cross default clause meant that if Ashanti was in default, or was anticipated to default, under any other agreement with any other lender or institution it would constitute an event of default under the proposed facility. Ashanti had to commit to raising $150m from new equity *or* an asset sale by 31 December 2000.

Tight financial covenants stipulated the maintenance of an interest cover of 4 (that is, AGC's earnings needed to be at least four times greater than the firm's interest payments) and a ratio of total debt to EBITDA of less than 3.25 (that is, the total amount of debt Ashanti could assume would be limited to just over three times its operating cashflow). Further preconditions were the receipt of satisfactory independent technical reports on Obuasi, Geita, Bibiani and Siguiri, the appointment of two directors approved by the banks to Ashanti's board and, last but not least, Ghana government approval. If Ashanti agreed, all the participating banks would receive internal credit clearance by 15 December; the legal documents would be drawn up by 7 January and signed by 14 January allowing the first drawdown shortly thereafter.

To accept the costs, the constraints and the invasion of outsiders into the company's operations and procedures felt ambivalently like volunteering to wear a straitjacket then consenting to be raped. Jonah and the Ashanti board accepted the proposal.

The need to restructure and strengthen the balance sheet

Barclays's liquidity solution, delivered and approved on 26 November, could now be incorporated into AGC's new corporate and financial restructuring plan and a five-year business plan to be presented, as a condition of the warrant agreement, on 1 December (the day before the RCF expired) to the hedge and RCF banks.

The essence of the plans was to build on Ashanti's tremendous goodwill and leadership example in Africa. The company had a stable of high-quality ore bodies, a good record on exploration, business development, work and training practices as well as processing expertise. The first priority was to reduce debt from the current $556m to $105m by 2004. To that end Ashanti would raise a minimum of $150m either through the sale of 50 per cent of Geita or from issuing equity by 31 December 2000. Geita's production start date remained on track for mid-2000. The rationalisation of Obuasi's operations would continue on a deeper scale by reducing capital expenditure and costs per ounce. There would be further redundancies and productivity improvement initiatives. New life of mine plans were being completed for each mine. Exploration and business development would now focus on areas proximate to existing properties, and no major acquisitions would be made.

Market capitalisation as a result of the hedge crisis had seriously undervalued the firm at $440m. Delivering on the business plan would see an expected rise to $620m by 2001. For each of the next five years Ashanti aimed to achieve a return on capital employed of 8–9 per cent. To strengthen corporate governance three new, independent directors with appropriate backgrounds were promised. With regard to hedging, the portfolio would become smaller and simpler with tighter management incorporating three levels of supervision: board level, a world-respected treasurer (who was in the process of being recruited), and the retention of independent consultants. Noticeably, the financial management section of the business plan did not mention the replacement of Mark Keatley as CFO. To the bankers' irritation Jonah's loyalty to him did not flinch.

To further bolster the balance sheet, the business plan also detailed the possibility of merging with another mine company (besides Lonmin) and re-organising Ashanti's group structure to improve the attractiveness of raising equity.

After these presentations Barclays outlined to the audience the four-tranche debt proposal at the core of Ashanti's short-term restructuring strategy. The occasion also served to drum up participants for the syndication of this facility.

To allow time for all those present to digest the plans it was agreed to rollover all existing debt facilities until 17 December. The government of Ghana would hear exactly the same presentations on Wednesday 8 December. If approval was not obtained from it by 17 December and if the RCF was not renewed then Ashanti would be trading insolvent. The cash forecast, now produced by Deloitte & Touche Debt Solutions, reported that just $1.2m would be available by 31 December. This should have been $8.2m but $7m due from Resolute Mines for the purchase of Ashanti's interest in a small mine in Tanzania, which the company had disposed of following the Samax acquisition, was no longer expected since Resolute was itself in a hedge-related financial crisis.

Jonah knew that his presence at the Accra presentation threatened to sabotage any chances of winning government support. Consequently, Andy Quinn travelled to Ghana to detail the restructuring and business plans. At the meeting, in a conference room at The Castle, were Vice-president Mills, the government advisers, ministers of state and the governor of the Bank of Ghana. Quinn reported back to Jonah that his audience appeared 'agreeable', an assessment that unnerved the chief executive. Quinn had laid bare the severity of the cash situation; he pressed the importance for the government to express its support in writing for the refinancing package almost immediately. Jonah decided to await the content of that letter before indulging in optimism.

In the meantime, the RCF bankers, particularly the three whose institutions did not provide Ashanti with hedging services (the Royal Bank of Scotland, HSBC and Standard Chartered) insisted on a share of the warrants. Under 'London Rules' they argued, they were creditors on a par with the hedge banks and therefore had to be treated equally. Since the Ghana government threatened legal action to prevent the issue of more warrants the only remaining option was to re-price and redistribute the existing ones. It was agreed with all the creditors – the hedge and RCF banks – that of the 19 835 001 warrants (15 per cent of the company), 13 223 334 would be allocated to the hedgers to apportion between themselves as they saw fit. The remaining 6 611 667 warrants would be divided on a pro rata basis between the RCF and bilateral lenders according to their share of Ashanti's aggregate debt. The strike price was reduced to $3 to make the redistribution as attractive as before, and because AGC's share price had plummeted to $2.75. Ashanti accepted the amendments – refusal would have killed off any prospects of concluding the Barclays deal.

The warrant agreement was not the only thing revised to Ashanti's disadvantage. Once Barclays had incorporated the comments it had received during the marketing of the new debt package, the bank returned on 15 December with an ossified term sheet. Participants had been identified for only $100m of the sought $125m of new debt. Selling 50 per cent of Geita had morphed from an option into an imperative. Ashanti would be in default if by 31 March 2000 it had failed to identify and formally approach a potential buyer. It would also be in default if by 31 August 2000 it had failed to provide all relevant information as well as allow site visits in connection with the sale; and if by 31 October 2000 it had failed to sign a binding sale agreement. As well as the written approval of the Ghana government in support of the Geita sale, the agreement of Lonmin was also now needed. Another new condition precedent was an audit by PricewaterhouseCoopers (PWC) at Ashanti's expense (estimated at $700 000) first to verify Ashanti's cash needs and then to act as reporting accountants for the banks over the ensuing three months.

Within a day the Ghana government and Lonmin responses arrived. The government would support an orderly sale of Geita or other assets. But its opposition to a larger stake in Obuasi, to allow the group to separate its Ghana and non-Ghana assets, remained entrenched – as did its objections over Ashanti assuming tranche D's new debt. Lonmin too delivered a double-edged sword. It felt unable to confirm that it would not oppose a partial sale of Geita, but was prepared to top up the proposed tranche D $100m debt facility by committing $25m.

The two largest shareholders diverged over Geita; the government disagreed with the principal element of the bank proposal – the new $100m debt; and on top of this the banks had hardened their terms.

When enough is enough

Jonah reacted instinctively to the feeling of being cornered, of having the incongruent wills of others imposed on him. It was time to dictate Ashanti's destiny – there were limits to being screwed and his threshold had been reached. Although Ashanti's cash and time were running out, Jonah rejected the onerous, revised term sheet. He returned it to Barclays for reconsideration, *inter alia* the removal of the Lonmin and government approval preconditions. Without waiting for a positive response he directed that a key person from a supranational agency should be found to act as a broker between the main shareholders in an attempt to align their interests with those of the company. Alternative bridging finance had to be found as immediate back up. Jonah instructed his friend and adviser, Quinn, to oversee this and to structure another refinancing term sheet to compete with Barclays. He ordered the start of auction procedures for 50 per cent of Geita in tandem with a capital gains avoidance tax plan. In addition, there was no harm, the CEO decided, in preparing a Registration Statement for a possible equity issue on the NYSE – raising equity could take several months, so it was as well to start the process even with the uncertainty of Ashanti's continued existence.

The bankers were caught on the back foot by Jonah's bullishness and were themselves in need of some respite. With just one week to go to Christmas, and with the welcome receipt of the overdue $7m cash owed by Resolute Mines to Ashanti, the banks agreed to rollover all debt facilities until the New Year.

Other plans afoot

There would be no respite over the millennium Christmas and New Year for Mark Horn. The lawyer was sick and tired of Jonah and the Ashanti board's refusal to fully involve his team and shareholders, such as Gandur, in the solutions process. He was also convinced that the banks were railroading the firm to disaster. Consequently, he spent the best part of the holidays sifting through Ghanaian and Commonwealth legal precedents to find a way to force Jonah to stop and listen. Horn uncov-

206

ered that Ghana's Companies Code allowed anyone holding 5 per cent of the shares in a company to order an extraordinary general meeting (EGM). But this could take twelve weeks or more, by which time the indomitable Jonah would, no doubt, have succeeded in borrowing more money. The government advisory camp believed that the latest terms for the debt facility were unduly harsh, which was true; but besides this it felt that the assumption of new debt was unnecessary, refusing to believe the severity of Ashanti's solvency situation. Despite reading in Ashanti's restructuring and business plans of the company's commitment to make board-level changes and its willingness to sell 50 per cent of Geita, Horn and his team were of the opinion that Jonah would not sell unless forced to. They were ignorant of the fact that the auction process for half of Geita had already been set in motion. The government team also felt that the most critical boardroom change – the removal of Jonah and Keatley – would not take place without intervention. Horn would de-light in unravelling the deal that the big bully Barclays appeared to have all but sewn up. What he needed was a court order to accelerate an EGM. With the government's 17 per cent of votes he was confident he could garner an additional 34 per cent, starting with Gandur and his affiliates, to unseat Jonah and the entire board. He already had one name for chairman – Jean-Claude Gandur.

Horn's millennium efforts were incommensurate with his relatively paltry fixed fee agreed with the government. He was not even in line to receive a success fee. (How the government might have defined a suc-cessful outcome as a basis for such a fee would have been interesting.) Unless Gandur had offered a carrot, Horn's extraordinary zeal reflected his passion to battle for the little man, the little firm, and the little coun-try against the big boys.

On 7 January a Ghana High Court summons, drafted by Horn, was served on Ashanti. The applicants were Adryx Mining and Metals Ltd, Stingray Ltd (both Gandur-related companies), Brown Brother Harriman and Jean Pierre Delker. They were pleading under Section 162 of the Companies Code to request, firstly, an expedited EGM to consider two resolutions: the election of a new board of directors and the removal of the existing board, and under Section 202(1) to permit the sale of all, any or part of the company's mining assets. Secondly, they sought an injunction restraining the current directors 'from entering into any agreement, contract, or understanding which may impair or substantially reduce the ability of any board of directors elected at the general meeting to deal with the company's affairs as they might otherwise have chosen'. In other words, they wanted to stop Ashanti from taking on any new debt.

CHAPTER 14

'Rain beats a leopard's skin, but it does not wash out the spots'

January–February 2000

Ashanti's general counsel, Merene Botsio-Phillips, took charge of the case and arranged defence. Her immediate plan of action was to challenge the application's legality. The sum of the applicants' stake in Ashanti totalled 4.2 per cent, less than the 5 per cent required under Ghanaian law to call an EGM. Apart from Stingray, the other parties did not even fit the Ghana Companies Code's explicit definition of a company member – only Stingray met the criteria as a beneficial owner of shares. The others held shares through nominees. Consequently, their names were not in the Register of Members and they did not hold share certificates as evidence of legal title. The Ashanti board felt reassured that the Ghanaian and international legal precedents on this point alone destroyed the plaintiffs' case. Ashanti was further bolstered by a legal opinion obtained from a leading British barrister at Lincoln's Inn concluding that the route taken by the applicants was illegal. Confidence in the outcome, however, did not reduce the distraction that fighting a legal action would cause during the refinancing and restructuring efforts.

Cash balances head into the red

Deloitte & Touche's latest cash flow forecast predicted a net position of negative $1.2m by the week ending 28 January 2000. Ashanti could not continue to trade legally after 18 February without new money. Leading Deloitte's team was an Indian restructuring expert, Srinivasan Venkatakrishnan, known as Venkat. Despite Jonah's visible stress, the CEO never failed to ask after Venkat's family and to apologise for taking him away from them with the long hours of work required. Venkat was taken aback by Jonah's concern, which was almost bizarre in the context of impending bankruptcy, where time ticked against the firm.

Payments were deferred to dam the outflow of cash. This created a backlog of unpaid supplier debt, and now the cement supplier to Geita threatened to withhold the essential material unless Ashanti settled its account. Standard Risk, an independent derivatives consultancy that was to add an additional layer of supervision as promised in the business plan, had commenced its work. It supported management's case to close out some in the money hedge contracts, which could raise $16m, but the hedge counterparties and banks disapproved.

While Quinn at CIBC pursued an alternative finance package, Barclays appointed PWC on behalf of all the RCF banks to verify independently Ashanti's need for new money. The PWC Phase 1 Report, as it was called, would not be completed before 31 January. There was no chance of the Barclays deal moving ahead without it, even if the government and Lonmin approval preconditions were removed or satisfied. Jonah's legal team fired back to Barclays some conditions of its own regarding the level of fees payable should Barclays fail to deliver.

With regard to the auction of 50 per cent of Geita, also being co-ordinated by Quinn, information packs had been sent to a list of interested parties, several of whom had conducted site visits and commenced the due diligence process. Significant amounts of regulatory and legal work had to be satisfied in Ghana, Tanzania, the United Kingdom and the United States to allow the sale to proceed (there were fourteen Ashanti companies linked to Geita), so Mark Bankes (of Norton Rose) made a start on that front. While various options such as bridge finance, an alternative syndicated loan and an equity issue were being examined, Jonah stressed the importance of pursuing steadfastly the preferred course of action: refinancing with Barclays on the best terms that Ashanti could negotiate and selling half of Geita.

Court proceedings start

In an attempt to preclude the minority shareholder suit, Jonah and Peprah accepted Gandur's offer to meet at Ashanti's London office in

Wood Street. The meeting on 12 January did not go well. Gandur demanded his own appointment as chairman, the executive appointment of Martin Martineau (also party to the action) and the immediate dismissal of Mark Keatley.

The requests were not onerous on the face of it. Martineau, in particular, was well regarded in the industry. But to Jonah they were completely unacceptable. Gandur's alleged closed-period trading and contempt for corporate procedures with regard to the awarding of contracts, made him, in Jonah's eyes, the least appropriate character to head a company. The CEO also despised the blackmail tactics being adopted; he would never concede to any demands made in that manner.

Two Ashanti non-executive directors, Michael Beckett and Nick Morrell, also met separately with Gandur and failed to persuade him to drop the case.

The first hearing at the High Court, in the heart of Accra's colourful Makola market area, took place on Thursday 13 January before Justice Richard Apaloo. The courtroom brimmed with journalists, many standing for the lack of space. The barrister defending Ashanti was the formidable Kwami Tetteh, a member of the Ghana Judicial Council (and future president of the Ghana Bar Association). The applicants, by contrast, arrived in court without any counsel to represent them. Tetteh shared Merene Botsio-Phillips's confidence that the case was a non-starter. However, to their dismay, Judge Apaloo granted the plea and the applicants' request for an adjournment, despite Tetteh's arguments that any delay would imperil the company. Apaloo instructed the plaintiffs to find legal representation and dismissed the parties until Wednesday 19 January.

It took Mark Horn several days to find a Ghanaian barrister to act as counsel. He took this as evidence of the fear that Jonah's power wielded, rather than any legal weakness in the case he had formulated. At last he found an eager young lawyer, Tony Lithur, who had only recently opened his own practice and was willing to take the case.

When the court re-adjourned, Tetteh opened his submission with the words: 'He who comes to equity must come with clean hands.'[1] Before detailing the numerous procedural, technical and legal faults in the plaintiffs' application, it was necessary to expose their dishonourable agenda. The last paragraph of the plaintiffs' affidavit in support of their application openly confessed the close support that they enjoyed from government. Tetteh went further; the plaintiffs and the government had, 'long before the application herein been in constant consultation, planning and scheming and the application is the outcome of their efforts … We have in this court the scenario in which the government stands in the background and urges the applicants on.'[2] Yet, confusingly, he continued, Richard Peprah, the government's own minister of finance who chaired the Ashanti board, opposed the plaintiffs. In a 'sordid' twist, he explained that the government, through the board presence of the minister of finance and the former minister of mines and energy and the Minerals Commission chief executive, shared collective responsibility for the actions and current consequences of that board. Furthermore, it was unjust and despicable for Gandur, the main appellant who had been until very recently a director of Ashanti, to now denounce the board and 'renounce his collective responsibility for decisions taken during his board membership'. Of great concern to Tetteh was the impact that the case would have on the foreign investor. 'How will he receive this scenario?' he asked. 'Surely he will say that the conduct of government is unbecoming of a regulator of the mining business in Ghana; he will say that the conduct of government is unbecoming of a partner in business; he will say the conduct of government is unbecoming of a trustee of the interest of Ghanaians in the company.'[3]

Besides their failure to show a 5 per cent share ownership of Ashanti, the applicants had not provided their addresses on the pleadings, in breach of Order 4 of the Ghana Rules of Court, which would make it difficult to pursue them for costs. Tetteh evoked a precedent of a case being dismissed on this ground alone. The plaintiffs were seeking to restrain Ashanti's directors but the directors were not before the court; they were not party to the action. Not only did this violate the principle of *audi alteram partem* rendering the directors unable to respond to the allegations of misconduct laid at them, but it also contravened a ruling of the Ghana Supreme Court in 1995 that, 'Directors were the only persons who should be joined as respondents in an action that sought to restrain them.'[4]

As they felt the legal ground beneath them weaken, the plaintiffs rushed to submit a share certificate dated 1998 in an attempt to meet the definition of a company member, as well as to reach the 5 per cent ownership threshold needed to call an EGM. However, checks with Ashanti's share registrar in Guernsey revealed that the particular share certificate offered by the plaintiffs as evidence of beneficiary ownership of Ashanti shares had been transferred to a Depositary Nominee on 11 March 1999. With the exception of Stingray, the plaintiffs were all holders of Ashanti global depositary receipts (GDRs), not shares. Judge Apaloo called expert witnesses from the Ghana Stock Exchange and Barclays Bank of Ghana who supported the defence that holders of global depositary securities were not, according to Ghana's commercial law, members of the company. GDRs were designed purposely so that holders do *not* directly own foreign securities. The depositary bank, or other institution, becomes the shareholder. Although German commercial law, for example, gave depositary holders the same rights as shareholders, there was no such provision in Ghanaian law, or in the law of many other countries in 2000.

In the middle of the case Judge Apaloo called the two barristers to his chambers. After offering them soft drinks and lighting a cigarette, he chastised Tony Lithur for his ignorance of court procedure. He admitted that the inexperienced barrister was receiving some bruising blows from the defence counsel. The judge declared his inclination to dismiss Lithur's case. Back in open court he asked again whether the parties wanted to continue. Tetteh unhesitatingly replied in the affirmative. From his point of view it was important for his client as well as for the reputation of Ghana's judiciary to smash the case by obtaining a judgment in Ashanti's favour. Lithur nodded.

The plaintiffs' main arguments were that the board's concurrence with the Lonmin merger proved that it was not sufficiently independent. The board had actually abandoned the Lonmin merger offer by November 1999. Lithur used Jonah's admission to recklessness from an article that appeared in the *Financial Times* on 8 November as an indictment of incompetence. In reply Tetteh submitted an affidavit from Jonah explaining that he had been misquoted and that his comments had been lifted out of context. The article read: 'I am prepared to concede that we were reckless. We took a bet on the price of gold. We thought it would go down and we took a position.'[5] During that interview, a rambling conversation conducted at the height of the crisis, Jonah had used the word 'reckless' in an analogy: suppose he had taken his family out to the beach, knowing that the security men he employed would be at home, but on their return they found that none of the security workers had turned up and the house had been ransacked; could he be called reckless for going to the beach? He would only have been reckless if he had known the security team would not come. In the same vein, he felt he would only be guilty of recklessness if he had known the gold price would boomerang as it did. Nevertheless, the CEO should have been more careful with his choice of words.

The plaintiffs also argued that the board had too many Lonmin members. In fact, although Lonmin had about twice the number of shares as the government, it only had three representatives: Sam Jonah (a Lonmin employee seconded to Ashanti in accordance with the Technial Services Agreement between the company and the government), Nick Morrell and Philip Tarsh. Until Rawlings's recent dismissals of Ohene-Kena and Ansah from their government jobs, Ashanti's board had had three government employees, including the chairman and finance minister, Richard Peprah.

When Tetteh in his opening submission gave assurances that, 'It will be demonstrated in this court that the applicants have come to this court with very dirty hands,'[6] no one in the audience could have imagined that the best evidence of this would be provided not by defence counsel but by Judge Apaloo himself. A handful of journalists including Kofi Coomson, editor and publisher of the best-selling tabloid, the *Ghanaian Chronicle*, were invited to the judge's chambers for a question and answer session. During this, Apaloo confessed, 'This is political. This case should never have been brought, but it is not my call.'[7] Unable to retract his momentary flash of honesty, perhaps induced by guilt for his involvement in the debacle, the judge threatened the pressmen not to publish that comment; he would deny he ever said it. 'Publish and be damned,' he warned.[8] After three weeks of submissions, a ruling was expected on Wednesday 9 February.

Only a few grains remain in the cash egg timer

Deloitte & Touche's solvency brink date of 18 February was corroborated by the bank-commissioned PWC Phase 1 Report. It confirmed the acute cash crisis and exhorted the banks to allow a speedy drawdown for Ashanti, as any delay would damage the business. Mark Bankes at Norton Rose continued to negotiate for more flexibility with Barclays's loan agreement terms.

The banks, having confirmed for themselves the urgency of Ashanti's situation, now demanded a further reduction in the price of the warrants from $3.00 to $2.80. Although advisers bleated that the company had no choice, Jonah and his board rejected the $2.80 outright. Furthermore, the CEO warned the bankers that they needed to draw down in days – not weeks. As Jonah boarded a plane from London to Cape Town he rued Ashanti's desperation, but the company was not yet down and out.

The Cape Town Indaba

Prior to the crisis Ashanti had been scheduled to deliver its operational results along with other senior gold producers at the annual Indaba, Investing In Africa Mining Conference in Cape Town, South Africa, from 7–9 February 2000. As one of the most prestigious mine industry forums the Indaba gathered over two thousand delegates from over fifty countries. Producers, investors, policymakers and financiers attended the talks, presentations, exhibitions and dinners. Jonah decided to attend the Indaba as planned. Ashanti's refinancing efforts needed a visible display of confidence in the mine's current and future operations. His absence would have signalled fear and failure. Not only would he attend the conference, but he also prepared a presentation for the Tuesday morning.

Michael Beckett, Ashanti's non-executive director, agreed to a request from the litigant minority 'shareholders', who were also attending the Indaba, to arrange a meeting with them and Jonah. If Jonah was prepared to listen to their offer, they said, then the court case would be abandoned; there would be no need for a judgment – expected on Wednesday 9 February – and everything could be normalised. Jonah agreed to listen. He took the invitation to meet as a sign of weakness and retreat on their part. Not only had Judge Apaloo admitted in chambers that Lithur's case should be dismissed, but the plaintiffs' legal argument was full of holes.

That weekend Jonah received what he thought was another massive boost to a positive outcome (for Ashanti) of the trial. His brother, Ernest, the owner of a petrol station a stone's throw from the High Court in Accra had excitedly passed on a message to him. On the morning of Saturday 5 February a High Court judge, a friend of Ernest's, had driven to his Mobil petrol station. 'Tell your brother,' the judge said, 'that he should have no fears.' Before the judge left, he repeated for emphasis, 'No fears!' Taking this trustworthy source's word, Ernest eagerly relayed the information.

It was thus with confidence that Jonah arrived at the meeting venue in Cape Town on Monday, but the sight of Mark Horn in the Cape Palace Hotel foyer disturbed him. The meeting had been arranged for Jonah, Gandur and Martineau; nobody had mentioned Horn. When Jonah entered the meeting room, Horn was sitting there. It was a brief and charged interchange. Since the litigants had been at pains to present themselves and their legal action as independent from the government, Jonah demanded to know in what capacity Horn was in attendance. He retorted that his client, the Ghana government, had requested that he act as a broker in the meeting.

'But you are not part of the resolution,' Jonah insisted, evoking the plaintiffs' own claims of independence. 'We don't need a broker,' he continued, 'unless of course you are acting in concert,' which they all knew full well to be the case. The unnecessary pretence irritated Jonah. The government with its 17 per cent direct shareholding in Ashanti could have legitimately demanded an EGM and tabled resolutions for directorship and refinancing changes to be voted on. But its feeble attempt to camouflage its involvement by hiding behind Gandur and fellow plaintiffs in a fatally flawed lawsuit appeared dishonest.

Horn reacted angrily: 'I have people on standby in Accra waiting to hear the outcome of this meeting. I have the judgment. If you agree to what the shareholders are asking today then I have the authority to set the judgment aside.' When Horn saw the total lack of fear in Jonah, he repeated, 'I have the judgment! I have the judgment, and it will be given against you!'

'And I don't want you in this room,' Jonah replied.

'Then you will have to face the consequences!' Horn shouted on his way out.

'So be it,' retorted Jonah, confident that he was calling Horn's bluff.

Gandur proceeded to make the same claims that he had made in London a month earlier: in addition to selling half of Geita, he insisted that Mark Keatley should be sacked immediately; he wanted Richard Peprah replaced by himself as chairman, a number of Ghanaian directors to be substituted, and Martin Martineau to take up an executive directorship role. He did not say to Jonah that his own job would go, but Horn had already approached Ashanti's COO, Trevor Schultz, about taking over the CEO role.[9]

Jonah again took offence at the manner of the request rather than the content. The facts that the auction process for Geita had already started and that Jonah had publicised the need to strengthen Ashanti's corporate governance with board level changes were beside the point. For a handful of shareholders who held less than 5 per cent of the company – even if the GDRs were equated to shares – to think that they could railroad demands on an entire PLC board infuriated him. That Gandur, in particular, who had proved in Jonah's opinion to be devious and opaque as a director, should now attempt to impose such orders was nauseating.

'I thought you were coming with fresh ideas,' Jonah sighed, exasperated. 'This is not the way these things are done. These are matters for a board to decide. I can't give you the assurances you seek.' With that he left the room.

At 11.00 a.m. on the Tuesday Jonah presented Ashanti's results. The operating results of 1999 before exceptional items were on a par with 1998. However, exceptional items incurred from redundancies, the May strike, as well as legal and professional fees associated with the hedge crisis hit the bottom line by $49m. The cessation of surface mining at Obuasi and the closure of treatment plants for surface ores created a $171m one-off asset write-off. As a result, earnings per share after exceptional items plummeted to negative 1.64 compared to positive 0.37 the previous year.

After the figures Jonah launched into the status of the crisis negotiations. He explained the various work-out options – those tried and those still under consideration, including the prospect of separating the group into a non-Ghana and a Ghana company. (Jonah had not dismissed the idea despite the Ghana government's objections.) He explained the litigation issues, his advisers' confidence in the illegality of the application, and the dangerous message it was sending out to the investment world that in Ghana just about anybody could hold a boardroom to ransom, and that, in Ghana, courts dictate whether a company can assume a loan or not. From a legal argument perspective, he assured his audience, judgment in favour of Ashanti was a slam-dunk. Jonah mentioned that at the forthcoming AGM in April, four directors would not be offering themselves up for re-election – William Ryrie and Henry Otoo had reached retirement and Fred Ohene-Kena and Kofi Ansah would step down. In fact, Ashanti's Remuneration and Nomination Committee had already commenced the recruitment of replacements. Jonah's speech was well received by his audience, particularly his assurances over the outcome of the minority shareholder court case.

The judgment

On the morning of Wednesday 9 November the High Court in Accra squeezed in even more spectators than usual. The tension was palpable. Judge Apaloo began to read the judgment. A few sentences in, he turned to his right and gazed through the large windows. After some moments he muttered under his breath, but in earshot of the lawyers less than six feet from the bench: 'My mind is wavering.' The judge then looked up. In the opinion of Tetteh's co-counsel, he appeared to be scanning the room, as if the presence or absence of an individual would decide for him whether to continue reading the judgment or to say something else. He looked down again and picked up the sentence from where he had broken off.

Notwithstanding Judge Apaloo's now public admission before a packed court that the plaintiffs' counsel had conducted himself and the presentation of his evidence in a manner unacceptable in legal practice, and despite his admission that the plaintiffs did not constitute 5 per cent of the company according to Section 162 of the Companies Codes (a threshold that he arbitrarily deemed irrelevant), and regardless of the court's agreement that only Stingray among the applicants met the definition of a company member with a shareholding of 0.02 per cent, Judge Apaloo ruled in favour of the plaintiffs. He did, however, dismiss the applicants' charges of incompetence brought against the directors since they were not party to the action.

He explained the basis of his ruling as follows. Stingray, an undisputed company member, had expressed serious concerns about Ashanti's board and since the share price had fallen from $20 at the IPO to the current $3 Stingray deserved a forum to express those concerns. Apaloo ordered an EGM of Ashanti to be convened within 21 days to consider two resolutions: the removal of the existing board and the election of a new one, as well as the sale of Ashanti assets. He granted an injunction restraining Ashanti from assuming any financial obligation. The courtroom gasped.

Afterwards Merene Botsio-Phillips called Jonah with the judgment. Jonah could not believe the cavalier treatment of the rule of law. With domestic and international media attention riveted on the case, the opportunity had arisen for Ghanaian commercial law to demonstrate maturity, to prove that a sound and impartial judiciary institution supported the country's nascent political freedoms. Instead, it exposed Ghana's democratisation as skin deep, and its investment promotion talk as boneless. The newspapers focused on these negative implications for Ghana. Yes, the public was angry about Ashanti's troubles, for which people blamed Jonah – blame that Jonah accepted as the CEO under whose watch the crisis had occurred – but they were equally angry at the government's obvious interference with the due process of law. If Rawlings and Jonah had personal issues they should resolve them without making a fool of the law, the public and the country.

Horn's words, 'I have the judgment!' rang in Jonah's ears. It was rumoured that Horn had written the judgment himself. Botsio-Phillips and Tetteh immediately prepared the grounds for appeal, of which there were many: the procedural defects, Apaloo's interpretation of Sections 162 and 297 of the Companies Code, the judge's method of weighing the evidence and his failure to consider the hardship the restraining order would cause to the company. Procedures for stay of execution would follow the application for appeal.

The climax of the Cape Town Indaba was the closing gala dinner hosted by Anglo American on the Wednesday evening. As the industry bigwigs and their partners donned black ties and ballgowns for the evening's glitzy dinner all the gossip centred on Jonah and Ashanti's de-mise – it was expected that the boardroom changes would remove him, and the loan sanction would ruin the company. Post-insolvency, Ashanti would be broken up; the company, as everybody knew it, would cease to exist. Nobody expected Jonah to turn up, not after his reassurances of the previous day had been humiliatingly shredded. But in he strolled – his broad smile gleaming as he caught the guests' astonished expressions. His presence was as much of a shock as his confident demeanour. He'd been dealt a career-destroying blow but there he was smiling and greet-ing just about everybody. One industry leader walked up to him. 'I give it to you, Sam, you've got the biggest balls in this industry!' He reached out for Jonah's hand, exclaiming again, 'Boy, have you got balls!'

The reaction of Ashanti's board of directors

An emergency board meeting was conducted in Cape Town the very next morning. Jonah's first words were an offer of resignation. If the board felt that his leadership was hampering rather than helping the crisis res-olution then he would walk. He deeply regretted the company's predica-ment, particularly the fact that his personal fallout with Rawlings had, he felt, directly caused the government's obstacle-stacking. He had earlier ten-dered his resignation to the board at the beginning of the crisis, and later he had told the banking group of his willingness to step down as CEO if it would help; on this third occasion his audience rejected his offer.

Mark Horn had been broadcasting divisions among the Ashanti dir-ectors. He claimed that he had the support of Michael Beckett and Trevor Schultz, the COO. When Jonah asked for a show of hands for those in support of the minority shareholders and those in support of the com-pany's stance, Beckett explained that while he had met with the govern-ment team on several occasions with a view to wrangling an amicable way out he was firmly on the company's side. Everyone declared likewise, except Schultz. He would not oppose any board decisions but he was 'neutral'. The word stabbed through Jonah's chest, deflating him. He was bitterly angry at what was in his book abject disloyalty.

Schultz was equally incensed and disappointed that no attempt had been made by Jonah or the board to give assurances that the executives would be taken care of in the now highly likely event of the firm going bust. Unlike Jonah, with youth and a reputation on his side, Schultz was nearing retirement and had to be pragmatic about his professional future. Jonah recalled Schultz's visit to his work-out flat months earlier. Schultz had returned from the United States with an approach on behalf of the American energy company Kinder Morgan about a possible leadership role for Jonah. His intent was all the more clear now: Jonah should prepare for life after Ashanti. Schultz revealed that the government advisers had asked him to run the company following Jonah's desired exit, but the COO believed that Ashanti, and all of them, not only Jonah, were finished.

Jonah had always been there for Schultz. He had backed him when, a year after his appointment, market analysts had questioned his capabilities. Schultz's response was that the CEO had been wrong, just as he was now wrong with Keatley. Whatever the market wanted, Jonah, as chief executive, ought to deliver. Schultz simply did not understand Jonah's obsession with loyalty. The COO, backed by Beckett on this, believed that Jonah had been too trusting of people whose actual capabilities did not merit such trust. They had Mona Caesar-Addo and Keatley in mind, whom they felt had not been as fulsome in their information given to the board as they could have been. But for the CEO loyalty and trust were (and continued to be) vital features of his management and team-building style.

With the exception of Philip Tarsh, who had been consistently nervous about hedging following unsuccessful dabblings by Lonmin into platinum derivatives, and who took an unwavering anti-hedging stance, all the other directors had been congratulatory and entirely supportive of Ashanti's hedging strategy over the years. Some of these people now felt that Jonah's preternatural bullishness, the company's growth quest, and Keatley's financial successes had carried them away. With the benefit of hindsight they should have contemplated more deeply what could potentially go wrong. Jonah's dominant character and Keatley's lucid explanations had always satisfactorily answered the queries raised, but perhaps they had been asking the wrong questions. But, criticisms and self-criticisms aside, they would not now shirk their collective responsibility, nor would they surrender to underhand tactics to remove any of them.

In Jonah's own words, the government's interference in the company's operations represented the 'de facto nationalisation' of Ashanti. The battered but united board considered the judgment and the company's cash status. Liquidity would be negative by 18 February. By the week ending 25 February it would be –$3.9m, falling to –$8.1m on 3 March.

The banks unite behind Ashanti

Two factors now served to narrow the differences among the banks. On the one hand, the realisation of the enormity and unevenhandedness of the opposition that the company faced from the Ghanaian government and, on the other, the fact that bankruptcy was no longer a threat, but was imminent. In stronger focus was the prospect of sustaining real – not paper – losses. The hedge banks agreed to consider a request from Ashanti to close out some hedge positions to realise $20m. The hedge steering committee promised to come back with an answer on this by 14 February. Standard Chartered Bank held $18m of Ashanti's money as collateral for Ashanti's Zimbabwean subsidiary. If another bank would counter guarantee the money, it was prepared to release the funds slowly to AGC. Neither option would constitute a loan obligation and would not therefore be in breach of the court injunction. The leader of the lending banks, Gerard Holden, agreed to meet the government of Ghana along with the deputy chairman of Barclays. Their aim was to persuade the government to lift the injunction to allow Ashanti a $10m to $15m bridging facility in view of the urgent cash needs until the $100m facility could be concluded.

Of the two parts of the ruling it was the injunction that mattered. As for the EGM, it could be expedited and the outcome of any vote would likely not favour the minority shareholders. Lonmin vouched its 32 per cent to Jonah and his board; Genesis, a 10 per cent shareholder, intimated the same. It would be easier for Ashanti to reach 51 per cent of the votes than for Gandur and the government.

It was not in Horn, Gandur or the government's interest to sack the whole board if Ashanti's survival was their goal. Operational discontinuity and the lack of experience of an entirely new board would create a deeper crisis than the current situation. Indeed, it was Horn's plan to use the injunction, his 'strongest card',[10] to negate having to call an EGM. If, as he now believed, Ashanti's need for cash was desperate enough, Horn could force an immediate agreement on boardroom changes. The government team was of the opinion that the only current board members worthy to stay were Schultz, Beckett and Morrell. Jonah would be 'up for consideration'.[11] In addition to the four lined up to leave at the next AGM, as Jonah had discussed in his Indaba presentation, the government team added Philip Tarsh, who was of retirement age, and Mark Keatley. With six going, the plan was to appoint Gandur immediately as co-chairman; Michael Martineau, two new government nominees, and two or three independent, non-Ghanaians, were also desired.

Jonah had no problem with the Remuneration and Nomination Committee assessing any new appointments in terms of the normal corporate procedures, but he baulked at changes by diktat. He wished to put it on the record at the emergency board meeting that Keatley's contributions to the company had been 'phenomenal' and that he personally wished to retain his services. As far as Jonah was concerned, the decisions and judgements made that led to the hedging crisis were borne jointly by management and the board, and were not solely on Keatley's shoulders. He would not treat him as a scapegoat. Things had certainly gone wrong, mistakes had been made, but never had Keatley shown mal-intent. For that Jonah would remain loyal to him. He persuaded the banks that Keatley would be needed to finalise any refinancing package, so on that basis alone it was appropriate for him to remain.

The lending banks, hedge banks and their lawyers expressed their dislike of Gandur to Ashanti.[12] They would not lend to a company with Gandur as a director.[13] Ashanti's lawyer, Mark Bankes, was asked to convey this to Horn and to request a list of the government team's nominations for directors in writing. Any potential appointees would be invited to submit themselves for election in the normal manner. But Jonah insisted that any outgoing board members must be afforded the dignity of retiring at the next AGM and not before.

Richard Peprah's resignation

In a show of power, on Friday 11 February, Rawlings called Richard Peprah into his office in The Castle. Soon after he entered the room an official walked in bearing a letter. Rawlings asked Peprah to sign it. To the finance minister's surprise he was reading his own resignation letter from Ashanti's board. Peprah should have been making his way to Gold House. Jonah and Keatley had arrived back in Ghana and an evening board meeting was scheduled with a teleconference link to directors and advisers based in the United Kingdom. But Rawlings detained Peprah at The Castle until he had signed the resignation letter and the news was announced on Ghana radio and delivered to international press agencies. The weary finance minister signed the letter reportedly drafted by Databank directors.[14] Between landing at the airport and arriving at Gold House Jonah received a call. It was Quinn in London: 'What the hell is going on?' He knew more than the CEO.

A member of the Databank team delivered 'Peprah's' letter in person to Gold House. When Rawlings finally released Peprah, he rushed to Ashanti's headquarters to relate exactly what had happened. In protest, the entire board considered resigning on the spot, but Bankes reminded them of their fiduciary duty to shareholders and creditors. At Peprah's insistence that they allow him to go with immediate effect for the benefit of appeasing the government, the board reluctantly accepted his departure – he had served on Ashanti's board for eighteen years. Philip Tarsh assumed the role of acting chairman.

The start of substantive negotiations

It was decided that Bankes and Quinn would join Barclays and representatives of the hedge groups at a meeting with the government on Valentine's Day. For the first time all the banks would be presenting one front with the company. Jonah would not attend because of the risk of his presence raising temperatures.

Vice-president Mills and his advisers met the delegation at The Castle. The bankers stressed that the court ruling was directly to blame for Ashanti's share price tanking. Since the judgment Ashanti shares had lost nearly two-thirds of their value, bottoming at $1.13 in intraday trading. Within days Ashanti would be insolvent. In reply Horn played and replayed his card: no new loans until the board is reconstituted as we want it.

It was perhaps just as well that Jonah was not in the room as he would have been unwilling to stand back from confrontation. After considerable bluffing and blustering the parties eventually agreed on a thirteen-man board to consist of four executives (the CEO, COO, CFO, plus another), one Lonmin nominee, three government nominees and five independent non-executives. The independents – Alex Ashiabor, Ekow Awoonor, Chester Crocker, Kwabena Duffour and Michael Martineau – were to join immediately. The timing dismayed Jonah when he learned of it. One executive (not named, but Keatley) and five non-executives from the old board were to retire, but, as Jonah had insisted to his negotiating team, not until the next AGM. In exchange, the minority shareholders would ask the court to cancel the order and lift the injunction. The bankers would not even consider losing Jonah; that was non-negotiable. What would happen to Gandur remained a sticking-point.

The government advisers agreed to meet with the banks and Ashanti board members, including Jonah, the following morning at the Labadi Beach Hotel. It was resolved that Tarsh would continue to act as chairman until the next AGM. A chairman would be chosen after that date from the new board (which excluded Gandur). The banks' refusals to have anything to do with Gandur put paid to his plans, and their stance on retaining Jonah as CEO thwarted Rawlings's hopes. That evening, Tuesday 15 February, a memorandum of understanding (MOU) was signed by Ashanti, Lonmin, the minority shareholders and the Vice-president's Office. It stated the board changes made, the vacation of the court judgment, as well as the unanimous approval for the sale of 50 per cent of Geita and the re-financing package. The MOU also promised a more cooperative relationship going forwards between the government and the company, and a cessation to the use of the media to air any misunderstandings.

At 11.00 p.m., a member of the Ashanti legal team delivered a draft court order to Kwami Tetteh's house. The lawyer was summoned to appear before Judge Apaloo the next morning along with Tony Lithur. There, Apaloo swiftly vacated the ruling. The ruling was not set aside and it was not reversed; rather it was vacated – as if it had never been given in the first place. Ashanti's internal legal team and Tetteh would have preferred to proceed with the appeal; a victory for Ashanti would have set an important precedent and restored some dignity to the judiciary.

The crisis ends

On Friday 18 February, Keatley signed a $100m bridging facility arranged by Barclays for Geita as a stopgap until the four-tranche re-financing package totalling $326m was concluded. The cost of the four-tranche package had been significantly trimmed to Libor +2.5 per cent rising to +4 per cent depending on the amounts drawn. The financial covenants were revised to give the company more headroom and the dividend prohibition now allowed scrip dividends to be paid. The banks retained the right to sweep Ashanti for cash balances in excess of $10m, and a minimum of $250m from the funds raised from the Geita sale was mandated to repay debt.

The financial crisis was over. It had been the most exhausting and excruciating five months of Jonah's life and career. The bankers also remarked that they had never experienced such a fraught and bitter financial crisis. The anxiety took a physical toll on Ashanti's investor relations manager, James Anaman, precipitating a stroke. Richard Peprah dates the start of his hypertension to the telephone call that he received from Jonah back in September 1999 that the company was in very deep trouble. The financial effects of the crisis were relatively minor when compared with the emotional and physical impacts.

None of Ashanti's creditors lost a penny. On the contrary, they made attractive fees and came out with 15 per cent ownership of a fundamentally sound and undervalued business. Ashanti lost $14.7m from closing out hedges in the run-up to the Geita sale and there were professional fees of $40m incurred directly by the crisis work-out.[15] In fact, for 1999 the company's hedge book earned greater net revenue than it had in 1998: $143m against $139m.[16] The financial consequences for Ashanti compare with the $1.3bn lost by Metallgesellschaft in 1993 and the $1.4bn lost by Barings in 1995 from their derivatives scandals.[17]

Ashanti's crisis had been primarily caused by a lack of cash, which in turn had been caused by a debt-heavy growth strategy, Geita's development expenditure, an unpropitious industrial strike and weather-related production problems in Guinea, which had all reduced cash reserves. A secondary level of explanation was the overly complex hedge book that now had to be simplified and slimmed.

The liquidity injection from the new refinancing deal had merely solved a short-term problem. Ashanti's balance sheet remained fragile. Even with cash from Geita's sale repaying a considerable chunk of debt, gross gearing in 2000 was expected to deteriorate, not improve, because of diminished shareholder funds from the Obuasi asset write-offs. Then there was the outstanding $216m of the $250m bond issue to redeem or refinance by March 2003. Some fundamental changes in the balance sheet were obviously needed for Ashanti's long-term survival.

The trauma of the last five months was strangely comforting to Jonah. If he had survived thus far, he told himself, then he would survive anything. He vowed to re-focus on what he did best: mining.

If only.

CHAPTER 15

'The moon moves slowly, but it crosses the town'

February–December 2000

Just as one legal case ended, others started. This time Ashanti was faced with three separate class actions from American shareholders. They soon joined forces as one class seeking hundreds of millions of dollars from the company as well as from Jonah and Keatley as individuals to compensate for their loss of wealth, caused, they alleged, by fraudulent representations made about the nature of the hedge book. The class included all purchasers of Ashanti's GDRs from United States exchanges between April 1997 and October 1999. The claimants' evidence hinged on Jonah and Keatley's own public statements before and during the crisis: in particular, Keatley's reassurances that the book could withstand a sudden hike in the gold price without margin calls and Jonah's misquoted 'reckless' interview with the *Financial Times*. Ashanti appointed an American legal team, Milbank, Tweed, Hadley & McCloy, to defend the action in collaboration with Ashanti's legal department. The grave charge levelled at the company of scienter, knowingly fraudulent dealing in securities, could result in a criminal trial by jury. It was an eventuality that had to be prepared for.

If that were not enough, whispers among Ghanaian lawyers and politicians grew in volume that the government also had plans to redress the obliteration of the value of its own Ashanti shares. Back in July 1993 the Criminal Code Act 458, Section 3 had been amended to define a new crime of causing financial loss to the state: 'Any person who by a wilful act or omission causes loss, damage or injury to the property of any public body or any agency of the State commits an offence' with sanctions of a fine or imprisonment for up to ten years, or both. It was suggested that the unused amendment could be deployed against Jonah for diminishing the value of the government's shareholding in Ashanti. The only snag was that the Act, as it stood, would require an incredulous stretch of interpretation to view Ashanti as a public body or agency of the state – but this could be remedied. And if Rawlings kept his promise to step down as stipulated by the constitution, he had just ten months left in office until the general election to do so. The word was that before he went, he wanted Jonah down.[1]

The latest in a long line of individuals to witness first-hand the president's unabated and violent jealousy towards Jonah was the Right Honourable Baroness Chalker of Wallasey. The respected Englishwoman with 30 years of service in the British parliament and 25 years of business and philanthropic experience in Africa was taken aback by Rawlings's vitriol at a meeting in The Castle following the 15 February settlement. This episode – added to the accounts of the Ghana ambassador to Britain, Britain's acting high commissioner in Ghana, Peter Munk, and others – paradoxically gave Jonah a feeling of protection. Public manifestations of Rawlings's hatred limited what the president could actually do with impunity, or so Jonah thought. He left Rawlings to stew in his insecurities. Hopefully, by December not only he but also his party would be out of power.

Selling 50 per cent of Geita

The bidders for half of Geita had been short-listed to Anglogold, Barrick, Homestake and Meridian Gold. Lonmin did not bid. CIBC's evaluation methodology looked at the cash component of each offer, spending commitments, management fees, as well as any assets offered; then there was the net present value calculation of each bid to Ashanti assuming a discount rate this time of 7 per cent, a gold price of $300 and taking Geita's production model into account. Last but not least, there was an important qualitative assessment covering cultural fit, the bidders' African presence and experience, and the degree of management control. An estimated valuation of the whole mine stood at $400m, so offers of at least $200m were expected. The mine's African situation and associated location risks as well as the potential view by the bidders that this was a fire sale did, however, reduce the chances of exceeding this starting figure.

By the beginning of April only two horses remained: Anglogold and Barrick. In terms of cash and total bid value there was little to separate them. Anglogold offered $205m cash up front and $130m project finance. Barrick's term sheet indicated the same amount of cash but $160m project finance at a similar rate. Barrick would generate superior investor confidence. However, although it had been persuaded to take a management fee out of its offer, the Canadian giant insisted on retaining voting control over Geita. Anglogold threw a neighbouring property, Ridge 8, into the joint venture. And there would be potential synergies from sourcing South African mine supplies for the Ashanti group on better terms. It was in the qualitative assessment that real differences appeared. Anglogold was seen as a better cultural fit; it would create an African alliance in line with Ashanti's continental outlook. Most significantly, Anglogold was offering a deadlocked joint venture – unanimity would be needed for all decisions. Equal management control was the deciding factor for the board. Its decision would be put the shareholders at the AGM at the end of April before signing heads of agreement.

New board members

The Ashanti board was disturbed to discover that Ekow Awoonor, one of the new government-nominated directors, had communicated to Barrick that the government preferred it to Anglogold and that it would not recognise CIBC's evaluation method. Awoonor denied this. However, his position became untenable after Tocqueville, a United States gold fund and asset management firm that held AGC shares, sent a fax to the company protesting his nomination for reasons of their own. Awoonor walked in April. That month two additional independent, non-executive directors, Baroness Chalker and Thomas Gibian of AIG's Africa Investment Fund, joined the board.

To strengthen corporate governance at AGC the roles and responsibilities of directors and committee members were documented. New corporate governance and risk management committees were established. Feedback from investors also highlighted the need for an independent chairman with no links to the government or to Lonmin. Having two co-chairs, as suggested by the government advisers, would create market uncertainty, and institutional investors advised against it. There was an immediate need for a strong financial director with a mining background, following Keatley's departure at the April AGM.

Long-term issues for Ashanti

Personnel needs could be satisfied relatively easily. However, Jonah was aware of the fundamental problems that would prove less tractable for Ashanti. The gearing level and bond repayment were top of the list, followed closely by the company's share ownership structure. Lonmin's 32 per cent and the government's 17 per cent holdings impeded liquidity in the stock and its value. The arbitrariness surrounding the use of the golden share had a similar effect. Each of these challenges would have to be surmounted; exactly how remained unclear, but efforts had to start immediately.

Two early remedies that were investigated included a $200m equity issue, provided that Lonmin and the Ghana government waived their right to participate. There were also merger discussions with Newmont and Gold Fields; the main advantage of combining would be to subsume Ashanti's balance sheet into a stronger one. Diversification into other African minerals such as copper and platinum would allow Ashanti to exploit its core competency – its knowledge, expertise and profile in Africa. These major and long-term structural and strategic changes needed debating.

Escaping bankruptcy had boosted staff confidence throughout the group. Good operating results had been maintained during the crisis, and now the exploration team at Obuasi reported exciting discoveries. Mining had reached Level 50, 5 000 feet below ground, but geological investigations below Level 50 revealed ever-richer ore. To appreciate the value of the find, the ore mined above Level 50 yielded on average just under 8 grams of gold per tonne,[2] but ore samples taken from 150 feet below Level 50 assayed 56 grams per tonne. The exploration team sought board approval and resources to extend the drill tests to Level 75, about 7 500 feet from the surface. If the preliminary results obtained were accurate, the life of this unique mine could be extended by decades. Exploration work intensified, within the resource constraints, to delineate the deep resources with more confidence. Good news from Geita indicated that the start of production would be earlier than scheduled and on budget. By mid-year, four of Ashanti's six operating mines headed for new gold production records.

A new finance team and hedging policy

The bank-commissioned PWC Phase 2 Report confirmed the satisfactory progress made by the firm in drafting a new hedge policy, which was accepted by all the banks. The main elements of this were to continue price protection but with simpler instruments, strengthened supervision, and decreasing levels of ounces committed so that by the end of the margin-free trading period in December 2002, the exposure to margin calls would be greatly reduced. The banks were confident in the appointment of Mark Arnesen, previously the treasurer for BHP Billiton, the global resource company, to fill the same role at Ashanti. Evidence of tighter financial management at the firm received commendation. Venkat, as part of the Deloitte & Touche Debt Solutions team, had implemented additional cash flow controls. He extended payments wherever possible without affecting the company's credibility, introduced strict capital expenditure monitoring, and reviewed the fees of the small army of professional service providers associated with the crisis and with the normal business. He also negotiated discounts and insisted on itemised billing. In so doing, no drawdowns were made from the debt facility in April and May, saving $4m in interest.

If the banks had formerly complained about a lack of information they were now liable to complain at the flood of it. Jonah instructed Venkat to tell them everything. Whatever Venkat knew, the banks knew too, and they knew at practically the same moment plus the time it took for Venkat to send the fax or click the email. Everybody received the same information. The new culture of openness built a huge amount of confidence in the banks over Ashanti's finances.

Headhunters had been appointed to find a CFO, but relocating to Accra limited the supply of the calibre of candidate wanted. At the same time, Jonah put feelers out for personal recommendations, his preferred recruitment method. It was Gerard Holden who had recommended Mark Arnesen, the new treasurer, and it was Arnesen who, when asked by Jonah, advanced Venkat's merits. Arnesen had seen him working superbly with Ghanaians, which was an imperative; he was capable, forthright and a great communicator. Arnesen humbly confessed that Venkat would be a better candidate than he would. Jonah bounced the idea off Quinn. While no one doubted Venkat's credibility and skills, he had never run the finances of a PLC and that concerned the banker. When the CEO went to speak to Venkat, the hardworking young man was flattered to be considered, but declined to apply because he had no CFO experience. Jonah, undeterred, focused on the skills that Venkat had demonstrated. His high emotional intelligence, as Jonah termed it, was exactly what the battered financial team needed. 'Chief, you are taking a big gamble with me,' the Indian warned. It was a gamble that Jonah was prepared to take.

When Jonah put Venkat's name to the board, the directors' immediate reaction was to dismiss the suggestion: Venkat did not have a mining background; he had never even worked as a financial director; he was a bankruptcy expert; and he was only 35 years old. But Jonah stubbornly sustained his pitch for him. In the six months since January 2000 when Venkat had arrived with the Deloitte & Touche team, his delivery of accurate and timely information had impressed; his interaction skills with Ashanti staff at all levels were second to none; he had grasped not only the fundamentals but also the details of the business enabling him to effect cost savings rapidly. Above all, his transparency, at a time when trust in management from international investors was weak, would be a tremendous bonus. Jonah encouraged the young man to apply formally for the post. The Remuneration and Nominations Committee, comprising three non-executive directors, recommended the application.

Venkat was appointed as CFO from 1 July 2000. While he himself viewed his selection as a leap of faith, and some board members saw it as another example of Jonah's misplaced confidences, the CEO had absolute belief in the young man. Jonah's total support energised Venkat to vindicate his selection before the entire board. The banks cautiously welcomed the appointment. They were glad that at least the post had been filled. Ashanti's board now numbered an unwieldy fifteen members.

Jonah and Venkat immediately set about restoring and sustaining Ashanti's status as a first-class gold producer, focusing on cost, efficiency and profitability in a safe work environment. Business for the two never ended – they enjoyed continuing their discussions and exchanging ideas well after office hours and over weekends. Their shared workaholism and sense of humour meant that working together was a real pleasure. The long-term challenges that had appeared so foreboding now excited them.

As the CEO, CFO and the entire company worked assiduously to dazzle the doubters with outstanding operational results, credence was given to the whispers that Rawlings had indeed not finished with Jonah.

A Serious Fraud Office investigation

On 30 May 2000, before the company had been notified, the *Daily Graphic* newspaper announced a Serious Fraud Office (SFO) inquiry into Ashanti. The letter that arrived a day after the headline coverage stated that the Office of the President had issued the directive to the SFO to proceed. The SFO investigator, Gabriel Dzandu, sought to uncover whether, under Section 3(1)(a) of the Serious Fraud Office Act 466 of 1993, any 'serious financial or economic loss to the State or to any State organization or other institution in which the state has financial interest' had been committed by management in general and by Jonah in specific relation to certain queries. The trigger for the investigation was not the depreciated government shareholding in Ashanti as had been rumoured, but Brigadier H.K. Anyidaho's 'Report of the Fact-finding Committee to Investigate Ashanti Goldfields Company Limited, Obuasi Mine Industrial Action' of May 1999.

Dzandu requested details of contracts awarded, procurement transactions, cashbooks, bank statements and stock registers. In addition, the Management and Technical Services Agreement between Lonmin and the firm, which had been in the public domain since the flotation in 1994, was summoned. Ashanti supplied all of the required information. In return it requested a copy of the much talked about but never seen Anyidaho Report, as well as clarification of the offence committed that had caused financial or economic loss to the state.

It would be some weeks before a copy of the Anyidaho Report was made available to Ashanti. By contrast, the allegations were quickly specified and were essentially the same as those broadcast by Rawlings to discredit Jonah prior to the crisis.[3]

The manner in which the investigation was publicised rocked the company's credibility again, just when it was on the path to rebuilding its reputation. Equally disturbing was the inference that Ashanti was viewed by the government as some sort of parastatal. Only weeks earlier, on 26 April, AGC had held an AGM at which government proxies had been received that, among other things, showed approval of the company accounts. Since the government was a major shareholder, any issues concerning Ashanti and meriting an SFO investigation could first have been queried with the company directly or tabled on the agenda for discussion at the AGM. The government's actions went against the spirit of the 15 February MOU to communicate first before exposing the company to public glare.

Jonah assured the board verbally and in writing of his own honesty. At his suggestion the board agreed to commission its own internal review of each of the Anyidaho allegations. The internal audit department along with the external auditors would carry this out and report directly to the chairman, Michael Beckett. The Corporate Governance Committee, chaired by Baroness Chalker, would review the results of the internal investigation.

Unfortunately, Jonah's clean conscience and confidence in the propriety of his own and the company's actions and procedures provided little assurance for his freedom. After the abuse of the interpretation of the law during the minority shareholder case, there was no telling how this 'causing financial loss to the state' offence would be pinned on Jonah or the Ashanti management team, irrespective of the evidence.

The prospect of permanent relief

There were fewer than six months to go before the general elections and there was no certainty that Rawlings would step down, despite British and American encouragement for him to respect the constitution.[4] Queen Elizabeth II had made British opinion uncharacteristically clear during her address to the Ghana parliament back in November 1999 when she reminded her audience that Rawlings's 'successor is to be chosen freely and fairly by the people of Ghana'.[5] The opposition benches cheered, 'Hear, hear!', grateful for the high-profile exhortation.

If Rawlings did step down and his party, the NDC, won with its newly selected leader, Vice-president Mills, then Jonah's torment would surely continue. The NDC party leadership contest had selected Mills over Kwesi Botchwey, the former finance minister. Botchwey had demonstrated strength of character and freethinking by leaving the NDC government back in 1995. Rawlings's support for his vice-president to replace him as leader augured a loss of independence for Mills. It was a perception transformed into fact by Mills's own admission that if elected he would consult with Rawlings on a daily basis.[6] Mills suited Rawlings's plans to direct from the shadows. The omnipresence of Rawlings during the campaign made it clear that he fully intended to continue to dominate the political arena.

It was difficult to call the outcome of the election. A significant proportion of Rawlings's votes in his previous two election victories had undoubtedly been for him personally rather than for his party. But Rawlings's rally cry for Mills could be enough to earn the NDC a third term in office. In the absence of Rawlings's charismatic leadership some pundits predicted victory for the opposition NPP, led by the mild giant and experienced politician, John Kufuor.

In Ghana's post-independence history there had never been a peaceful change from one democratically elected political party to an opposition party. The NDC, feeling the pressure, obtained a court ruling dismissing the Ghana Electoral Commission's decision for each voter to carry a compulsory photo identification card. This strategy, it was hoped, would help to eradicate the 1.5 million 'ghost voters'. These extra names, 8 per cent of the total population, appeared on the electoral register but did not tally with the demographic statistics on the number of Ghanaians of voting age.[7] Rawlings vociferously objected to photo identification claiming that it would prevent rural people from voting even though the cost and distribution of the cards were effectively financed and executed throughout Ghana's villages and cities by the United Kingdom's Department for International Development.[8] The inference was that the NDC planned to stay in power by whatever means possible.

For these reasons Jonah expected Mills to win. His fear, then, was of continued victimisation through Rawlings's actions from the sidelines. Jonah's NDC friends, Peprah and Ohene-Kena, insisted that contrary to public opinion, Mills was his own man and nobody's lapdog. They advised their friend to help Mills directly and vouched, rather unconvincingly, that the political change that Jonah, and Ghana, desperately wanted would come with Mills. Jonah's next calculation was that if he didn't help Mills and Mills went on to victory, then he would have marked himself as an enemy and opened himself, his family and Ashanti to continued harassment. Throughout Ghana's political history, change in government had been accompanied by change in patronage. Allies of the outgoing leaders saw their fortunes dwindle while friends of the newcomers received new favours. AGC had experienced the same: Nkrumah's friendship with General Spears was followed by a harsh treatment by the NLC that backed Lonrho to usurp Spears. The NLC's supportive relationship with Lonrho was then followed by Acheampong and his NRC's contempt for the firm and expropriation of majority control. Instead of continuity and development, political junctures disrupted business. The immature state of party politics in sub-Saharan Africa threatened the same for Ghana in 2000.

Jonah's own views of party politics are controversial. He advocates research and debate into a ten-year political experiment for Ghana to test what he calls a coalition government of national unity. This would be a consultative, representational, command government benefiting from continuity, which is conducive to growth, rather than four-yearly upheavals. His hope is that such an institution would promote nation-building and streamline the size and decision-making process of government; while political parties could continue to exist, this alliance government would minimise the marketing machinery surrounding them, which diverts money away from production into politicking.

His reasons for this are many. In his opinion, first-past-the-post party politics are a luxury of the developed world. Not only is sub-Saharan Africa unprepared and ill-equipped for party politics but, he feels, the system itself, because it requires expensive marketing machinery, becomes an instrument of corruption. Ghana has a 27-person executive compared to the United States's 17, and the latter country's economy is 770 times larger with a population 13 times bigger.[9] Landing a political post in Ghana is seen as akin to winning the lottery and patronage unnecessarily expands the size of government.

Ghana's elections are not fought on policy. There is no substantial policy difference between the parties since the country's development path is to a significant degree dictated by foreign funds, foreign conditions and foreign trade policies. As for the electorate, in a situation of mass poverty and in some cases hunger, along with 40 per cent illiteracy,[10] the majority cannot and do not assimilate or debate the policies of different parties, assuming there were any. They vote on other issues: T-shirts and bicycles distributed by campaigners, as well as family and ethnic affiliations.

Economic history supports the fact that a multiparty system is not a prerequisite for rapid economic growth: Communist Russia 1950–65, the miraculous growth of the East Asian Tigers 1960–90, and China today have transformed themselves from economic backwardness under authoritarian governments. However, history also shows that at a point of development, command governments instead of nurturing growth begin to inhibit it. In Jonah's opinion, Africa is far from that stage; at present, the level of development demanded by the continent requires strong, authoritative leadership. He argues that the decision-shackling, resource-wasting aspects of Western democracy harm Africa's early development efforts more than help them. Therefore the introduction of such a system should, ideally, be postponed until literacy is near-universal and the standard of living of the majority improved; only then could the benefits of the most liberal and direct form of democracy outweigh the costs.

Ghana, indeed most of Africa, is in an emergency situation. In circumstances such as war, parliaments temporarily increase the powers of the executive, abandon their differences and coalesce in order to concentrate their efforts on overcoming whatever peril is facing the nation. Jonah calls for similar drastic political measures for the duration of a decade to give Ghana the chance to fight and win the war on poverty.

Faced with the realities in 2000 Jonah decided to hedge his bets with the party political system. He made a donation to Mills through Ohene-Kena. But his best hope for a quiet life for himself and his company would be an NPP win, however remote the chances of that were. Unlike Mills, John Kufuor was a family friend of the Jonahs and close to Nana Prah. Desirous of real change in the country and motivated by self-preservation Jonah met Kufuor to offer his financial assistance. He made a large financial gift to him personally rather than directly to the NPP. Jonah did not hide his reasons for his actions: he was not endorsing NPP political views, nor was he about to sign up as an NPP party member, but it was in his and his family's interests for the opposition to defeat the NDC. Kufuor welcomed the funds – the donation would help to level the playing field since the incumbents had an unfair campaign advantage in their use of government vehicles, personnel and other resources.

The general election

Jonah's overtures were viewed with suspicion by many opposition party members when they later learnt of them. They saw Jonah as an NDC man despite his fallout with Rawlings. In most people's eyes, his friend-ships with key NDC personnel, such as Peprah, and his former closeness with Nana Konadu were not simply private relationships but political ones. They therefore interpreted his private donation to Kufuor as Machiavellian.

The days leading up to the election were marred by violence and intimidation, particularly in Kumasi, Berekum, Wenchi and Alajo.[11] Jonah was warned that his elimination could easily be engineered by a stray bullet during the helter-skelter expected at polling stations on election day.[12] His enquiries from sympathisers in the intelligence ser-vices confirmed the severity of the threat. A lack of evidence had checked any hopes that Rawlings may have entertained of seeing Jonah on trial for causing financial loss to the state, but the CEO's demise re-mained in his reach. Jonah desperately wanted to cast his vote, knowing that his freedom, his life even, depended on an NPP victory, but he lis-tened to his family's pleas and left Ghana for the safety of London.

The outcome of the 7 December presidential poll was inconclusive. Neither Mills nor Kufuor had the requisite 50 per cent plus one vote to be declared winner. Mills achieved 44.8 per cent and Kufuor 48.4 per cent, with the remaining votes scattered among five minority party leaders.

Kufuor's NPP won 100 out of the 200 seats in the parliamentary poll to the NDC's 92, but there would have to be a presidential run-off. The date was set for 28 December.

The failure of either leader to win convincingly made Jonah re-evaluate his assessment of Kufuor's chances. Victory was indeed possible. He redoubled his efforts by fundraising among friends and pumping more of his own money into Kufuor's fighting fund.

In the three weeks to the run-off, the minority parties clubbed with Kufuor, sharing their disillusionment at the derailed economic reforms and the scorched earth policy that NDC functionaries appeared to be following in their final days. Corruption, unemployment, inflation and a fast depreciating cedi led the smaller parties to conclude that it was high time for change.

Unrest escalated in pockets. On 28 December an NDC supporter stabbed the NPP member of parliament for Alekuma North. Opposition voters were also responsible for some episodes of harassment. The deployment of army personnel, vehicles and aircraft by the incumbents heightened the sense of anxiety. Nevertheless, undaunted, 60 per cent of the electorate – including Jonah – came to the polls to choose between Mills and Kufuor.

Despite Theo's objections, Sam had returned to Ghana to cast his vote. He was aware of the danger and arrived at his local polling station as soon as it opened to avoid any crowds. Immediately after voting he drove with his friend Alhaji Yusif to Kotoka International Airport. They completed departure procedures and boarded a private plane only to disembark under the cover of baggage trolleys to slip into a waiting car. Kofi Ansah drove them to his house in Saltpond, a sleepy town about three hours west of Accra. The men ensconced themselves there, anxiously awaiting the results.

The 2000 election would later be described as Ghana's most critical election since independence in 1957 because it demonstrated a major shift in voting alliances, if less so in policy direction.[13] It was the first time that a change in administration had occurred without the creation of a new republic or a coup d'état. Kufuor took 57 per cent of the votes.

The defeat was explained by the NDC's complete dominance by Rawlings and his wife, its lack of internal democracy, the public view of

Mills as a puppet, corruption, and the people's economic hardship. Rawlings had been Ghana's longest serving head of state. His flaws aside, his nineteen years of rule had brought a period of continuity unknown since independence. His greatest legacy was the bold and brave step to stay along the path of Structural Adjustment (albeit with varying degrees of compliance). Much credit for the initial paradigmatic shift made in 1983 from a state-led, communist-leaning economy to a free market one was owed to Kwesi Botchwey. This in itself highlighted another of Rawlings's strengths – fully aware of his own deficits, he skilfully surrounded himself with capable intellectuals. Despite these positives, an air of fear had pervaded those nineteen years of economic breakdown and recovery.

In contrast, Kufuor's NPP quickly repealed the criminal libel and sedition laws dating from the colonial days but used extensively by the NDC to convict journalists and other civilians for speaking against the government.[14] One of the new government's priorities was to establish a South Africa-type National Reconciliation Commission. In view of the constitutional immunity granted to the ex-president and all military personnel, it was hoped that a forum for people to voice their experiences of abuse and violence under dictators and military governments since 1957 would provide emotional redress. It could help to heal wounds and draw a line under Ghana's bloodiest period in history – Rawlings's AFRC and PNDC rule. As the *Ghanaian Chronicle* front-paged when the results were announced, 'Free at Last! Great God Almighty, We are Free at Last!'[15] Jonah shared the sentiment in a very real and private way. He felt that he could rest easy for the first time since Tiny Rowland's death back in July 1998.

A long road back to credibility

The election result was the cherry on the top of a successful year of operations for Ashanti. Gold production hit a record of 1.7 million ounces, up 11 per cent, and average costs per ounce fell by 9 per cent. On 15 December Geita's 50 per cent sale achieved $335m, which was well above expectations. Gross debt peaked that year at $693.3m, but thanks to the money from Anglogold and the new cash-saving controls put in place, total debt was reduced by 47 per cent to $365.7m at the end of the year. A smaller hedge book showed a positive mark-to-market value of $29.1m and again contributed revenue, although at a reduced amount of $97m.[16] Nevertheless, profitability remained negative due largely to another write-off of $193.5m on tangible fixed assets. The annual report for 2000 attributed this to lower than expected gold prices reducing future projected cash flows and therefore net asset values. Ashanti's share price still bobbed around the crisis level of $2.00. The absence of profit, the dividend moratorium imposed by the warrant agreement and the class action hanging over the company could forseeably be resolved in the short-term, but Ashanti's still high levels of indebtedness, the dominance of the Lonmin and Ghana government stakes and the unrestricted golden share were also reflected in the share price. In a nutshell, the market had little to be positive about in terms of Ashanti's *long-term* structure and future.

CHAPTER 16

'Wood already touched by fire is not hard to set alight'

2001–04

The focus on rebuilding operational and financial credibility returned Ashanti to profitability in 2001 with earnings per share of $0.53 compared to a negative $1.25 the year before. Savings were squeezed from every quarter. Natural shedding and redundancies reduced the workforce by 7 per cent. Merrill Lynch was replaced with Williams de Broe as corporate brokers, saving $400 000 per annum. Head office staff numbers were pared. A complicated group structure following the spate of acquisitions was heavily pruned, and Ashanti de-listed from the Australian and Zimbabwean bourses. While expenses were lopped, gold production hit targets without risking health and safety. In 2001 Obuasi earned a modest but significant industry safety rating of three stars (out of a possible five) and the Group Health and Safety Coordinator, Sean McGinley, received the top Safety Professional of the Year in Africa award for the improvements made in this area.

PWC continued to act as the banks' reporting accountants, producing monthly and quarterly reviews checking Ashanti's compliance with loan covenants and the revised hedging policy. The banks were content with the short-term recovery but shared management's concerns about the medium to long term.

Ashanti's 2001 five-year business plan forecast diminishing fortunes for the group. Bibiani, Freda Rebecca and Iduapriem were nearing the end of their mine lives unless neighbouring properties were acquired or exploration work delineated new resources. Without the financial and technological resources to develop Obuasi below Level 50, now referred to as the Obuasi Deeps, management predicted a peak in gold output in

2004 followed by a decline thereafter in terms of ounces, operating profit and earnings.

The need to restructure the balance sheet

The next major milestone for Ashanti would be to deliver a strong balance sheet to boost the share price and attract investors. This would allow equity capital to be raised to address the production growth constraints. A healthier balance sheet would also attract merger suitors. The gold industry was transforming into fewer, larger entities, but Ashanti risked being demoted as an inconsequential player if it stood still and alone.

In December 2002, the margin-free trading period would end. One month later, the RCF would have to be repaid. Thanks to the 50 per cent sale of Geita to Anglogold, the bulk of the $326m RCF secured at the end of the crisis had been repaid, leaving just $88m due in January 2003. Two months after that, in March 2003, the $216m bond debt would mature. To restructure the balance sheet comprehensively required dealing with three groups of creditors: the hedge banks, the RCF banks, and the bondholders. Jonah and Venkat discussed the ideal scenarios: they wanted permanent margin-free trading; they wanted a debt facility with longer tenor, lower costs and greater flexibility; and they wanted to repay the bonds on time and at par to reduce gearing and to earn the respect of the credit market. Conscious of the enormous difficulty in obtaining their preferred outcomes in this trilemma, they confronted the bond debt first.

Addressing the creditors

After a bank selection process, Houlihan Lokey Howard and Zukin with Close Brothers were retained to help tackle the bond problem. The experts advised Ashanti to negotiate with the bondholders to restructure the debt sooner rather than later. The closer the negotiations approached the maturity date, the more onerous the terms would be for Ashanti. It was hoped that the bondholders, aware of Ashanti's recent difficulties, would prefer to negotiate rather than insist on redeeming their notes at par and in cash at the peril of pushing the company back towards insolvency. Since a little of something always beats all of nothing, Ashanti assumed that the bondholders would come to the table. Once face to face there would only be three options for discussion.

If Ashanti offered to repay the bondholders in cash, they could perhaps be persuaded to accept a discount. But cash was tight and Ashanti's borrowing capacity low. If it paid the creditors with brand new bonds, it would preserve cash but, on the downside, this would not reduce Ashanti's over-gearing. The best option would be to repay the debt in equity but this would demand a premium and demonstrable, long-term strategic achievements. In Ashanti's favour, the shares were significantly undervalued in comparison to its peers if comparing market capitalisation to net asset value. So an equity aspect to a bond refinancing package could be attractive.

A roadshow to bondholders indicated a willingness to receive new bonds on better terms and with an equity component. Ashanti offered to replace 75 per cent of the old 5.5 per cent debt with new 7.95 per cent convertible bonds to mature in five years from June 2003. The remaining 25 per cent of debt would be paid in shares at the highest closing share price in the 30 days preceding the conclusion of the deal, but capped at $3.75. The conversion price would be set at 130 per cent of the trading peak in the 30-day run-up to completion. The bondholders would also receive a 2 per cent cash fee upon successful conclusion of the restructuring. Houlihans secured signed irrevocable undertakings from 60 per cent of the bondholders for the deal and were confident of persuading the remainder. There was, however, one precondition demanded by this group of creditors: Ashanti had to extend its margin-free trading for the new bond duration, that is, up to June 2008.

Jonah and Venkat turned their attention to the hedge banks. On an individual basis, the company had been negotiating with each hedge bank to grant permanent margin-free trading. With the exception of Goldman Sachs and Credit Suisse First Boston, each hedge bank had bilaterally signed an agreement suspending rights to call margin for as long as other hedge counterparties did too, and provided that Ashanti was not in breach of any covenants. The hedge contracts of Goldman Sachs and Credit Suisse First Boston could be assigned to parties prepared to sign a new bilateral agreement, a process known as novation. Once all had signed, the company's plan was to reveal the redundancy of the three-year December 1999 Margin-Free Trading Agreement, and to propose a collective, substitute agreement for permanent suspension. This would satisfy the bondholders.

One angle of the balance sheet restructuring trilemma remained: refinancing the existing RCF. For the first time Ashanti considered a non-syndicated option. Rothschild, Bayerische Hypo Vereinsbank and Standard Bank indicated that they would be prepared to underwrite a new facility for five years at 2 per cent with a $1.75m arrangement fee. Ashanti was encouraged by the fact that Bayerische, a bank with which it had no previous relationship, was eager to get involved. Just as an inattentive husband begins to appreciate his wife at the sight of another man admiring her, Barclays elbowed in. It made a similar offer, but at a reduced fee of $1.25m. By playing the two parties against each other, Ashanti managed to bring the competitors together to offer an overall package, in the end syndicated and arranged by Rothschild, of $200m and on attractive terms. The only condition was that Ashanti would purchase political risks insurance to protect the banks. This was duly obtained.

An alternative solution to refinancing the bond debt

Venkat anticipated that Lonmin would object to the equity dilution that would result if the bond restructuring proceeded. Consequently, he encouraged a discussion of alternatives. If Lonmin wanted to, it could provide Ashanti with cash rather than face dilution. Lonmin's 43 per cent stake at the time of flotation in 1994 had whittled to just under 28 per cent. Many on Lonmin's board were angry at the company's treatment by Ashanti over the years in this regard. They were horrified at the thought of further dilution if new options were awarded to the bondholders as part of the refinancing plan. If this went ahead, Lonmin's shareholding in Ashanti would drop to below 25 per cent, the critical threshold needed to block any unwanted corporate changes. Jonah and Venkat made a formal presentation to the Lonmin board in which they compared the bond refinancing package with an alternative cash injection, and the effects of both on Ashanti's financial health. Some felt that to provide this cash to Ashanti would be throwing good money after bad. It was with great difficulty that the arguments of Sir John Craven, Lonmin's chairman, about the long-term advantages of maintaining a 28 per cent stake of a financially rehabilitated Ashanti, carried the day. Lonmin reluctantly agreed to inject $75m through a private equity placement.

If the hedge and RCF banks that held warrants for 15 per cent of the company could be persuaded to exercise them early for shares, it would raise a further $45m cash. Together with the $200m loan and Lonmin's $75m, a cash chest of $320m could redeem the $216m bonds in full, repay the remainder of the existing RCF, and leave a little for working capital.

This cash redemption alternative was preferred by the board to the bond restructuring package, as it would significantly improve gearing. It didn't take much effort to persuade the banks to exercise their warrants early. The conclusion of the $200m enlarged RCF and the prospect of Ashanti repaying its bonds in full meant that the only way the share price would go was up, so now was as good a time as any to convert the warrants.

By early June 2002, Houlihans had secured 91 per cent of bond-holders' approval for the note restructuring. Since the bondholders had signed irrevocable undertakings in favour of the original restructuring offer, they would need to be consulted over the cash alternative. With no major objections raised, Ashanti repaid all the bonds at par and in cash on 28 June 2002. At a time when few borrowers in the bond market were redeeming in cash, and if they were, only at a discount, Ashanti's feat signalled that the company was back to market-winning ways. In a masterful display of negotiating prowess, Jonah, Venkat and Arnesen had achieved margin-free trading, obtained $200m debt refinance on softer and more flexible terms, reduced total debt by $70m to $257m, brought gross gearing down to a respectable 56 per cent *and* redeemed the bonds at par and in cash. The timing and execution of the balance sheet re-structuring exceeded market expectations. Venkat had more than repaid Jonah's confidence in him. And in the eyes of all parties – banks, hedge counterparties and shareholders – Ashanti's treasury and finance team had regained credibility.

With a healthy balance sheet and good operational momentum, the share price responded approvingly by breaching $6. To re-establish

Ashanti as an attractive investment opportunity it was critical that the next eighteen months delivered consistently improved earnings and efficiency, and no bad news.

A time of positive change at Ashanti and in Ghana

Out of twenty-six major gold mining companies existing in 1997 only thirteen remained in 2002. A few had gone bankrupt, but most had been absorbed. Ashanti was the smallest of the world's senior producers by market capitalisation and would have made an obvious target for absorption were it not for the political risks linked to the firm, although Ghana's political environment had improved somewhat under the new regime.

Following Kufuor's inaugural promise of 'zero tolerance for corruption', his own youth and sports minister, barely warmed in the post, was trialled and convicted of misappropriating bonus money of $46 000 that was owed to the national football team. In the crackdown on financial misdemeanours, the new administration unearthed $100m of IMF loans wrongly obtained by Rawlings's government on the basis of false information. The governor of the Bank of Ghana and the finance minister, at the least, would have known that data on money growth and supply had been hugely misreported, misleading the IMF.[1] Court proceedings against Rawlings's former ministers occupied significant media space. A former deputy finance minister was successfully tried for the disappearance of $1.2m marked for the computerisation of Ghanaian courts. Three others, including the minister of finance and Jonah's friend, Richard Peprah, were convicted for two to four years for their role in facilitating the transfer of $22m to an African-American woman for a fictitious rice farm. It appeared that the men were simply following verbal orders from Rawlings as none of them had benefited personally from the scandal. Ironically, it was the NDC's amendment to the Criminal Code of 'causing financial loss to the state' that condemned the men.

Rawlings had justified his 1979 executions in the name of justice against corruption, although none of those shot received a just trial. Even if a fair trial had indicted those men, the appropriateness of capital punishment is difficult to defend. Thankfully, the NPP got off to a good start (maintaining it, however, would sadly prove more difficult). But Kufuor won international acclaim for initially backing anti-corruption words with action *and* respect for human rights.

In the matter of the SFO investigation, its conclusions chimed with the results of Ashanti's own internal enquiry into the Anyidaho allegations. The SFO failed to establish 'any act of financial mismanagement or manipulation, irregularity or impropriety, commission of fraud, that has caused or [is] likely to cause financial or economic loss to Ashanti Goldfields Company Limited (Obuasi) in which the Government of the Republic of Ghana has financial interest'.[2] Jealous of his own reputation, the *Daily Graphic's* front-page exoneration pleased Jonah so much that he framed it and mounted it on his living room wall.

Rawlings has, as expected, attempted to stay in the limelight. He remains popular and is able to pull the crowds, but his antics, such as calling President Kufuor 'an armed robber' and veiling his wish for a coup to overthrow the NPP,[3] reveal a severe power hangover. His ill-considered rants and opulent obesity now create something of a spectacle rather than a sense of danger.

Anxieties from the United States

Across the Atlantic legal proceedings progressed less straightforwardly. A motion filed by Ashanti to dismiss the class action was rejected. In May 2002, a United States District Court for the Eastern District of New York ruled that the action should proceed to trial. At an interim hearing after that, the judge encouraged the parties to reach an out of court settlement. So while pre-trial processes continued and Ashanti vigorously rebutted all the charges, attempts at mediation commenced. Ashanti's counsel appointed a damages expert with the cooperation of the firm's liability insurers to attempt to minimise the plaintiffs' initial demand of hundreds of millions of dollars. However guilt-free it was, Ashanti felt that the risks of a jury verdict going against the company in a get-rich-quick-by-lawsuit culture were to be avoided if possible. (The case was eventually settled in December 2005 for a modest sum to the relief of the company and its insurers.)

In February 2001, the United States SEC launched an inquiry into

Ashanti's 1999 regulatory filings, specifically the Obuasi asset write-offs, the hedge policy and Geita's drilling results. The company responded to the copious list of detailed questions only to receive in return a new and longer set of queries throughout 2002. This time the list concerned the company's change from United States to United Kingdom accounting practices back in 1996, further hedge book disclosures, inventory treatment and other accounting issues. Jonah was confident that Ashanti had acted appropriately on all counts and assured the board to that effect. The SEC investigations were, however, an information and time burden. If not handled with absolute transparency and accuracy they threatened to undermine the trust that Ashanti had been carefully reconstructing. This was the time of the ruination of Enron, Worldcom and Arthur Andersen. Corporate America was under detailed scrutiny with AOL Time Warner, Citigroup and others facing serious censures. For Ashanti, the first African operating company on the NYSE, to be upbraided or fined in any way would have plunged the company back into a crisis of credibility and extinguished for good the trail-blazing reputation heralded back in 1996. As it was, when the exhaustive SEC investigations eventually concluded, Ashanti was found to be snow-white.[4] All told, 2002 had been a satisfying, profitable year, and it ended with a tingle of excitement.

The Anglogold merger

Ashanti had been considering merger combinations since 1998, and in earnest following the crisis. Lonmin, Newmont, Gold Fields and Randgold had all eyed Ashanti and been eyed in return. But now that the balance sheet was on an even keel, Ashanti could really begin to flirt. In fact, whether the company liked it or not it was in play: Lonmin, the largest shareholder, had broadcast that following the failed merger it now viewed Ashanti as a passive investment, and it was looking for an exit, which attracted suitors.

The Geita joint venture between Ashanti and Anglogold had worked extremely well, unlike many such unions where, despite contracting for equality on paper, the reality of a more powerful partner invariably sours the relationship. In this instance, communication, problem-solving and results satisfied both parties. Friendship and mutual respect between Jonah and his counterpart, Bobby Godsell, set the tone for discussions over greater cooperation. Initially talks focused on a joint venture for exploiting the Obuasi Deeps. Anglogold, through its Anglo American heritage, had decades of experience in exploring, planning, developing and operating deep level gold mines and the financial wherewithal to bring the Deeps into production. Early in 2003 the preliminary talks extended into discussions over a full merger.

Godsell had not forgotten his vision before Ashanti's crisis broke, to create, together with Jonah and Oliphant, giant gold-producing units. The hedging crisis had interrupted the plan, but now there was an opportunity to fulfil it in a way. It was Godsell who proposed the iconic name Ashanti for the post-merger mega-producer. He also offered the CEO position to Jonah, intimating that he wished to return to academia (he is a published sociologist). Jonah declined; he would only step up if Godsell remained. At 54 years old Jonah had planned to relinquish executive responsibilities at the age of 57, a key threshold in Ashanti's succession planning. But the prospect of working with Godsell excited him. Godsell acquiesced – he would be prepared to take the chairmanship with Jonah as chief executive. They shook hands on this. The companies signed confidentiality agreements and started to conduct due diligence on each other.

The attractions for Anglogold were that Ashanti was undervalued; the company was financially rehabilitated and its shares were on the up. Full control of Geita and the addition of Obuasi would add two long-life mines with high-volume ounces and tremendous future potential. Of particular interest too was Kimin, Ashanti's advanced exploration site in the Democratic Republic of Congo, which awaited the settlement of ownership disputes and a window in that region's turmoil for full exploitation. Ashanti also gave Anglogold strong African senior and middle management, and useful pan-African political relationships.

The advantages for Ashanti were Anglogold's strong finances. It had the cash to invest in the long-term development of Obuasi and Kimin. The merged entity would benefit from Anglogold's superior credit standing, improved procurement and other cost synergies. Anglogold's record of paying the highest dividend yield of all the major gold producers promised a restart of dividends for Ashanti shareholders. The single most important factor though was Anglogold's deep mining expertise.

On 17 April 2003 the South African company offered in an all paper transaction 26 Anglogold shares for 100 Ashanti shares. This valued the company at just under $1bn, equivalent to $7.20 per share and representing a 43.9 per cent premium on the closing share price of the day before. This was in line with recent premiums paid in the acquisition of Acacia by Anglogold, Battlemountain by Newmont, and Homestake by Barrick.

Acutely aware of the need to carry all shareholders, with the Lonmin debacle still painful in his memory, Jonah asked the aged and respected Ghanaian gold industry academic, T.E. Anin, who had joined the board a year earlier, to interface with the government. Jonah expected difficulties because of the public emotions surrounding Ashanti and the golden share.

The government supported the merger in principle. In a letter sent to Ashanti it expressed delight at the potential investment injection and raised no objections to continued negotiations. However, the support came with qualifications. The government would insist on keeping its golden share and the historic name, Ashanti; it also required a continued listing on the Ghana Stock Exchange of the merged entity, a regional head office in Ghana for West African operations to promote Ghana as a major investment destination, and the retention of jobs. Société Générale was appointed to advise the government on the merger proposal, which would also be subject to review by a parliamentary committee for mines and energy.

On 4 August Anglogold and Ashanti agreed the principal merger terms by signing a Transaction Agreement. If the government, as a major shareholder and golden shareholder, did not formally approve the merger by 1 October, Anglogold could pull out without penalty. Ashanti's board unanimously recommended the offer and a press release was issued.

After the public announcement Jonah met Godsell at the Grosvenor House Hotel in London. The South African looked morose and he apologised to his friend for what he was about to say. 'I can't deliver on the name, Sam.' At best they would have to marry the two names and in order of financial superiority: Anglogold Ashanti. 'And I can't deliver the

CEO, nor offer you the chairmanship.' Anglogold's principal shareholders and the board of directors had rejected Godsell's propositions.

No blow-softening reasons followed. Jonah didn't doubt his friend; he knew he would have done his best and he could see Godsell's pained countenance from having to renege on his word. The market frowned on co-CEO arrangements, so that was a non-starter. Jonah had first-hand experience of the problems caused by shared leadership when Tiny Rowland and Dieter Bock attempted it at Lonrho. Upstairs at Anglogold were prepared to cede the co-deputy chairmanship – a non-executive post – to the African.

Jonah did not mind. With or without him in the driving seat, the compelling operational and financial rationale for the merger continued to hold. He subjugated his pride. This merger was not about his career; it was about Ashanti's survival. What was important for him was to oversee the integration of the companies post-merger, and to ensure continuity, which could be achieved from a non-executive position. After all, this would allow him to follow through on his retirement plan. A non-executive status for him would not be a deal breaker. The fact of the matter was that Anglogold was taking Ashanti over. None of the chief executives of the companies acquired by Ashanti had survived or joined Ashanti's board in executive capacities. Consequently, Jonah, had it not been for Godsell's earlier generous offer, could not have expected anything different.

Randgold starts a bidding war

The public announcement of Anglogold's deal encouraged other unsolicited offers. One received from a Theodore Roxford, described as a 'corporate raider',[5] offered $9 per share via email, which was not taken seriously. Randgold, which had been in tentative merger talks with Ashanti back in August 2002, re-emerged on 23 September 2003 offering one Randgold share to two Ashanti, or $11.14 per Ashanti share ($1.5bn in total). Between the date of Anglogold's offer and Randgold's offer, Ashanti's share price had jumped from $5 to $11.25. Pertinent aspects of the Randgold deal included changing the name of the merged entity to Ashanti and moving its headquarters to Accra – tactics guaranteed to please the Ghanaian public. Randgold would appoint the CEO and CFO and allow Ashanti to fill the COO, legal counsel and chairman roles, the last going to Jonah.

It paid to be wooed by several admirers. In October, Anglogold revised its offer upward to 29 of its shares for every 100 Ashanti shares, valuing Ashanti at $1.43bn. This was intentionally pitched below Randgold's $1.5bn.[6] Bobby Godsell would not be lured into a bidding war. Anglogold had two advantages over Randgold that could not be easily matched in money terms: technical know-how and Lonmin sewn up. Sir John Craven's foresight to maintain a Lonmin stake in AGC above the critical 25 per cent level paid off. It was now in Lonmin's power to call some important shots in this merger. Lonmin, which held 27.6 per cent of Ashanti, had given an irrevocable commitment to support Anglogold unless Randgold could buy it out for cash – which Randgold could not do. Anglogold's paper, because of its liquidity, was superior to Randgold's and Lonmin planned to use the merger as an exit from gold to focus on its platinum operations.

Furious at the aspersions cast on the quality of its paper, Randgold's chief executive, Mark Bristow, vowed to match Anglogold 'cent for cent'.[7] Ashanti's board maintained its recommendation for shareholders to support the Anglogold bid. The execution risks were greater with Randgold, a smaller company with less financial capacity and weaker technical ability to accelerate the development of Obuasi Deeps.

In a belligerent mood, Randgold responded to Anglo's improved price by upping its paper offer to a whopping $12.57 per share ($1.7bn). Although this would provide greater short-term cash, the board concluded that in the medium and long term Randgold could not sustain the capital expenditure needed at Obuasi. To Bristow's shock, Anglogold remained the preferred partner.

While waiting for the green light from government, Godsell returned to Jonah about the latter's post-merger status. Godsell had remained aggrieved that Anglogold Ashanti would not benefit as fully as possible from Jonah's hands-on knowledge, experience and leadership with him in a non-executive capacity. Godsell drew on the model used by Newmont following its merger with Franco-Nevada when the latter's CEO was retained in an executive presidency role to persuade the

Anglogold powers-that-be to create a similar position for Jonah. As president Jonah would be responsible, with Godsell, for the group's strategic leadership. Jonah accepted.

The government's position

The Transaction Agreement deadline for government approval had been extended from 1 October to 4 November. Based on advice from Société Générale and the parliamentary committee's consultations with the firm, the ministry of mines, the Environmental Protection Agency, the Bank of Ghana and the Mine Workers' Union, the government released a public statement on 28 October in support of the board's recommendation for a merger with Anglogold.

From the government's perspective, as a shareholder, the advantages of the deal were plain. Anglogold had offered the government an additional 1 per cent of the merged entity, to be called Anglogold Ashanti, in exchange for limiting the golden share to the Ghanaian assets and liabilities. This 1 per cent represented an additional 2.6 million Anglogold Ashanti shares on top of the government's 6.3 million shares for its existing 17.2 per cent ownership of AGC. The government's total stake in the new company would be 3.4 per cent. The additional shares were worth $100m on 28 October and were likely to appreciate. If Anglogold paid the same dividend rate as it had in 2002, the government would earn $11m, which would be the highest dividend paid to the state in Ghana's mining history. Furthermore, Anglogold had committed to spending $220m on the existing Obuasi mine in the first four years, $44m on exploration of the Obuasi Deeps, and thereafter, depending on the exploration and feasibility studies, $570m on the development of the Deeps.

As a regulator, the government was satisfied with Anglogold Ashanti's promises not to implement new job cuts in the first two years (indeed, if expansion plans at Obuasi were achieved it was envisaged that more jobs would be created over a longer time frame); the merged entity would designate 1 per cent of Ghanaian profits for community works in Ghana; and commitments were given to expand training as well as health and safety initiatives. Corporate tax revenue stood to increase with

Obuasi's growth. The new company's listing on the Ghana Stock Exchange and the creation of low denomination Depositary Securities especially for the small Ghanaian investor also met with approval. The government was to be commended for its non-sentimental consideration of the proposal, which was no easy feat in view of the public uproar.

Some called for re-nationalisation rather than selling out. Despite the talk of a merger, Anglogold, by virtue of its sheer size, was clearly taking over Ashanti, and to many the idea of facilitating this usurpation by a South African firm, given the history of apartheid, was horrifying. The government's insistence on maintaining the golden share helped to assuage the discontent, as did Ashanti's public relations campaign that echoed the potential long-term economic advantages.

Another worried group of stakeholders was the staff at Ashanti. Feelings of dejection and uncertainty clipped morale. The economic and strategic explanations made sense, but it was one thing to talk about long-term aggregate benefits and quite another to talk about individuals. As one human resources manager, with tears in his eyes, put it to Jonah at a group meeting to explain the merger, 'But what about us, Chief?' The questioner was one of many who had taken advantage of Ashanti training opportunities at home and abroad to work his way up the ranks. It was a frightening thought that the mighty Anglogold would arrive with its hordes of staff. Even if Ashanti was spared an invasion of people, what guarantees could be given that Anglo's culture would not subsume Ashanti's? Other staff commented that Jonah had instilled in them a can-do attitude, but this merger smacked of defeat. They had crawled back from the edge of bankruptcy; whatever operational problems lay ahead could surely be overcome too. '*We* should be taking over Anglogold!' someone remarked to whoops and nods. They had also heard with dismay that Jonah would be moving to Anglogold's headquarters in Johannesburg. If Jonah went, the heart of Ashanti would leave with him.

Their comments touched Jonah to the quick. He did his best to enthuse the team without disparaging people's feelings. It was his and Godsell's plan to fuse the best of Ashanti's culture with the best of Anglogold's to create a new culture altogether. For example, the South Africans were impressed with Ashanti's top-down indigenisation policy, which it hoped to emulate in all its country subsidiaries. But Ashanti could also learn something from Anglogold's efficiency. As for job security, the enlarged group, present in eleven countries, offered greater training and career opportunities for anyone who strove for them. Both Jonah and Godsell fiercely defended meritocracy and that principle would dictate an individual's success. Never one to be emotional, Jonah reiterated the bare facts that made the merger the best option for Ashanti – the industry was changing and Ashanti had to change with it.

Autonomy comes to an end

The penultimate step to completing the merger was the important matter of negotiating a Stability Agreement with the government in its capacity as regulator. After considerable negotiations with the parliamentary committee overseeing the merger, it was agreed to extend Obuasi's mine lease from 2024 to 2054, and to cap Anglogold Ashanti's royalties at 3 per cent and corporation tax at 30 per cent for fifteen years. The company would be exempt from any adverse changes in laws affecting its operations. It would be allowed to retain foreign currency offshore without any restrictions on dividend payments. Finally, the agreement confirmed that the golden share would be limited to Ghanaian assets and liabilities. On 12 February 2004 the Ghanaian parliament ratified the Stability Agreement. Other legal approvals from the ministers of mines and finance, the Bank of Ghana and the Ghana Stock Exchange were duly supplied.

Finally, the scheme of arrangement process, ably led by Ashanti's general counsel and her tireless internal and external legal teams, went through the Ghanaian courts. On 26 April 2004 the High Court announced the cancellation of all Ashanti Goldfields Company Limited shares, their reissue to Anglogold Holdings PLC, and the creation of Anglogold Ashanti. In a historically neat coincidence 26 April marked the tenth anniversary of Ashanti's return to the London Stock Exchange, one of the most important junctures in the company's history. It was also poetic that during South Africa's tenth anniversary of the end of apartheid, the country's largest gold company, and the world's second largest,[8] should have an *African*, a former shovel boy, as president.

'When you follow an elephant you do not get entangled with creepers'

Africa is richly endowed with lucrative and strategically important mineral resources: platinum, gold, oil, vanadium, chromium, uranium, titanium, copper, bauxite and others. Yet, as Tony Blair bleakly stated in February 2004:

> Africa is the only continent to have grown poorer in the last 25 years. Its share of world trade has halved in a generation and it receives less than 1 per cent of direct foreign investment. Forty-four million children do not go to school, millions die through famine or disease or conflict and Africa risks being left even further behind.[1]

If anything, the abundance of natural resources has so far been a multifaceted curse: non-renewable assets are depleted without being replaced by adequate investment in the best alternative long-term asset – human capital. Alongside this depletion mines have caused environmental and health damage; and instead of broadening linkages with the wider economy all too often foreign capital exploits Africa's resources in the form of enclave investments, shipping in foreign expertise and shipping out the gains. To ensure this easy entry and exit, the palms of a few Africans are oiled while many others abandon productive pursuits in an attempt to get the smallest piece of this illicit action, causing the neglect of other sectors of the economy.[2] It does not have to be this way; there can be a more equitable exploitation of the continent's mineral wealth.

The transformations at Ashanti Goldfields under Sam Jonah's stewardship show that a better balance can be struck between capitalist profit

and the socio-economic needs of host countries. The continent's liberal-
ised mining codes, including Ghana's, now need fine-tuning to improve
that trade-off. Ring-fencing a fixed percentage of the gross revenue of
Africa's mines, for example, 2 per cent, exclusively for education would
be a good start.

It is also not unreasonable to impose targets on mines for the managerial training of Africans. Indigenous ownership control of AGC in
1972 did not usher in any fundamental changes at the firm; it was only
in 1986 with the appointment of an African as MD that welfare, the
environment and training received priority attention. Ashanti even included the willingness of foreign supply firms to establish local offices
and workshops in Ghana as part of Obuasi's contract award criteria. In
this way the linkages to the wider economy were fostered while improving the level of service received by the mine.[3] The lesson here is
that African management training and opportunities will make a huge
difference to the behaviour of mine companies on the continent. But,
as many state-owned mines have experienced, the best local management without cash will lead to failure. The winning combination that
Ashanti achieved was to marry Jonah's leadership with foreign investment. And in order to attract this sort of capital, the political environment must give investors absolute confidence.

Even at the present low levels of African economic development, I
don't share Jonah's despair for the current party political system. It may
be an imported, ill-fitting mantle, but with time – as Ghana's 2000 elections demonstrated when for the first time in the country's history there
was a peaceful change from one civilian administration to another –
African states will grow into it.

With political and judicial transparency there can be a win–win outcome: high returns for investors because of the immense untapped opportunities (next to Antarctica, Africa is the continent least explored for
minerals)[4] twinned with rapid human capital development for African
nations.

Jonah's life as recounted here was not faultless. Mistakes were made,
for example, with the quest to extract a million ounces a year from
Obuasi and with the hedging crisis. But Jonah cannot be criticised for
conducting his business affairs with probity. None of Rawlings's many

attempts to pin some illegality on Jonah could hold; a Serious Fraud Office investigation and detailed SEC enquiries into Ashanti's affairs all delivered a clean verdict.

Queen Elizabeth II conferred an Honorary Knighthood on Jonah in June 2003. This award was made in recognition of Jonah's contributions as an African businessman and for his philanthropic work, especially in education, an aspect of his life not explored in this business biography. His feats in the international mining industry were similarly recognised in December 2004 at the Mining Journal World Congress when he was awarded a Life-time Achievement Award. World leaders have drawn on Jonah's unique experiences of international business and the challenges faced by Africa by appointing him to advisory roles. He has served on the advisory councils of the president of the African Development Bank and the International Finance Corporation. Currently he advises President Thabo Mbeki of South Africa, President Obasanjo of Nigeria and President Kufuor of Ghana, as well as contributing to the United Nation's Secretary-General's Global Compact Advisory Council. These advisory posts focus on governance, investment and the role of business in economic development.

To broaden the benefits of his knowledge and experience to the continent, Jonah stepped down as president of Anglogold Ashanti in June 2005. Once he had satisfied himself with a smooth post-merger transition, he took up a non-executive role that would allow him more time to commit to his next challenge. Jonah plans to act as a viaduct to increase foreign investment to the continent by helping private investors to understand, assess and more easily negotiate their way to the motherlode of opportunities that Africa holds. The future is bright for the dark continent.

Abbreviations

31st DWM	31st December Women's Movement
ACSM	Associateship of the Camborne School of Mines
AFRC	Armed Forces Revolutionary Council
AGC	Ashanti Goldfields Corporation
AGM	annual general meeting
AIG	American International Group
Amep	Ashanti Mine Expansion Project
Biox	Bio-oxidation
Cast	Consolidated African Selection Trust
CEO	chief executive officer
CFO	chief financial officer
CIBC	Canadian Imperial Bank of Commerce
COO	chief operating officer
CPP	Convention People's Party
CSM	Camborne School of Mines
EBITDA	earnings before interest, tax, depreciation and amortisation
EGM	extraordinary general meeting
ERP	Economic Recovery Programme
GDP	gross domestic product
GDRs	Global Depository Receipts
Glamco	Ghana Libyan Arab Mining Company Limited
GM	general manager
Goil	Ghana Oil
HSBC	Hong Kong and Shanghai Banking Corporation
IFC	International Finance Corporation

IGR	International Gold Resources
IMF	International Monetary Fund
IPO	initial public offering
Laaico	Libyan Arab African Investment Company
Lafico	Libyan Arab Foreign Investment Company
Libor	London Inter-Bank Offered Rate
Lonrho	London and Rhodesia Mining and Land Company
MD	managing director
MIT	Massachusetts Institute of Technology
MOU	memorandum of understanding
NDC	National Democratic Congress
NLC	National Liberation Council
NLM	National Liberation Movement
NPP	New Patriotic Party
NPV	net present value
NRC	National Redemption Council
NYSE	New York Stock Exchange
OTC	over-the-counter
OSC	Obuasi Sports Club
PDCs	People's Defence Committees
PLC	public limited company
PNDC	Provisional National Defence Council
PP	Progress Party
PWC	PricewaterhouseCoopers
RCF	revolving credit facility
RSM	Royal School of Mines
SEC	Securities and Exchange Commission
SFO	Serious Fraud Office
SMC	Supreme Military Council
SU	Students' Union
UBS	Union Bank of Switzerland
UGCC	United Gold Coast Convention
UN	United Nations
WDCs	Workers' Defence Committees
WGC	World Gold Council

Glossary

Ghanaian terms[1]

Adansihene Chief of the Adansi; this chieftaincy was of second-tier importance in the Asante kingdom. In the last quarter of the nineteenth century the Adansi sought British help to secede from Asante.

Akan A large ethnic group found in West Africa, predominantly in Ghana, where it makes up the single largest ethnic group. The Akan consists of several subgroups including the Asante and Fante. The Akan people have a matrilineal system of descent.

Asante The Akan spelling is used throughout the book to refer to the people of this Akan subgroup and their former kingdom. Ashanti is the English translation and is used as a short form of Ashanti Goldfields Corporation (AGC) or to refer to the geographic region of that name after its conquest by the British.

Asantehemaa Although translated in English as the Queen Mother, the Asantehemaa is not necessarily the Asante king's mother. She is usually the most senior woman in the royal household, so could, for example, be the king's grandmother or aunt.

Asantehene King of the Asante.

Assin An Akan subgroup. The Assin people occupy territory in between the Fante to their south and the Asante to their north. Over history several wars were fought on Assin land as they switched allegiances between these neighbours.

Bekwaihene Chief of the Bekwai; this chieftaincy was one of five core polities at the centre of the Asante kingdom.

cedi The Ghanaian currency. One cedi is divided into 100 pesewas although pesewas are no longer in use.

chop bar A food shack where local food is cooked and sold at reasonable prices.

Ewe An ethnic group found to the east of the Volta River in Ghana.

Fante An Akan subgroup occupying the central coastal area of present-day Ghana. The Fante people were conquered by the Asante in 1807 but later aligned themselves with the British. The Fante town of Cape Coast became the administrative centre for the British until 1876. Fante is also the name of an Akan dialect.

fufu A West African food made from pounding cassava, yam or plantain. Fufu is moulded into balls and eaten with soup or stew.

Golden Stool The stool, or throne, of the Asante king. Besides being a physical object, the Golden Stool symbolises the Asante king's supremacy over lesser chiefs as well as Asante ideologies such as the king's divine selection.

kalabule A colloquial word that emerged during the late 1970s in Ghana, a time of severe economic hardship. The word means corruption.

kente An expensive cloth made from woven, narrow loom strips using traditional, labour-intensive technology.

pesewa One one-hundredth of a cedi.

stool Literally, the seat, or throne, of a chief, carved out of wood and sometimes overlaid with precious metals, but can also refer to the chief's area of influence and chieftaincy as an institution.

Twi A dialect of the Akan language spoken by Asante people.

zongo Urban, migrant quarters that spring up in a town along ethnic lines.

Gold mining and financial terms[2]

Biox Bio-oxidation; a patented process where bacteria are used to break down ores containing sulphides.

bond issue The sale of a corporate debt instrument. Issuing bonds is one way for companies to borrow money. The company promises to repay the amount borrowed (the principal) with interest by a specified date.

Bretton Woods system An international financial management system adopted by the world's industrial nations after the Second World War until 1973. Fixed exchange rates were a key element of the system – the currencies of participating countries were pegged to the dollar and to gold.

bullion Precious metals in the form of bars or ingots.

bull market An optimistic investment market where prices are rising over a long period. The opposite is a 'bear' market where sentiment is pessimistic and prices are falling over a long period.

capital gains The increase in the price of an asset between the time it is sold and when it was originally bought.

cash cost An indication of the average cost of producing one ounce of gold. The cash cost is arrived at by dividing the direct costs associated with mine production – mine labour, extraction costs and processing costs – by the ounces produced in a given period.

Chapter 11 Part of the United States Bankruptcy Code providing indebted companies with court protection from creditors to allow them time to reorganise.

City, the Financial centre of the United Kingdom situated in the oldest part of London.

commitment fee A fee imposed by lenders for holding funds for a borrower.

convertible bonds A corporate debt instrument used by companies to borrow money. Interest is usually paid, but the holder, rather than receiving repayment of the principal, has the right within a certain time frame to convert the bond into equity shares in the borrowing company.

derivatives Financial instruments whose behaviour and value are determined by the behaviour and value of an underlying asset such as a commodity or currency. Options are a type of derivative.

discount rate The rate used to adjust future expected income streams to a present value. Discounting reflects the effects of inflation on the value of money as well as borrowing rates. The higher the discount rate used, the lower the present value of the future cash flows.

dotcom bubble The unprecedented bull market in technology stocks that peaked towards the end of 2000.

Dow The Dow Jones Industrial Average, an index of the United States's top 30 firms.

downside protection Protection from falling prices.

drawdowns Disbursements from an agreed loan.

due diligence The investigation of a company before making an investment.

EBITDA Earnings before interest, tax, depreciation and amortisation. EBITDA reflects a company's operating cash flow.

exotic derivatives Complex financial instruments whose behaviour and value are determined not only by the behaviour and value of the underlying asset, but also by other contingent factors. Barrier options would be an example of an exotic derivative.

forward selling market A market where the price of goods are fixed today even though the goods will not be delivered until some point in the future. Forward selling attempts to avoid adverse price movements in the future.

FTSE 100 The index of the largest 100 companies – measured by market capitalisation – on the London Stock Exchange.

GDP Gross domestic product; the value of a country's goods and services produced in a given year. GDP gives an indication of a country's wealth.

gearing The proportion of a company's capital that is made of up debt as opposed to equity. The higher the gearing, the greater the risk of difficulty in meeting interest payments and therefore the risk of bankruptcy. Gross gearing is calculated by dividing total borrowings by shareholders' funds, whereas net gearing subtracts from the total borrowings figure the amount of cash and other liquid assets the company may hold.

gold derivatives market The market for financial instruments whose behaviour and value are determined by the behaviour and value of gold.

grade In the case of gold mining, the relative gold content found in ore.

hedge book/hedge portfolio A collection of investments in derivatives.

hedge funds Sophisticated investment funds that generally follow aggressive trading strategies.

hostile takeover A takeover that proceeds without the support of the target company's board of directors.

interest cover The calculation of a company's pre-tax income or cash flow divided by its total interest expense. It shows how many times income can service debt payments.

intraday During a single trading day.

IPO Initial public offering; the first sale of a company's stock to the public.

Libor London Inter-Bank Offered Rate; the interest rates that banks charge each other to borrow money.

Lincoln's Inn One of four prestigious inns of court in London where barristers are trained.

liquidity risk The risk of being unable to raise cash quickly, or dispose of assets quickly.

margin call A demand for a collateral payment from a counterparty, usually in the form of cash, to cover an adverse movement in the price of a financial instrument.

market capitalisation The value of a company as measured by the share price multiplied by the number of shares in issue at a given point in time.

net present value (NPV) calculation Net present value is one way of assessing investment opportunities. The calculation looks at future cash flows from an investment and based on the cost of borrowing and inflation, adjusts these income streams to a current value. See also 'discount rate'.

ore Rock containing at least one mineral of commercial value that can be economically extracted.

political risks insurance Insurance cover for events caused by or involving the action of governments such as expropriations, confiscations and so on.

proven reserves The existence of ore where the physical character, continuity, size, shape, quality, mineral content as well as tonnage have been defined, and detailed technical and economic studies justify extraction.

refractory ores Ores whose mineral composition make the gold extraction process more difficult. Intermediary processes are required to deal with the refractory elements before satisfactory levels of gold can be recovered.

reserve asset Assets such as gold and foreign currencies held by central banks that can be used to rectify imbalances in the national accounts.

revolving credit facility A form of flexible corporate borrowing whereby the company can draw on funds as and when needed within a certain limit and time frame.

rollover In the case of derivatives contracts, instead of delivering the underlying asset by the maturity date of the contract, the obligation is renewed or transferred to a new contract with a new maturity date.

scheme of arrangement An agreement between a company and a group of shareholders or creditors arrived at by majority vote but which is then endorsed by a court.

scrip dividends Dividends paid in new shares rather than in cash.

SEC The Securities and Exchange Commission; the United States federal regulator for securities markets.

shaft A vertical excavation used to transport miners, equipment, waste and ore to and from underground mine faces.

share dilution The fall in a shareholder's percentage ownership of a firm caused by the increase in the number of new shares issued to others.

spot price The cash price for a financial product if traded immediately rather than at some point in the future.

standstill agreement A legal contract binding all parties not to take specific actions outlined in the contract for a limited time period.

stope The mining face; an underground area that has been blasted and from which ore is taken.

strike price The price at which the right to buy an underlying asset can be exercised.

syndicated revolving credit facility A revolving credit facility (see above) where the funds are provided by a group, or syndicate, of banks.

tailings The residue following ore processing. Tailings are stored in hopes of future technological processes allowing re-treatment and economic recovery of the remaining ore content.

Acknowledgements

My thanks go to Ernest Abankroh, Akwasi Acheampong, Janet Acheampong, Kwaku Acheampong, John Addaquay, Marian Addaquay, Ben Adoo, Frank Adu Jnr, Christine Afrifa, James Aggrey-Orleans, Nana Prah Agyensem VI, Joe Amanor, Daniel Adzesiwor Ametepey, David Ampofo, Y.B. Amponsah, James Anaman, Kofi Ansah, Kwaku Antwi-Boasiako, Reverend Canon Garnet Prah Arthur, James Assan, Keith Atkinson, Gareth Austin, Mark Bankes, K. Bartells, Michael Beck, Michael Beckett, Vincent Kizito Beyou, Merene Botsio-Phillips, Tim Brew, Dawnette Brown, Cleo Campbell, Baroness Lynda Chalker, John Clark, Kofi Coomson, Sir John Craven, Dr Chester Crocker, Josephine de Graft Johnson, Anthony Tengey Djokoto, Robert Elliott, Victor Flores, Anthony Forson Jnr, Jojo Fosu, Professor Ron Gaskell, Thomas Gibian, Isaac Glover, Bobby Godsell, Barbara Harris, Vince Harris, Joyce Koryo Hogarth, Gerard Holden, Alhaji Yusif Ibrahim, Hamid Ibrahim, Nat Ishino, Ben Jonah, Ernest Jonah, Sam Jonah, Victor Jonah, Mark Keatley, Paul Kusi, Naana Kwakye, Robert Lea, Bob Leatham, Tim Leunig, Michael Martineau, Nick Morrell, Terry Morris, Pat Mundon, Craig Murray, Andrea Nattrass, Rosaline Nutsugah, Fred Ohene-Kena, Randall Oliphant, Anthony Orchard, Robert Orleans-Pobee, Reverend Colonel J.K. Otoo, John Owusu, Christopher Paterson, Richard Kwame Peprah, Reindorf Perbi, John Pott, Michael Price, Joyce Quigley, Andrew Quinn, John Robinson, Charles Russell, Onno Rutten, Sir William Ryrie, Kwame Sakyi, Captain Andy Sam, Trevor Schultz, Kwamena Sekyi-Yorke, Dusanka Stojakovic, S. Kwami Tetteh, Chris Trueman, Ken Tshribi, Otumfuo Osei Tutu II, Srinivasan Venkatakrishnan and Robin Wade, as well as to all of those people who requested anonymity.

Notes

Author's Note

1. North (1990); Knack and Keefer (1995).
2. Kaufmann et al. (1999); with regard to the importance of institutions for sustained economic growth see Crafts (1999).
3. The English translations of Asante proverbs are drawn from Rattray (1916) or www.cogweb.ucla.edu/Discourse/Proverbs/Ashanti.html.

Introduction

1. World Gold Council, 2002 estimates, www.gold.org, accessed 3 March 2005.
2. C. Premoli, Sydney Mineral Exploration Discussion Group, 'African Gold: Potential, Problems and Opportunities': 79, www.smedg.org.au/premoli. pdf, accessed 6 September 2004.
3. R. Bromby, 'World is Good as Gold Again', *The Australian*, 29 September 1999, www.factiva.com; www.gold.org/value/markets/supply_demand/ mine_production.html, accessed 3 March 2005.
4. Unless otherwise specified 'African' is used throughout the text to describe black Africans (as opposed to European or Asian Africans, for example).
5. GL MS24659; Dumett (1988); McCaskie (1978).
6. GL MS24669.
7. GL MS24669.
8. Anin (1990: 3–6).
9. Anin (1990: 3–6).
10. Anin (1990: 3–6).
11. Dumett (1998).
12. 'Tribe' is used throughout the text to denote a subunit of people within an ethnic group who share well-defined cultural characteristics such as dialect,

customs and dress. 'Ethnic group' is defined as a group of people sharing a common root language, broad physical attributes and broad cultural values. The terms are used primarily to convey solidarity and levels of social cohesion rather than stages of economic or political development.

13. For explanations of Ghanaian terms appearing in the text, for example, 'Fante' and 'Asante', see the Glossary that starts on page 263.
14. Dumett (1998: 35).
15. GL MS24666; Wilks (1975: 568–75).
16. For an excellent exposition of the Asante kingdom see Wilks (1975).
17. Asanteman Council of North America website, www.acona-usacanada. org/aconahistory1.html, accessed 15 July 2005.
18. Wilks (1975: 112, 271, 412).
19. Turner (1947: 1–3).
20. GL MS24666: 28.
21. Turner (1947: 3).
22. The following details are taken from GL MS24669 and GL MS24666.
23. GL MS24666: 8.
24. GL MS24666: 6.
25. GL MS24666: 6.
26. McCaskie (1978: 42–43).
27. GL MS14164/1, 8 July and 12 July 1897; MS24669: 7–9.
28. GL MS24666: 22.
29. ARG 7/5/60/1, letters dated 14 February, 12 May, 13 March 1944 from Adansihene to District Commissioner.
30. Silver (1981: 514–16).
31. AGC Annual Report, 1973.
32. Huq (1989: 2).

Chapter 1

1. Quoted in J. Phaceas, 'Europeans Hand Australian Gold Index Best Day in Decade', *Australian Associated Press*, 27 September 1999, www.factiva.com.
2. P. Pank, 'Gold Surges on Pledge of Central Bank Sales Restraint', *Agence France-Presse*, 27 September 1999, www.factiva.com.
3. Quoted in P. Kennedy, 'Gold Rush', *British Columbia Bureau*, 29 September 1999, www.factiva.com.
4. The World Gold Council website, www.gold.org/value/reserve_asset/ gold_as/background.html, accessed 4 March 2005; *Golden Sextant*, 'Real Gold, Paper Gold and Fool's Gold: The Pathology of Inflation', 12 October 1999, www.goldensextant.com/commentary4.html, accessed 10 March 2005.

5. *Financial Post*, 1 September 1999; *Business Wire*, 14 September 1999, www. factiva.com.

6. *Reuters News*, 14 September 1999, www.factiva.com.

7. 'Gold Bullion Price to Remain Subdued – Australian Forecaster', *Asia Pulse*, 15 September 1999, www.factiva.com.

8. *Reuters News*, 'Gold Price Flat Despite Lease Rates Hike', 3 September 1999, www.factiva.com.

9. Quoted in P. Pank, 'Gold Surges on Pledge of Central Bank Sales Restraint', *Agence France-Presse*, 27 September 1999, www.factiva.com.

10. V. Dragomanovich, 'Gold Seen at $300/oz after European Central Banks Limit Sales', *Dow Jones Commodities Service*, 27 September 1999, www. factiva.com.

11. Quote from Philip Klapwijk, managing director of Gold Fields Mineral Services Ltd, in S. Wyatt, 'Gold Sits on Knife Edge as Hedge Funds Fuel Chaos', *Australian Financial Review*, 30 September 1999, www.factiva.com.

12. *Golden Sextant*, 'Real Gold, Paper Gold', as per Note 4 above.

13. *Golden Sextant*, 'Real Gold, Paper Gold', as per Note 4 above; Hathaway (June 2000).

14. *Golden Sextant*, 'Real Gold, Paper Gold', as per Note 4 above; Hathaway (June 2000).

15. 'Lessons from the Ashanti Debacle', 20 February 2000, www.eikos.co.za, accessed 14 December 2004; 'The Great Black Hope', *The Economist*, 11 November 1999.

16. A. Secombe, *Reuters News*, 22 September 1999, www.factiva.com.

17. AGC Board Minutes, 19 August 1990.

18. P. Chalmers, 'N. American gold miners not threatened by hedging', *Reuters News,* 7 October 1999; *Financial Times*, 8 November 1999, www. factiva.com.

19. *The Economist*, 11 November 1999.

20. The following calculations are derived from the 1999 and 2000 AGC Annual Reports. As noted in the 1999 Annual Report, the hedge book at 31 December that year had not materially changed from 30 September. The hedge book analysis in the 1999 report was provided by external consultants, Standard Risk and Treasury Management Services (Pty) Limited of South Africa.

21. As per Note 20 above. The Annual Reports themselves distinguish be-tween 'protected' and 'committed' ounces.

22. Internal document, Gold House, undated.

23. See, for example, Shepherd (1999). See also *The Economist*, 11 November 1999.

24. *Corporate Finance*, January 1999.

25. Keatley, 'Paper on the Management of the Hedging Portfolio', April 1999, AGC internal document.

26. See, for example, Grinblatt and Titman (1998: Ch.20). For empirical arguments for and against the benefits of hedging to shareholders of gold companies see Callahan (2002) and Wixley (2002).

27. See, for example, the opinion of the Australian government's chief commodities' forecaster (in Note 7 above); that of Ted Arnold, Prudential-Bache's minerals strategist, in *Metals Week*, 13 September 1999, www.factiva.com; and Gold Fields Minerals Services Ltd in *Dow Jones International News*, 14 September 1999, www.factiva.com.

28. Hathaway (February and September 1999).

29. Hull (2003: 693).

30. Laws of Ghana, National Redemption Council Decree 132, December 1972.

31. International Centre for Settlement of Investment Disputes, Case No. ARB/92/1:Vacuum Salt Products Ltd vs. Government of the Republic of Ghana in *Yearbook of Commercial Arbitration* 20, 1995: 11–34.

32. Gilbert (2000: 13).

33. *The Express*, 6 October 1999, www.factiva.com.

34. Gillian O'Connor, *Financial Times*, 8 October 1999.

35. Barry Fitzgerald, *Sydney Morning Herald*, 8 October 1999, www.factiva. com.

36. As a result of the crisis Ashanti was forced to divest its small but profitable investments in manufacturing, farming, banking and hotels. The diversity of interests mirrored that of Lonrho's operations across the continent. See also *The Economist*, 11 November 1999.

37. Rawlings and his administration have been incriminated in the ruin of the following businessmen: J.K. Siaw, Safo Adu and Appiah Menka; and in the murder of three High Court judges in 1982: Cecilia Koranteng Addow, Justice Sarkodee and Justice Agyepong. See Amnesty International, 'Ghana Briefing on the Death Penalty', 17 July 2000, www.web.amnesty.org/library/Index/ENGAFR280012000?open&of=ENG-GHA, accessed 21 July 2005.

Chapter 2

1. Stockwell (2000: Ch.1).
2. Public Record Office, Kew, Colonial Office 847/36/1 no.9, Papers prepared by the Agenda Committee on the Conference of African Governors, no.2, 'Constitutional Development in Africa', May 1947, cited in Stockwell (2000: 1).
3. Killick (1966: 274 Table 12.1).
4. Reindorf (1966 [1898]: 57); Williams (1994).
5. Stockwell (2000: 80).

6. BBC World Service, www.bbc.co.uk/worldservice/people/highlights/ 000914_nkrumah.shtml, accessed 23 October 2004.
7. The following details are mostly derived from McLean Amissah (1980).
8. McLean Amissah (1980: x).
9. Killick (1978: 229–33).
10. 253 Memorandum from Robert W. Komer of the National Security Council Staff to the president's Special Assistant for National Security Affairs, Washington DC, 27 May 1965: 'We [USA] and other Western countries (including France) have been helping to set up the situation by ignoring Nkrumah's pleas for economic aid.' Johnson Library, National Security File, Country File, Ghana, Vol. II, Cables, 3/64–2/66.
11. Rimmer (1992: 7, 71–72).
12. Interview with Vince and Barbara Harris, London, 8 September 2004.
13. See, for example, *Bulletin of the International Commission of Jurists*, March 1964, December 1965.
14. As per Note 10 above.

Chapter 3

1. Federal Research Division of the Library of Congress, www.country-studies.com/ghana/the-national-liberation-council-and-the-busia-years,-1966-71.html, accessed 3 June 2004.
2. Egremont (1997: 309–10).
3. Egremont (1997: 309–10).
4. Egremont (1997: 309–10).
5. Stockwell (2000: Ch.6).

Chapter 5

1. Rimmer (1992: 134).
2. Text of speech by Col. I.K. Acheampong (Acheampong, 1973, Vol.2: 119–25).
3. Acheampong (1973, Vol.2: 119–25).
4. AGC Annual Report, 1972: Note 1; AGC Annual Report, 1974: 7.
5. Cited in Konings (1980: 13) from Cliffe (1977: 130–33).
6. AGC Annual Report, 1973: 20.
7. AGC Annual Report, 1974: 8; AGC Annual Report, 1975: 8.
8. Huq (1989: 16, 26).
9. Rimmer (1992: 136).
10. Inflation in 1977 was 116.5 per cent; money expansion between 1976 and

1978 rose 165.7 per cent (Boahen 1989: 10); export volumes drastically declined, see Rimmer (1992: 143 Table 7.1).

11. Huq (1989: 26).
12. Calculated from AGC Annual Reports by dividing total fixed assets in 2002 values by the number of employees.
13. Jonah (1979).
14. *Daily Graphic*, Ghana, 16 June 1979.
15. *Catholic Standard*, 24 June 1979.
16. Testimony of Joss Aryee, former senior reporter of the Ghana News Agency, 5 July 2004, Accra, to the National Reconciliation Commission, www.nrcghana.org/pressdetails.php?q=2004-07-05, accessed 5 October 2004.
17. See Shillington (1992: 52–55).
18. Boahen (1989: 17–18, 23, 39).
19. Text of broadcast by Flight-Lieutenant Jerry John Rawlings, Chairman of the PNDC, 'No Turning Back', 29 July 1982.
20. Federal Research Division of the Library of Congress, www.country-studies.com/ghana/the-second-coming-of-rawlings,-1982–87.html, accessed 3 June 2004.
21. Text of broadcast by Flight-Lieutenant Jerry John Rawlings, Chairman of the PNDC, 'No Turning Back', 29 July 1982.
22. See K. Yankah, 'Under Arrest!', originally published in the weekly Accra paper *The Mirror*, *c.*1986, and reprinted in Yankah (1990).
23. Text of broadcast by Flight-Lieutenant Jerry John Rawlings, Chairman of the PNDC, 'No Turning Back', 29 July 1982.
24. Amnesty International, 'Ghana Briefing on the Death Penalty',17 July 2000, www.web.amnesty.org/library/Index/ENGAFR280012000?open &of=ENG-GHA, accessed 21 July 2005.

Chapter 6

1. Huq (1989: 5).
2. World Bank Statistics, www.worldbank.org/data/, accessed 21 January 2005.
3. Huq (1989: 1–32).
4. Huq (1989: 1–32).
5. Huq (1989: 1–32).
6. Frimpong-Ansah (1991: Ch.5).
7. Beckman (1976: 279 Table 1) and Boahen (1989: 46).
8. Boahen (1989: 45).
9. Adams (1990).
10. Herbst (1993: 62).

11. Herbst (1993: 45–46).
12. 'Investment Inflow into the Mining Sector', Finance and Research Unit, Minerals Commission, Accra, Ghana, April 2004.
13. James Capel Bank, 'Ashanti Goldfields Flotation Marketing Document', February 1994, AGC internal document.
14. By reducing the size of the state in economic activity Structural Adjustment contributed to 20 per cent unemployment. Other criticisms of the IMF programme were that in 1998 GDP per capita was still lower than in 1975, and Ghana's external debt had increased from $1.4bn in 1980 to $7bn by 1999 (Ismi, 2004).

Chapter 7

1. Collier and Gunning (1999: 67).
2. Collier and Gunning (1999: 67).
3. Freedom in the World Survey 1998–99, www.freedomhouse.org/survey99/country/ghana/html, accessed 17 January 2005.
4. Ethno-Net Africa Database, www.ethnonet-africa.org/data/ghana/genpop.htm#lingue, accessed 18 January 2005.
5. For example, this was the topic of a speech delivered by Jonah to the Rotary Club in Kumasi, 29 July 1995, AGC internal document.
6. Federal Research Division of the Library of Congress, www.country-studies.com/ghana/presidential-elections.html, accessed 18 January 2005.
7. Federal Research Division of the Library of Congress, www.country-studies.com/ghana/parliamentary-elections.html, accessed 18 January 2005.
8. Federal Research Division of the Library of Congress, www.country-studies.com/ghana/parliamentary-elections.html, accessed 18 January 2005.
9. Botchwey stepped down after the government had to withdraw a new 17.5 per cent value added tax, which was aimed at increasing treasury revenue but resulted in violent urban protests costing five lives. The episode highlighted the growing political challenge of sustaining economic reforms that were increasing the cost of living and aggravating poverty (see Donkor, 1997).
10. Gold House internal document, 'Sir Sam's Contribution to Health, Safety and Environment Initiatives' (not dated, but May 2005).
11. AGC website, www.g-ir.com/ashantigold/culture/agchistory.jsp?subsection=3, accessed 2 February 2004.
12. Amnesty International, 'Ghana Annual Report 1995', www.web.amnesty.org/library/eng-gha/index, accessed 1 February 2005.

13. Interview with Mark Bankes, corporate lawyer, Norton Rose, London, 16 and 20 April 2004.
14. 'Ashanti Chief Learns Harsh Lessons of International Listing', *Evening Standard*, 18 December 1996.

Chapter 8

1. *The Times*, 8 December 1995, www.factiva.com.
2. 'Still Gold-crazy after 23 Years', *Financial Times*, 5 January 1996, www.factiva.com.
3. K. Gooding, 'Prospects Fade for Rival Cluff Bid', *Financial Times*, 14 December 1995, www.factiva.com; *The Times*, 5 January 1996, www.factiva.com.
4. 'Still Gold-crazy after 23 Years', *Financial Times*, 5 January 1996, www.factiva.com.
5. Dow Jones & Company, 'Emerging Markets Report', 21 February 1996.
6. AGC Annual Report, 1996.
7. AGC Annual Report, 1996.
8. Interview with Richard Kwame Peprah, Takoradi prison, 13 May 2004.
9. Interview with Professor Keith Atkinson, University of Exeter, 13 October 2004.
10. See The Environmental Law Institute, 'The Africa Programme Activity Report', June 2004.
11. For a selection see: ARG 7/5/60/1 letter dated 3 January 1940 from the Chief Conservator of Forests Office to The Hon. Colonial Secretary, Victoriasborg, Accra regarding AGC's deforestation; and 13 September 1940 from the Akrofuomhene to the District Commissioner Obuasi regarding pollution of the River Jimi by AGC; ARG 9/5/2 letters dated 11 and 20 November 1951 from local chiefs to the District Commissioner Bekwai regarding the death of cocoa trees in the vicinity of the mine allegedly from the smoke emitted by AGC's treatment plant; ARG 7/5/42 Akrofuom Rate Payers Association formal protest dated 15 September 1953 to the minister of local government, Accra and copied to the Akrofuom local council and elders, the press, and forestry personnel in Accra and Kumasi opposing the concession of new lands to AGC for the purpose of firewood; more recently the environmental degradation of open pit mining: *Ghanaian Chronicle*, 14 April 2000; *Public Agenda*, 17–23 April 2000; A. Darimani, 'Putting the First Last – the Case of Public Hearing at Kubi, Ghana', Third World Network-Africa, 25 July 2003, www.twnafrica.org/news_detail.asp?twnID=437, accessed 19 October 2005.

12. For example, in response to villagers' complaints about the foul-smelling black substance in the River Jimi rendering it undrinkable, AGC retorted that the substance was only coal tar and was 'not unhealthy' – ARG 9/5/2 letter from the Assistant District Commissioner Obuasi to the District Commissioner Bekwai dated 25 August 1951 concerning the petition made by local chiefs to the Adansi Banka Member of the Legislative Assembly regarding the contamination of the River Jimi.

13. AGC Annual Report, 1996: 7.

Chapter 9

1. T. Nicol, 'The Ultimate Showdown: Ghanaian Leader, Jerry Rawlings and Kow', *The Week*, 1 July 1996, www.findarticles.com/p/articles/mi_ hb4398/is_199607/ai_n15308331, accessed 1 February 2005; G. Ayittey, 'Stop Appeasing Rawlings', *Profile Africa*, 18 July 2004, www.profileafrica. com/commentary.ayittey.041004.htm, accessed 19 October 2005. See also the comments of Lord Rea, Lords Hansard Text, United Kingdom Parliament, 16 October 1996, Col.1722; Ayee (1998: 17).

2. *Free Press*, December 1994, www.web.amnesty.org/library/Index/ENGA FR280011999?open&of=ENG-GHA, accessed 1 February 2005.

3. As per Note 2.

4. Other examples include Haruna Atta, *The Weekend Statesman*; Kweku Baako, *The Guide*; Bunmi Aborisade, *The Independent*; and Lewis Asubiojo, *The Independent*.

5. Amnesty International, 'Ghana: Imprisonment of Journalists', 12 November 1999, www.web.amnesty.org/library/, accessed 1 February 2005.

6. Text of Bill Clinton's Speech, Independence Square, Accra, 23 March 1998, Federal Document Clearing House.

7. *Dick Davis Digest*, 23 March 1998: 3.

8. Newspaper clipping, Gold House public relations files, date and name of the paper missing.

9. J. Ford, 'Ashanti Gives Green Light to Anglo', *Evening Standard*, London, 3rd edition, 22 May 1997, www.factiva.com.

10. *Forbes Global Business and Finance,* 19 April 1999: 68–9.

11. Letter dated 2 November 1998, Gold House internal documents.

12. See Kenneth Barry's interview with Godsell in *Reuters News*, 23 September 1999, www.factiva.com.

13. 'Gold Miners Their Own Worst Enemies', *Reuters News*, 20 September 1999, www.factiva.com.

14. See, for example, Gassman and McConvey (1998).

Chapter 10

1. Wilks (1975: 411–13).
2. Wilks (1975: 411–13).
3. Wilks (1975: 327–31).
4. *Africa News*, 1 June 1999, www.factiva.com.
5. See the entry for Asantehemaa in McFarland (1985).
6. *Guardian*, 4 November 1999, www.factiva.com.
7. Interview, interviewee's name withheld on request, Accra, 9 April 2005. The information is supported by Jonah's knowledge.
8. Published in www.ghanaweb.com/GhanaHomePage/NewsArchive/artikel.php?ID=11042, accessed 28 February 2005. See also *Independent* (Ghana), 14 March 2000; *Ghanaian Chronicle*, 21 March 2000; *Weekend Chronicle*, 23 March 2000.
9. As per Note 8.
10. These problems were exposed following the change in administration in December 2000. See www.afrol.com/Categories/Economy_Develop/dev013_ghana_noncomplying.htm: 'IMF Grants Waiver on Non-complying Disbursement to Ghana', 23 August 2000; www.afrol.com/News2002/gha003_tricked_imf.htm: 'Ghana Tricked IMF into Payments', 7 February 2002, both accessed 1 March 2005.
11. Bentsi-Enchill (1998).
12. 'Report of the Fact-finding Committee to Investigate Ashanti Goldfields Company Ltd, Obuasi Mine Industrial Action', 1 September 1999.
13. 'The State vs. Sam Jonah', *Free Press*, 25–31 August 1999; 'Rawlings at it Again', *Independent* (Ghana), 24 February 2000; 'SFO Digs into Sam Jonah's Skin', *Weekly Insight* (Accra), 19 June 2000.
14. As per Note 13. See also C. McGreal, 'Gold Crisis Exposes Seam of Suspicion', *Guardian* (London), 4 November 1999, www.factiva.com.
15. *Crusading Guide*, 12 August 1999; 'Vendetta against Sam Jonah ... Peprah's Neck on the Line', *Independent* (Ghana), 24 August 1999.
16. As per Note 15.
17. *Dow Jones Commodities Service*, 24 August 1999, www.factiva.com.
18. *Accra Mail*, 3 April 2000.
19. Richard Kwame Peprah's submission to the Anyidaho committee.
20. AGC Board Minutes, 19 May 1995.
21. CFO meeting notes, Gold House internal documents, September 1999.

Chapter 11

1. AGC Board Minutes, September 1999 to April 2004, are the source of most of the information reconstructed in Chapters 11 through to 16.
2. Hathaway (October 1999).
3. Meeting at Goldman Sachs, Fleet Street, 9 October 1999.
4. AGC press release, 5 October 1999.
5. Name and address have been omitted here for anonymity; the letter was received at Gold House on 2 November 1999.
6. I was unable to uncover this article, but Jonah was adamant in his recollection of it.
7. Interview with Gerard Holden, global head of mining and metals at Barclays Capital, the investment banking division of Barclays Bank PLC, London, 19 March 2004.
8. Gross gearing calculated as debts due after one year divided by total equity.
9. *Reuters News*, 14 October 1999, www.factiva.com.
10. Interview, interviewee's name withheld on request, London, 17 February 2005.
11. J. Kibazo, 'Three Omissions that May Cost Lonmin', *Financial Times*, 15 October 1999.

Chapter 12

1. This is because the Libyan Sanctions Order had been suspended, with a few exceptions, in April 1999.
2. File note on proposed loan from Libyan Arab Foreign Investment Company (Lafico)/Libyan Arab African Investment Company(Laaico) from Norton Rose to Mark Keatley, 1 November 1999, Gold House internal document.
3. Interview with Mark Horn, London, 17 February 2005.
4. Interview with Mark Horn, London, 17 February 2005.
5. *Reuters*, 14 October 1999, www.factiva.com.
6. *Reuters*, 14 October 1999, www.factiva.com.
7. *Financial Times*, 2 December 1999, www.factiva.com; interview with Mark Horn, London, 17 February 2005.
8. *Financial Times*, 2 December 1999, www.factiva.com; *The Financial News*, 6 December 1999, www.factiva.com.
9. Interview with Mark Horn, London, 17 February 2005.
10. Interview with Frank Adu, managing director of Cal Merchant Bank, Accra, 19 April 2005.
11. Interview with Frank Adu, managing director of Cal Merchant Bank, Accra, 19 April 2005.

12. *Financial Times*, 29 October 1999, www.factiva.com.
13. *Africa News Service*, 24 November 1999, www.factiva.com.
14. Letter delivered 16 October 1999 from the Saudi prince to President Rawlings, Gold House internal documents. *Reuters English News Service*, 19 October 1999, www.factiva.com.
15. *Financial Times*, 29 October 1999, www.factiva.com.
16. *Africa News Service*, 24 November 1999, www.factiva.com.
17. Letter delivered to Jonah on 30 October 1999.
18. Interview with Craig Murray, former acting British High Commissioner in Ghana, London, 17 May 2005.
19. Interview with Craig Murray, former acting British High Commissioner in Ghana, London, 17 May 2005.
20. Interviews with Michael Beckett and Sir John Craven, London, 1 and 16 March 2004. See also *Reuters*, 6 October 1999, www.factiva.com.
21. Hathaway (May 2000).
22. *Reuters*, 14 October 1999, www.factiva.com. Rawlings's withdrawal of ministerial support from AGC's board during the negotiations was a particularly dangerous tactic for the future of the firm. Similarly, the firm's existence was threatened by the leaked titbits from the unpublished Anyidaho report of alleged criminal conduct by AGC management as a whole – and not only Jonah.
23. Letter to Lonmin from the Ghanaian ministry of mines and energy, delivered 4 November 1999, Gold House internal document.
24. Letter from the Ghanaian ministry of mines and energy to AGC threatening legal action if the government's stake was further diluted by the granting of more warrants; discussed at the AGC board meeting of 26 November 1999.
25. Interview with Craig Murray, former acting British High Commissioner in Ghana, London, 17 May 2005; interviews, interviewee's name withheld on request, Accra, 12 May 2004 and 15 April 2005.
26. *BBC World News*, 8 November 1999, www.news.bbc.co.uk/1/hi/world/africa/509599.stm, accessed 16 May 2005.
27. Interviews, interviewee's name withheld on request, Accra, 12 May 2004 and 15 April 2005.

Chapter 13

1. *Daily Graphic*, 16 November 1999.

Chapter 14

1. Copy of transcript of opening submission obtained from Tetteh & Co, Accra.
2. Copy of transcript of opening submission obtained from Tetteh & Co, Accra.
3. Copy of transcript of opening submission obtained from Tetteh & Co, Accra.
4. Quoted from AGC Board Minutes, 3 February 2000; the specific case was not cited.
5. *Financial Times*, 8 November 1999.
6. Copy of transcript of opening submission obtained from Tetteh & Co, Accra.
7. Interview with Kofi Coomson, editor of the *Ghanaian Chronicle*, Accra, 23 March 2005.
8. Interview with Kofi Coomson, editor of the *Ghanaian Chronicle*, Accra, 23 March 2005.
9. Personal correspondence with Trevor Schultz, dated 18 July 2005.
10. M. Horn, Memorandum, 'Ashanti – the Start of Substantive Negotiations', 10 February 2000.
11. From Quinn's report to the AGC board of his meeting with Gandur in Cape Town, 10 February 2000.
12. Bankers' contributions at board meeting, AGC Board Minutes, 11 February 2000.
13. Bankers' contributions at board meeting, AGC Board Minutes, 11 February 2000.
14. *Ghanaian Chronicle*, 15 March 2000.
15. AGC Board Minutes, 30 May 2000.
16. AGC Annual Report, 1999.
17. Gilbert (2000).

Chapter 15

1. 'The State vs. Sam Jonah', *Free Press*, 25–31 August 1999; 'Rawlings at it Again', *Independent* (Ghana), 24 February 2000; 'SFO Digs into Sam Jonah's Skin', *Weekly Insight* (Accra), 19 June 2000. See also C. McGreal, 'Gold Crisis Exposes Seam of Suspicion', *Guardian* (London), 4 November 1999; *Crusading Guide*, 12 August 1999; 'Vendetta against Sam Jonah ... Peprah's Neck on the Line', *Independent* (Ghana), 24 August 1999.
2. AGC Annual Report, 2000
3. See Chapter 10 for details of these allegations.

4. Interview with Craig Murray, former acting British High Commissioner in Ghana, London, 17 May 2005; *BBC World News*, 8 November 1999, www.news.bbc.co.uk/1/hi/world/africa/509599.stm, accessed 18 May 2005.

5. As per Note 4.

6. Ayee (2002: 172).

7. Gyimah–Boadi (2001: 104).

8. Interview with Craig Murray, former acting British High Commissioner in Ghana, London, 17 May 2005.

9. www.allghanadata.com/how2/gov.htm; www.firstgov.gov/Agencies/Federal/Executive.shtml; World Bank 2003 GDP statistics, www.unstats.un.org/unsd/snaama/SelectionCountry.asp, all accessed 19 May 2005.

10. Unesco, Illiteracy Rates in Sub-saharan Africa 2000–2004, www.uis.unesco.org/ev.php?ID=4927_201&ID2=DO_TOPIC, accessed 19 May 2005.

11. Ayee (2002: 153).

12. Interview, interviewee's name withheld on request, Accra, 20 March 2005.

13. Ayee (2002: 148–74).

14. See Amnesty International Report 2002, Ghana, www.web.amnesty.org/web/ar2002.nsf/afr/ghana?Open, accessed 19 May 2005.

15. *Ghanaian Chronicle*, 3 January 2001.

16. AGC Annual Report, 2000.

Chapter 16

1. *BBC News*, 6 February 2002, www.news.bbc.co.uk/1/hi/business/1803198.stm, accessed 15 June 2005.

2. Letter dated 5 July 2001 from the acting executive director of the SFO to the attorney general and the minister of justice, Gold House internal document.

3. *Ghanaian Chronicle*, 23 March 2005; *Daily Guide*, 14 April 2005.

4. These SEC investigations ended in 2003.

5. AGC Board Minutes, 28 July 2000.

6. *Financial Times*, 16 October 2003, www.factiva.com.

7. *Dow Jones Newswire*, 14 October 2003, www.factiva.com.

8. Anglogold Ashanti produced 6.052 million ounces of gold in 2004, compared to Newmont's 7 million.

Epilogue

1. Tony Blair's speech at the launch of his Africa Commission in February 2004, www.govnet.co.uk/printMagazine.php?magazine=5&ID=568%20, accessed 21 July 2005.
2. Sachs and Warner (2001); Sala-i-Martín and Subramanian (2003).
3. Jonah and Nti (1993: 8).
4. C. Premoli, 'African Gold: Potential, Problems and Opportunities', Sydney Mineral Exploration Discussion Group, undated, www.smedg.org.au/premoli.pdf, accessed 6 September 2004; and R.W. Ogden, 'Why Africa?', 6 February 2003, www.kitco.com/ind/Ogden/feb062003.html, accessed 6 September 2004.

Glossary

1. Ghanaian terms are adapted from McFarland (1985).
2. Some of the gold mining and financial terms are derived from AGC's 1997 Annual Report and www.investorwords.com.

Select Bibliography

Primary sources

Gold House, Accra
AGC Annual Reports, 1969–2003 (some years missing).
AGC Board Minutes, 1972–2004.
Ashanti Goldfields Flotation Marketing Document, James Capel Bank, February 1994.
Finance Director's Meeting Notebooks, 1998–2000.
Keatley, M. Paper on the Management of the Hedging Portfolio. AGC internal document, April 1999.

Parliament of Ghana, Accra
Laws of Ghana, National Redemption Council Decree 132, December 1972.
Minerals and Mining Law (Amendment) Act of 1994.
Official Report of Parliamentary Debates, 12 February 2004.
PNDC Law 153, The Minerals and Mining Law of 1986.

Public Records and Archives Department, Accra
Colonial Secretary's Office Files, various on AGC pertaining to health, welfare and the environment: CSO 5/1, CSO 19/1–9.

Public Records and Archives Department, Kumasi
ARG 7 Series: Records of the Commissioner's Office, Obuasi.
ARG 9/5 Series: Records of the Commissioner's Office, Bekwai.
ARG 1/5 and 1/37 Series: Records of the Chief Commissioner of Ashanti.

Guildhall Library (GL), London, AGC documents

MS14164/1, Minutes of the Board of Directors Meetings, 1897.

MS24659, Papers on Establishment, 1896–97.

MS24661,Vols.1–7,Annual Reports and Report of Proceedings of Shareholder Meetings, 1901–05, 1908–28, 1963–68.

MS24666, E.A. Cade to Directors of the Cote d'Or Co. Ltd: Report on Obuasi Gold Mine Estate, Cape Coast, August 1895.

MS24669, T. Rowe, The Early Pioneers, 1895–1905, 1991.

MS24670, E. Cade letters, 1897–98.

Secondary sources

Abbey, J. Ghana's Experience with Structural Adjustment. In J. Pickett and H. Singer, eds., *Towards Economic Recovery in Sub-Saharan Africa*. London: Routledge, 1990: 32–41.

Acheampong, I.K. *Speeches and Interviews by Col. I.K.Acheampong*. Accra: Ghana Government, 1973.

Adams, J., ed. *Background Notes: Ghana*. Washington DC: Office of Public Communication, Bureau of Public Affairs, United States Department of State, February 1990.

Ahiakpor, J. The Profits of Foreign Firms in a Less Developed Country: Ghana. *Journal of Development Economics* 22, 1986: 321–35.

Anin, T.E. *Gold in Ghana*. London: Selwyn Publishers, 1990.

Aryeetey, E., J. Harrigan and M. Nissanke, eds. *Economic Reforms in Ghana: The Miracle and the Mirage*. Oxford: James Currey, 2000.

Ayee, J. The 2000 General Elections and Presidential Run-off in Ghana: An Overview. *Democratisation* 9(2), Summer 2002: 148–74.

―――. Assessing the Progress of Democracy and Good Governance in Africa: The Ghanaian Case. Addis Ababa: The Development Policy Management Forum, 1998.

Ayensu, E.S. *Ashanti Gold: The Legacy of the World's Most Precious Metal*. Accra: Ashanti Goldfields, 1997.

Bardhan, P. Corruption and Development: A Review of Issues. *Journal of Economic Literature* 35, 1997: 1 320–46.

Beckman, B. *Organising the Farmers: Cocoa Politics and National Development in Ghana*. Uppsala: Scandinavian Institute of African Studies, 1976.

Bentsi-Enchill, N.K. Tough Times Ahead for Ghana. *Africa Recovery* 11(3), February 1998.

Boahen, A. *The Ghanaian Sphinx: Reflections on the Contemporary History of Ghana 1972–1987*. Accra: Ghana Academy of Arts and Sciences, 1989.

Callahan, M. To Hedge or Not to Hedge . . . that is the Question: Empirical Evidence from the North American Gold Mining Industry 1996–2000. *Financial Markets, Institutions and Instruments* 11(4), November 2002: 271–88.

Cliffe, L. Lonrho. *Review of African Political Economy* 8, January–April 1977: 130–33.

Collier, P. and J. Gunning. Explaining African Economic Performance. *Journal of Economic Literature* 37, 1999: 67–111.

Crafts, N.F.R. Implications of Financial Crisis for East Asian Trend Growth. *Oxford Review of Economic Policy* 15(3), 1999: 110–31.

Donkor, K. *Structural Adjustment and Mass Poverty in Ghana*. Aldershot: Ashgate, 1997.

Dumett, R.E. Sources for Mining Company History in Africa: The History and Records of the Ashanti Goldfields Corporation (Ghana), Ltd. *Business History Review* 62, Autumn 1988: 502–15.

———. *El Dorado in West Africa: The Gold-mining Frontier, African Labour, and Colonial Capitalism in the Gold Coast, 1875–1900*. Athens: Ohio University Press, 1998.

Easterly, W. The Lost Decades: Developing Countries' Stagnation in Spite of Policy Reform 1980–1998. *Journal of Economic Growth* 6, 2001: 135–57.

Egremont, M. *Under Two Flags: The Life of Major General Sir Edward Spears*. London: Orion Publishing Group, 1997.

Ewusi, K. *Structural Adjustment and Stabilization Policies in Developing Countries: A Case Study of Ghana's Experience in 1983–1986*. Tema, Ghana: Ghana Publishing Corporation, 1987.

Executive Intelligence Review. *Tiny Rowland: The Ugly Face of Neo-colonialism in Africa*. Washington DC: Executive Intelligence Review, 1993.

Fitch, B. and M. Oppenheimer. *Ghana: End of an Illusion*. New York: Monthly Review Press, 1966.

Frimpong-Ansah, J. *The Vampire State: The Political Economy of Decline in Ghana*. Trenton: World Africa Press, 1991.

Gassman, A. and D. McConvey. Goldman Sachs US Equity Research. New York: Goldman Sachs, January 1998.

Gilbert, C.L. Derivatives: Use and Abuse. Inaugural lecture given at the Vrije Universiteit, Amsterdam, 26 October 2000.

Greer, J. and K. Singh. *A Brief History of Transnational Corporations*. New York: Global Policy Forum, 2000.

Grinblatt, M. and S. Titman. *Financial Markets and Corporate Strategy*. Boston: Irwin McGraw-Hill, 1998.

Gyimah-Boadi, E. A Peaceful Turnover in Ghana. *Journal of Democracy* 12(2), 2001: 103–17.

Hansen, E. *Ghana under Rawlings: Early Years*. Lagos: Malthouse Press, 1991.

Harriss, J., J. Hunter and C. Lewis, eds. *The New Institutional Economics and Third World Development*. London: Routledge, 1995.

Hathaway, J. Bullion Dealers: Spin Meisters of the Gold Market. New York: Tocqueville Asset Management, February 1999.

———. Gold Bulletin. New York: Tocqueville Asset Management, 24 September 1999.

———. Simple Math and Common Sense: A $66bn Problem. New York: Tocqueville Asset Management, 7 October 1999.

———. JP Morgan to the Rescue. New York: Tocqueville Asset Management, 16 May 2000.

———. Conspiracy and the Gold Market: A Clarification. New York: Tocqueville Asset Management, 1 June 2000.

Herbst, J. *The Politics of Reform in Ghana, 1982–1991*. Berkeley: University of California Press, 1993.

Hopkins, A.G. *An Economic History of West Africa*. Harlow: Longman, 1973.

———. Imperial Business in Africa, Part 1: Sources. *Journal of African History* 17(1), 1976: 29, 30.

———. Imperial Business in Africa, Part 2: Interpretations. *Journal of African History* 17(2), 1976: 267–90.

———. Big Business in African Studies. *Journal of African History* 28, 1987: 119–40.

Hull, J.C. *Options, Futures, and Other Derivatives*. Upper Saddle River, NJ: Prentice Hall, 2003.

Hutchful, E. From 'Revolution' to Monetarism: The Economics and Politics of the Adjustment Programme in Ghana. In B. Campbell and J. Loxley, eds., *Structural Adjustment in Africa*. Basingstoke: Macmillan, 1989: 92–131.

Huq, M. *The Economy of Ghana: The First 25 Years Since Independence*. Basingstoke: Macmillan, 1989.

Ismi, A. *Impoverishing a Continent: The World Bank and the IMF in Africa*. Ottawa: Canadian Centre for Policy Alternatives, July 2004.

Jeffries, R. Ghana: The Political Economy of Personal Rule. In D. O'Brien, J. Dunn and R. Rathbone, eds., *Contemporary West African States*. Cambridge: Cambridge University Press, 1989: 75–98.

Jonah, S.E. An Evaluation of the Effects of Ghana's Present System of Mining Taxation on the Local Mining Industry. M.Sc. Thesis, Royal School of Mines at Imperial College, London, 1979.

Jonah, S.E. and K. Nti. Mine Management into the 21st Century: Perspectives from Ashanti. Accra: AGC internal paper, 1993.

Kaufmann, D., A. Kraay and M. Mastruzzi. Governance Matters. World Bank Policy Research Working Paper No. WPS2 2196. Washington DC: World Bank, 1999.

Killick, T. Manufacturing and Construction. In W. Birmingham, I. Neustadt and E.N. Omaboe, eds., *Study of Contemporary Ghana*. London: Allen & Unwin, 1966.

————. *Development Economics in Action: Economic Policies in Ghana*. London: Heinemann, 1978.

————. *IMF Programmes in Developing Countries: Design and Impact*. London: Routledge, 1995.

Kirkpatrick, C. and F. Nixson. Transnational Corporations and Economic Development. *The Journal of Modern African Studies* 19(3), 1981: 367–99.

Knack, S. and P. Keefer. Institutions and Economic Performance: Cross-country Tests Using Alternative Institutional Measures. *Economics and Politics* 7, 1995: 207–27.

Konings, P. *The Political Potential of Ghanaian Miners: A Case Study of the AGC Workers at Obuasi*. Research reports No.9, Leiden: African Studies Centre, 1980.

Lall, S., ed. *The New Multinationals: The Spread of Third World Enterprises*. Chichester: Wiley, 1983.

Lall, S. and P. Streeten. *Foreign Investment, Transnationals and Developing Countries*. London: Macmillan, 1977.

Lecraw, D. Direct Investment by Firms from Less Developed Countries. *Oxford Economic Papers* 1977: 442–57.

McCaskie, T.C. The Creation of Ashanti Goldfields Corporation, Ltd., ca. 1890–1910: An Episode in the Colonial Impact upon Asante. *Asantesem* 9, 1978: 37–55.

McFarland, D.M. *Historical Dictionary of Ghana*. Metuchen, NJ: Scarecrow Press, 1985.

McLean Amissah, G. *Reminiscences of Adisadel: A Short Historical Sketch of Adisadel College*. Accra: Afram Publications, 1980.

Mireku, E. *Which Way Ghana? Restoring Hope and Confidence in the Ghanaian*. Accra: Asuo Peabo Ltd, 1991.

Mishkin, F. Understanding Financial Crises: A Developing Country Perspective. In *Annual World Bank Conference on Development Economics*, Washington DC: World Bank, 1997: 29–62.

Murphy, K., A. Shleifer and R.W. Vishny. Why is Rent-seeking so Costly to Growth? *American Economic Review Papers & Proceedings* 1993: 409–14.

North, D. *Institutions, Institutional Change and Economic Performance*. Cambridge: Cambridge University Press, 1990.

Nugent, P. *Big Men, Small Boys and Politics in Ghana: Power, Ideology and the Burden of History, 1982–1994*. London: Mansell, 1995.

Olson, M. Big Bills Left on the Sidewalk: Why Some Nations are Rich and Others Poor. *Journal of Economic Perspectives* 10(2), 1996: 3–24.

Oquaye, M. *Politics in Ghana 1972–1979*. Accra: Tornado Publications, 1980.

Pobee, J.S. *Religion and Politics in Ghana*. Accra: Asempa Publishers, 1991.

Rathbone, R. Ghana. In J. Dunn, ed., *West African States: Failure and Promise*. Cambridge: Cambridge University Press, 1978: 22–35.

Rattray, R.S. *Ashanti Proverbs (The Primitive Ethics of a Savage People) Translated from the Original with Grammatical and Anthropological Notes*. Oxford: Clarendon Press, 1916.

Reindorf, C.C. *The History of Gold Coast and Asante*. Accra: Ghana Universities Press, 1966 [1898].

Rimmer, D. *Staying Poor: Ghana's Political Economy 1950–1990*. Oxford: Pergamon, 1992.

Rodrik, D. Understanding Policy Reform. *Journal of Economic Literature* 34, 1996: 9–41.

———. Where Did All the Growth Go? External Shocks, Social Conflict and Growth Collapses. *Journal of Economic Growth* 4, 1999: 385–412.

Sachs, J. and A. Warner. The Curse of Natural Resources. *European Economic Review* 45, 2001: 827–38.

Sala-i-Martín, X and A. Subramanian. Addressing the Natural Resource Curse: An Illustration from Nigeria. *Economics Working Papers* 685, Department of Economics and Business, Universitat Pompeu Fabra, 2003.

Shepherd, B. The Art of Hedging Gold. *Global Finance*, March 1999: 6–7.

Shillington, K. *Ghana and the Rawlings Factor*. London: Macmillan, 1992.

Silver, J. The Failures of European Mining Companies in the Nineteenth-century Gold Coast. *Journal of African History* 22, 1981: 511–29.

Skinner, W.E. *The Mining Manual and Mining Year Book*. London: Walter Skinner and *Financial Times*, 1925–1972.

Smith, D. Ghana's 2000 Elections: Consolidating Multi-party Democracy. *Electoral Studies* 21, 2002: 473–533.

Stockwell, S.E. *The Business of Decolonization: British Business Strategies in the Gold Coast*. New York: Oxford University Press, 2000.

Turner, G.W.E. The Ashanti Goldfields Corporation. *The Mining Magazine* June 1932.

———. *A Short History: Ashanti Goldfields Corporation Ltd., 1897–1947*. London: Ashanti Goldfields, 1947.

United Nations Department of Economic and Social Affairs. *Multinational Corporations in World Development*. New York: United Nations, 1973.

Widstrand, C., ed. *Multinational Firms in Africa*. Uppsala: Scandinavian Institute of African Studies, 1975.

Wilks, I. *Asante in the Nineteenth Century: The Structure and Evolution of a Political Order*. Cambridge: Cambridge University Press, 1975.

Williams, H.A. A Political History of Assin Kushea in the Seventeenth Century. BA Thesis, University of Cape Coast, Cape Coast, 1994.

Wixley, J. Is Gold Hedging Bad for Shareholders? Paper delivered at the Euromoney Gold Investment Summit, 6 September 2002.

World Bank. *Ghana: Policies and Program for Adjustment* (2 vols.). Washington DC: World Bank, 1984.

Yankah, K. *Woes of a Kwatriot: Reflections on the Ghanaian Situation*. Accra: Woeli, 1990.

Yeebo, Z. *Ghana: The Struggle for Popular Power: Rawlings, Saviour or Demagogue?* London: New Beacon Books, 1991.

Index

292